PROFESSOR ARTHUR VENO was born in the US and has lived in Australia since 1974. Most recently director of Monash University's Centre for Police and Justice Studies, Veno has studied the clubs for seventeen years. But he's no ordinary academic – he attends club nights, field days and runs, and counts members of the Gypsy Jokers, Hell's Angels and Coffin Cheaters as his friends (they call him the Mad Professor). Veno now grows trees on his farm in rural Victoria, and is a consultant to various groups on human rights and criminal justice issues, as well – of course – as the bikie clubs.

THE BROTHERHOODS

INSIDE THE OUTLAW MOTORCYCLE CLUBS

ARTHUR VENO
with Ed Gannon

A SUE HINES BOOK
ALLEN & UNWIN

First published in 2002
This revised edition published in 2003

A Sue Hines Book
Allen & Unwin
83 Alexander Street
Crows Nest NSW 2065
Australia
Phone: (61 2) 8425 0100
Fax: (61 2) 9906 2218
Email: info@allenandunwin.com
Web: www.allenandunwin.com

National Library of Australia
Cataloguing-in-Publication entry:

Veno, Arthur, 1945– .
   The brotherhoods: inside the outlaw motorcycle clubs.
   Rev. ed.
   Includes index
   ISBN 1 74114 137 0.
   1. Motorcycle gangs – Australia. I. Gannon, Ed. II. Title.
   364.10660994

The poems on page 150 and 159 are reproduced with permission from *Some Biker Bitches Poetry* by Kimberley Manning, Author's Choice Press, 2000.

Text design by Phil Campbell
Typeset by Pauline Haas
Printed by McPherson's Printing Group

10 9 8 7 6 5 4 3 2

To Veronica Veno, my mother, poet and person extraordinaire, who has been my friend and support all my life. Thanks Mum.

We are modern day heroes, like Ned Kelly. Mr Average would be happy being told by the government what to think, when to drink, when to fuck. That's not us. We are the last free people in society.
Hell's Angel

CONTENTS

CHAPTER ONE THE MAD PROFESSOR

'Let's go get a cup of coffee at Maccas,' they said.

Who was I to argue? The guys suggesting it were only the kingpins in one of the meanest bikie clubs in the land who had asked me along to a meeting to 'discuss' a few things.

As I tentatively climbed into what turned out to be an extraordinarily loud car I somehow knew there wasn't going to be any coffee. My arse is grass, I thought.

There was some small talk – they talked, I felt small. Then they told me what was going on. I was at once relieved and frightened. They didn't want to kill me, they only wanted me to do the next best thing – grass a bikie. They told me how they had a problem with one of their members and his amphetamine factory. They wanted me to act as a go-between to dump him in it.

At that point I became one of the few outsiders to be not only privy to, but actually involved in, outlaw club business. This was incredible stuff. To dob in a brother in the bikie world is the greatest sin. Yet, here I was being asked to do just that. I'd lay a bet I was the first professor to ever be asked to do such a thing. I'd also bet I was the first professor mad enough to get myself into that situation.

I tell that story, which I'll expand on later, to answer the most common question people ask me – what does a middle-aged professor know about outlaw motorcycle clubs? Or, more specifically, what can someone who's never been a club member and who doesn't ride a motorcycle reveal about bikie clubs?

I'd ask the same question. My answer is that things are not always what they seem. Gangs and bikie clubs are my professional and personal passion. I am often referred to as Australia's foremost independent expert on the outlaw motorcycle clubs as I've been studying them for nigh on 20 years. This currently makes me the only academic in the world who has made it their focus.

However, before I get into all that I'd better tell you a bit about myself and how I fell into the world of the outlaw motorcycle clubs.

I'm a Yank, and was born in Burlington, Vermont, just below the Canadian border, in 1945. These days I live in Australia and hold dual Australian–American citizenship.

No sooner could I walk than Dad, a sergeant major in the US army, began his round of international postings. By the age of 12 I'd lived in Greece, Germany, Italy, France and Turkey, before we returned to the US, to a town called Monterey, about 106 km south of San Francisco. An incident was to occur in that town a few years later that changed the image of motorcycle clubs forever. That event also changed my life, for I was caught up right in the thick of it.

I suppose my life was headed toward the gang culture the moment we moved to Monterey. By this time, Dad had retired from the army due to ill health, and was supporting his family on an army pension, so as you can imagine, we weren't destined for the flashiest part of town. We settled on the edge of a black ghetto, a part of town characterised by heavy gang activity.

The Hispanic and black gangs were the kings of the neighbourhood. Many of my mates joined these gangs, and I'd occasionally hang out with them. But I never joined a gang myself.

I discovered I had an aptitude for American football, or gridiron, as Australians call it. I was pretty good at it, to the point where it enabled me to gain sporting scholarships all the way through high school and junior college in Monterey, then on to San Francisco State University where I completed a Bachelor of Arts in psychology. However, I never made it to the pros. I did try out for the San Francisco 49ers, but I was only good enough to be a 'practice dummy' – the guys the good players batter around at practice.

I enjoyed the few bucks I earned, and I got the chance to rub shoulders with a few of the big names. Joe Montana arrived after I was in my final year in the 'meat squad', as we called it. Nathan Johns, the great all-pro defensive back, lived just around the corner from me in the Monterey ghettos.

My first contact with motorcycle clubs was at the Labor Day rally of 1964, held in Monterey. As I mentioned earlier, it was a weekend that left a scar on the reputation of all bikies across America.

I was home from university that weekend and heard that the Hell's Angels were in town. A few mates and I decided to go and check them out. We'd heard about the demonic bikers, so when we got there we hung back cautiously for some time, just checking them out. We eventually joined their party and were surprised to discover they were merely people committed to Harley-Davidson motorcycles and having a good time. We didn't find it at all threatening. To a 19-year-old they weren't a bad bunch of people to party with. However, the Hell's Angels' reputation was notorious enough for the police to organise a camp for the club at the beach on the outskirts of town.

That night there was a party at the camp, so my mates and

I thought we'd check this out too. Unbeknown to us, there were two under-age girls at the party, one aged 14 and the other, 15. One girl was black, the other white and pregnant. The girls accompanied between two and five Hell's Angels down to the beach, away from the party, where it was later claimed a series of sexual attacks took place.

There were conflicting stories about the girls' willingness for sexual activity. However, the girls appeared back at the campsite looking extremely distressed. We jumped to our feet and rushed over to the girls to find out what was wrong. I also remember many of the Hell's Angels gathering around to comfort the girls – it's an image that has stuck with me as it was so at odds with the image of the club.

When the police arrived the girls identified a number of people, who were arrested.

The media was soon onto it, portraying the Hell's Angels as 'dirty stinking thugs . . . repeatedly raping . . . girls aged 14 and 15'. Some stories said the girls were on a date with two boys and were in the middle of roasting weenies (sausages) on the beach when 4000 Hell's Angels appeared over the dunes and, according to one account, said to one of the boys, 'Don't worry son, we're just going to break the girls in for you.' The boys were alleged to '. . . have fought like tigers to save the girls'.

The three US television networks covered the event, and reporters from the *New York Times*, the *Saturday Evening Post*, *Time*, *Newsweek*, *The Nation* and other national newspapers descended upon Monterey. Emotions in the town ran high.

Four Hell's Angels members were arrested and charged with rape, only to have the charges later dropped. However, by this time it was too late. The legend of the outlaw motorcycle club had been forged indelibly in the minds of the public. Another 'Folk Devil' had been created.

It also made a huge impression on me. I could really see how the bikies were vilified, with the media trying to make them seem evil. I was there and I just couldn't see that they were as evil as they were made out to be. I didn't discount that they *could* be, but I needed to know more before I made up my own mind. I suppose my life-long academic search started that weekend.

A few years later, when I was studying for my PhD at the University of California at Berkeley, near San Francisco, I had my next formative experience with the bikie clubs.

The local Hell's Angels and the university students had been getting along fine until the anti-Vietnam war issue arose. At the time Berkley was a hotbed of anti-war protest in the United States and the club members, with their military roots, took umbrage at the students' constant barrage of criticism of the Vietnam War. This led to a violent confrontation between the Hell's Angels and the students at a Berkley campus protest. When student and hippy demonstrators marched from People's Park towards City Hall they encountered a line of police at City Hall. As they approached it a group of Hell's Angels roared in on their bikes and parked (this was shortly after Sonny Barger had written to the President offering a platoon of Hell's Angels for service in the war). The Angels got off their bikes and starting abusing the marchers, who were quite surprised and shocked by their arrival. As they approached the bikies, who were standing in front of the police, things got ugly and a few of the marchers got chain-whipped and stomped.

Once more, I found myself in the thick of it all. Luckily I wasn't in the firing line when the scuffles started, and it didn't turn into one of those real stompings the clubs are capable of; it was more a political statement of support for the armed servicemen overseas.

It proved to be another watershed experience, not just for me, but also for the United States, and it consolidated the country's views of the bikie clubs.

So, now I had been involved in two remarkable events in outlaw motorcycle club history. Whether I liked it or not, I suppose I was being drawn towards the bikies, through both my studies of criminal psychology, my personal experiences and the circumstances in which I had grown up.

I was forever running into various club members around San Francisco, and even went on a few runs. A best mate of mine was in the Gypsy Jokers and I'd go to open nights at his club and others, where I'd get to know more about them. I was even the marriage celebrant at a bikie wedding, officiating at the marriage of my Gypsy Joker friend after I bought a lifetime preacher's licence in the Universal Life Church for a dollar. It's a legitimate religious order in the US. Many Hell's Angels and other club members are part of it. I actually joined for taxation purposes, as well as to have the ability to marry and bury friends. Being a member of the church also entitled me to visit prisoners to 'save their souls', which led me to become even more heavily involved in the clubs.

As part of my PhD in social psychology, I worked as a research psychologist in the prisons on a program called the Prisoners Union, a prisoners' rights advocacy group. The union ran the San Quentin Train, a van that took prisoners who had been released from the notorious San Quentin Prison to Berkeley or San Francisco. Many of them were hard cases who'd been inside for a long time, so the union also offered them short-term accommodation in a halfway house. My work involved looking at violence and family background. It meant I was forever coming across bikies in prison.

After finishing my PhD, I had three choices: I could go to Cambridge University in the UK to do some post-doctoral study, or to the University of Queensland in Australia for a tenured academic position, or I could stay in the United Sates where I had a post-doctoral fellowship at the Langley Porter Neuro-Psychiatric

Institute. This would have allowed me to continue my research but there were virtually no academic jobs available. I chose Australia.

I arrived in Australia in 1974, ready to begin my new career. However, I immediately encountered something I was not prepared for – Queensland. I'd arrived at the height of Premier Joh Bjelke Petersen's reign. From San Francisco, the centre of the counterculture, free love and dope-smoking, I had moved to an incredibly tight, right-wing regime that seemed to outlaw any sort of public thought, let alone the slightest whiff of counterculture. Man, that was tough.

I endured it for four years, before I decided to escape to Sydney and the NSW Bureau of Crime Statistics, where I was appointed senior research fellow. From there I moved to the University of Zambia, Africa, for three years, where I was to head the department of psychology, philosophy and religion. Well, that was the plan. They changed their minds about letting me teach religion on the first day on the job because they didn't want me filling students' heads with any crazy Quaker notions.

I had a great time there, but I eventually found myself back in Queensland, where I set up my own private practice as a Human Relations Consultant.

I then spent some time in Perth at Curtin University as Director of Community Psychology, before moving to Charles Sturt University in Bathurst. I finally settled at Monash University, where I held a number of roles including Director of the Centre for Police and Justice Studies. In 1999–2000 I spent 12 months in South Africa working for Technikon SA and the University of South Africa working as a visiting research fellow studying violence among street gangs. It was a great experience and led to my appointment as Dean at Monash University's new South African Arts Faculty. However, the campus was put on the back burner for a while due to low enrolments, so I decided to take a retirement package and am now growing trees on my farm and pursuing my professional and personal passion for the bikie clubs. I also act as a consultant to various groups in relation to the clubs, human rights and criminal justice issues.

My most recent professional involvement was as a consultant to a group called the Freedom Forum. They wanted my input on the implications of Western Australian legislation aimed at curbing the activities of local outlaw clubs.

The Australian motorcycle club scene kicked in just as I arrived in Australia, so I naturally kept an interested eye on what was happening. However, it wasn't until 1981 that the professional interest I maintain today actually developed.

That year I went to Bathurst for the annual Australian Motor Cycle Grand Prix, only to find myself in the midst of yet another watershed event for the motorcycle movement. Tension between the police and the bikers, which had been brewing for years, finally boiled over into a massive riot. Boy, was it a blue. Ninety police were injured and 100 arrests were made. It turns out there had been rioting between the bikers and the police at the races on and off since an incident in the late 1970s, when police had driven over a woman who was sleeping on the ground, scalping her. In an already highly charged atmosphere it proved to be the trigger that caused the situation to explode.

After my experiences at Bathurst I applied for a grant from the Australian Institute of Criminology to study why the riots were occurring and how the event could be run more peacefully. They jumped at my offer, even offering me more money than I'd asked for. Of course, I accepted.

My wife, Elizabeth, and, later into the project, a student of mine, Rudi Grassecker, joined me in looking at the problem. We were an interesting team. Elizabeth has a BA in psychology; however, more importantly for the study, she had served in the police force for three years. Rudi, on the other hand, is a dedicated biker with a thirst for understanding what's going on around him.

We interviewed and surveyed bikers, police and townsfolk. For three years we studied the event, sending people in to mingle with the bikers and to see what was going on. In that time we felt we'd worked out the problem. Our report to the Australian Criminology Research Council – which is comprised of the most senior bureaucrats of the justice system in all states and territories – indicated that it was the policing style that was the fundamental cause of the violence. Their heavy-handedness was like a red rag to a bull for the bikers. We suggested they back off a bit and consult with the bikers before the event to set a few rules that everyone could live with.

The report fell upon deaf ears in the NSW police force. Instead, they chose to take the opposite path, adopting a get-tough stance. This only served to produce the most violent clashes ever seen at Bathurst, with more than 525 charges laid after a massive riot broke out in 1985.

By this time, many bikers had grown sick of the violence and decided to boycott the following year's event. Crowds dropped to less than a quarter of previous years, eventually driving the Grand Prix out of Bathurst, and down to Phillip Island in Victoria.

In contrast, the Victorian Police took our recommendations on board, and Liz, Rudi and I were appointed as advisers to the Major Incident Planning Unit, which was designing the Phillip Island event.

Our plan worked fantastically. For instance, when the Coffin Cheaters flew their flag from the island's major hotel we were able to talk to all the clubs to make sure it wasn't a problem. A senior Hell's Angel member from the club's Nomad chapter was able to meet with the police and sort out the issue in a few minutes.

Without this level of consultation the action probably would have led to violence between the clubs. It was great for those first few years. We had cops and bikies riding together to make sure everyone kept the peace at the event. Both sides agreed it was one of the best-run biker events ever held. Unfortunately it went off the rails a few years after our involvement, because these sorts of initiatives need constant tweaking. However, by 2000 it was back on track when the police realised they had to get the clubs and bikers involved again.

My work with the Grand Prix opened up many doors to the clubs. In 1986 the Hell's Angels asked my team to monitor the police roadblocks at their annual Broadford concert, north of Melbourne.

The club has been staging the event since 1976, and attracts about 4000 people each year. At least 15 outlaw motorcycle clubs attend the 25 hectare campsite, where each club has its own camp.

After our Grand Prix work, the police welcomed our involvement. They regard the outlaw motorcycle clubs as a serious problem. The outlaw motorcycle clubs hold the reciprocal view of the police. To have someone in the middle liaising was perfect for both groups.

The major problem at Broadford was the Hell's Angels' view that the concert was a private event, meaning police were not permitted on site. The police disagreed, saying that as alcohol was being served at the venue they did have the right to enter. However, they had never actually entered the property, preferring to sit at the gates and monitor the comings and goings of the bikies.

Up to 50 extra police converged on the town for the event each December. I went along to the briefing for these police and was staggered to find the Australian Federal Police had sent a contingent of officers who were carrying photos of outlaw motorcycle club members wanted by police. It was believed they might show at the event.

On the Friday, the first day of the concert, the police set up a roadblock, complete with sniffer dogs, on the only sealed road leading from Broadford to the concert venue, 10 km from town. Every car, motorcycle and occasional pedestrian was stopped and thoroughly searched for drugs, weapons and even explosives. The roadblock was in place 24 hours a day for the duration of the concert.

We saw one or two arrests for possession of cannabis from the Friday morning to Sunday afternoon, but that was about it.

Apart from that, there was one moment of excitement, when at about 5 p.m. on the Friday, as cars and bikes slowly inched their way through the roadblock, one biker made a run for it. He was close to being searched when he suddenly gunned the bike and made a break for it. He shot off the road and headed for a small gap beside the roadblock. The cops got such a shock when they saw him roaring past towards the entrance to the concert ground. The rider didn't realise that waiting further down the road, around a corner, were two police cars. When he saw them, he did a U-turn and headed back toward the roadblock.

The police were ready for him this time round, and had posted a strong young male sergeant on the path where the biker had evaded the roadblock only minutes before. It was pretty tense as it was clear the biker meant to burst through the blockade again but was blocked by the police who were frantically waving their arms in the hope that they would stop him.

Meanwhile, the young sergeant had decided to take a different course of action. Next to the path lay some freshly chopped saplings. He grabbed one and held it across the path to stop the rider. The biker could still see some light beneath the now overhanging sapling, and decided to gun for the narrow passage at full throttle. As he reached the path around the roadblock the sergeant dropped the tree, smacking the bloke fair in the face at about 80 km/h. The cops jumped on him and searched him thoroughly before carting him off to hospital with a broken collarbone. He was clean, which puzzled the police. They later discovered he'd recently been released from a mental hospital to which, I hope, he was returned upon recovering from his injuries.

It was always a game of cat and mouse between the clubs and police at Broadford. It didn't take long for the bikies wanted by police to figure out a hassle-free way to get into the concert – turn up a day early. There were some more sophisticated strategies. One year in the mid-1990s, a helicopter was used to ferry a band onto the site. It also carried a few extra passengers who may have otherwise had trouble arriving in the conventional way.

Strangely enough, there was a second unpaved road that gave access to the concert site, but it meant a 60 km long and rough detour on an unsealed road. Enduring 60 km of bone-jarring gravel and ruts was considered a better option than facing 60 days in the slammer if someone was on the police wanted list. The police never patrolled it until the late 1980s, when they finally cottoned onto what was happening.

We completed our report, which went to both the police and the Hell's Angels. The gist of it was that the police were remarkably restrained in the light of the briefing they received. From the club's side, the bikers were well behaved so self-policing at the event was all that was required.

The police no longer roadblock the entry to Broadford, which seems a sensible strategy. They were getting poor returns for their efforts, and only really succeeded in pissing off the clubs and driving an unnecessary wedge between the bikers and the police.

Who knows, our work there may have played a part in the police realising that their efforts weren't working.

Another event we studied was the rally to celebrate the 100th Anniversary of Motorcycling, held at Phillip Island in 1986.

It was a real cock-up both by the police and the organisers, making the event a total farce. The police did the right thing and met the organisers before the event. The pair running it weren't club members, although one was an associate of the Hell's Angels. The balls-up started when the organisers told the cops there would be 70 000 people attending the three-day event. This figure was plucked from a place I can't even begin to imagine.

The organisers also allegedly told them there would be many outlaw clubs attending. On the basis of this, the police deemed the event a high threat priority and erected roadblocks at the entry to Phillip Island with the intention of finding wanted criminals. At the roadblock there was also an Environment Protection Authority unit to bust anyone with an unroadworthy vehicle (including dirty licence plates!). Soon enough, the word got out that getting to the event was like running a medieval gauntlet, forcing people to turn around in droves. Ultimately fewer than 3000 attended. There were almost more police than attendees. We did a report outlining exactly what we thought about the situation. The police and the Australian Institute of Criminology received it without comment.

Most of my research work is done not to find out how the clubs operate but to look at events such as Broadford where there is friction between the bikers and the police, in particular. The goal of the research has been to understand the clubs well enough to be able to develop a viable and appropriate form of policing them.

Naturally, over the years I've got to know the clubs pretty well, attending club nights and field days of clubs such as the Coffin Cheaters and Hell's Angels.

It takes a long time to get to know the clubs, and there is no one easy way to get to know them. Some clubs approach me because they've heard of my work advising other clubs. With others, I'll make the first move because they have some information I'm after. My relationship with all the clubs is initially built on what I can offer them. In many cases it has developed into my making friendships with the members. As I get to know them they become trusted sources of information.

I'll give you an example of how I work with the clubs. The Gypsy Jokers are a notoriously hard bunch to deal with. However, I've developed a pretty good relationship with them, based on what we can do for each other.

In early 2001 they found themselves in a fair bit of trouble in South Australia. Eight club members were arrested in connection with the assault of three special operations police at a coastal tourist town.

Seven roadblocks were set up, manned by 100 police to search the 100 or so club members as they travelled back to their clubhouse in Adelaide. About 90 motorcycles were issued with defect notices and eight members were arrested and charged with offences ranging from carrying offensive weapons to traffic breaches and possession of drugs. Another 50 police followed the bikies back to the clubhouse. The political heat then started; there were calls from the South Australian Opposition to bulldoze the clubhouse, and the local council came under fire for allowing the club to set up in the area. It was a heavy time indeed.

I made contact with the South Australian Gypsy Jokers' president who asked if I could look at how the club was being policed. I set about finding out what had actually happened when the assaults took place. I gathered police statements, spoke with club members, and interviewed independent witnesses.

I discovered that the club was considered to be a major criminal risk by the South Australian Police, with significant police resources being used to monitor the club. I was surprised to find these resources included a helicopter circling above the Gypsy Joker Adelaide Clubhouse during a party to celebrate the 24th anniversary of the club.

Yet, I also found the club posed a clear danger to the community because of the number of weapons it had in its possession. They were clearly ready for inter-club violence, and that's where the problem lay. The police thought that if the club would attack police officers, God knows what they'd do to poor Joe Blow on the street. However, what the police didn't realise was that the Gypsy Jokers actually regarded the police as a rival club – 'the big blue gang', as some clubs call them. The violence came from a belief the club was being challenged by this other group and that they needed to protect their honour.

I reached two conclusions from the episode. The first was that the Gypsy Jokers should expect more police harassment in South Australia and Western Australia. This was due to the political and social forces that drive police funding to target high profile cases like the bikie clubs.

The second conclusion was that the 'bad boy' publicity generated by the incidents would actually attract new members to the Gypsy Jokers, assuring the long-term survival of the club. I don't think the police wanted to hear that.

You might think that sounds a bit sympathetic towards the club, but I call it as I see it. I take the time to get the straight story because to be straight is so important to me. I'm not pushing the bikies' line, nor am I pushing the police line. I just want to get the real story so the clubs and the police can work things out harmoniously. I suppose I'm in the unique position of being able to do that.

Twice I've been asked to act as a go-between for clubs in their dealings with the police. This was something I never expected I'd be asked to do. In 1990, out of the blue, a large research organisation sent me an FBI report on outlaw motorbike clubs. The report pointed the finger at one particular club as being a major player in making and dealing amphetamines. It actually identified one of the three Australian chapters as being a major producer. Out of courtesy, and so I could get their reaction, I mailed the report to the chapter in question. About two weeks later I received a phone call from the club. They wanted to see me. This is the case I referred to at the start of this chapter. I arranged to meet the sergeant-at-arms, the bloke who would bust your balls, at the Queens Bridge Hotel in South Melbourne, opposite where Crown Casino now stands, at 11 a.m. one cool April Thursday.

We met in this sleazy hotel, and then he suddenly asked me to go for a drive with him.

'Let's go get a cup of coffee at Maccas,' he said. I knew something serious was happening, which could possibly end up with me being stomped.

We went outside and got into his car. It was a Ford. A loud Ford. In fact, it was a bloody loud Ford. I was very worried by this stage. I knew what I'd sent were sensitive documents, but they could only be of benefit to the club.

We set off, and he began to talk about things in general. The conversation then shifted to the documents. The gist of it was that he wanted to know if I had any more. The club was very keen to get its hands on them. I said I didn't, but I'd see what I could do. We arrived back at the hotel, me feeling very relieved. I was getting out of the car when he suddenly changed his mind and told me to get back in. I began to panic again. When the car was moving and at a sufficient noise level, he blurted it out.

'Look, I won't bullshit you. We've got a member with a problem up in [a country town] and the club's about to take care of him. We're going to expel him.'

The problem was amphetamines. He went to great lengths to explain that the club didn't sanction what the member was doing. They didn't like it because it was obviously drawing too much attention towards them.

'It's not a club thing, it's a person thing,' he said.

'If you can find a way to communicate it ...' There was no

need for him to expand. They were grassing the member. They'd kick him out, and then provide the details to me to pass on to the police. I didn't have a problem with what he was asking of me. However, it certainly wasn't the standard researcher role. Academia doesn't adequately prepare you for mysterious drives in loud cars with burly men discussing police deals.

If it helped bring peace and get some drugs off the street, then I figured it was OK. I asked for assurance that they weren't using this to scare the bloke into getting rid of his goods.

'No,' he said, 'I'll guarantee we will get the factory closed down.'

His word was good. I spoke to a contact in the police force. Both the club and the cops did their part. The member was expelled, and his place was raided soon after. He got 10–15 years.

I never heard another word from the club on the matter – until the next time.

About a year later the same club had another member involved in manufacturing amphetamines. What made this case a bit sticky was the small matter of a corrupt cop entwined in the deal.

The president and vice-president of the club came to my house and asked me to go for a drive. Again, it was a very loud car. They explained the deal, including the issue of the corrupt cop. They gave me names, the location of the amphetamines factory, and asked if I'd be willing to handle the matter for them. Obviously, with a corrupt cop involved they couldn't just bowl into the local cop shop and spill the beans. It had to be handled delicately, by someone with a contact in the police hierarchy and who could be trusted. I said I'd help. I initially intended to talk to a close contact in the taskforce that deals with amphetamines, but decided against it. Who was to know how wide the tentacles of corruption had spread?

I was fortunate enough to know an assistant commissioner,

known for his policy on cleaning up the force. He listened respectfully and moved on the matter quickly. Arrests were made, and prosecutions of all parties were successful. The club thanked me for my help, and said they owed me a favour, which I've never had to call on.

Some may have criticised me for becoming involved, but I was happy with what I had done. It was a legitimate research tool, known academically as action research, where a researcher becomes involved in their research area. The late Professor Daniel Wolf, the only other academic that I know of who did similar work with the clubs, did the same thing by riding with the Rebels in Canada to find out more about the clubs. The university ethics committee initially freaked out when I told them what had happened, but they eventually calmed down and agreed with my strategy.

Interestingly, a while after these incidents the clubhouse was raided by the police. They took their safe and eventually blew it open. Inside it was the FBI report I'd handed on to them. On its cover was scrawled: 'Art, have you seen this?' It wouldn't have taken too long for the police to work out who Art was. God knows what they thought. I never heard a word about it from either the police or the club, and I didn't suffer any repercussions in my work with the police.

That amused me, as it stands in stark contrast to the time I spoke out in the media in 1998 about the spate of shootings by the Victorian Police in the mid-1990s, in my role as head of the Police and Justice Studies Centre. I basically said the police were overreacting by pulling their guns too hastily and that they needed to retrain the force on firearm use.

The police freaked. They were so sensitive about the situation that I suffered severe repercussions. They shut off my access to grants and wrote to my boss indicating that unless I pulled my head in, they'd cut all contact with the university.

The Vice Chancellor asked me to explain what had happened, which I did, and that was the end of it from the uni's side of things. I eventually called the guy in charge of police training, bought him lunch and sorted out our differences over a bottle of red wine. I agreed to shut up, and he agreed not to shoot me (just joking), so the issue was resolved.

Being asked to act as the go-between by clubs was a major landmark event in my work. I was in a position where I could collect real information on what it was like to be a member. I got to know various club members and attended open houses and runs, which are basically organised group rides. I became interested in making some sort of definitive statement about bikers and club members. I was also developing a reputation as an authority on the clubs. I don't know whether the label of being Australia's foremost outlaw motorcycle club expert is technically correct, as I actually consider myself a distant outsider to the outlaw club scene.

Some of my best information comes from close insiders. The clubs all use many of the same strippers, bands, photographers, bike painters and tattooists, who act as conduits between clubs that may not be speaking to each other. These people are invaluable resources, as they know more than anyone – often more than the actual bikies.

As an academic making bikies the centre of my study, I'm a bit of a rarity. I'm now in a position that if I want to know something I know who to ask and who will be on the ground at that point to give me the true story. I've been criticised because I'm not part of a club. All I can say to my critics is that I've done the research thoroughly, checked my sources, and that I know the fundamentals of the clubs. I also have a fair idea whether something rings true or whether it's too outlandish.

I'm now in constant contact with Australian outlaw biker clubs, whether it's for research, through my work liaising between the clubs and the police, or personal friendships. I'm now known among the clubs as the Mad Professor.

I have strong friendships with club members from the Gypsy Jokers, Hell's Angels and Coffin Cheaters, including national executive members of many of the clubs. I'm also a friend of members of the God Squad and other clubs that hang around the fringes of the outlaw scene. It's important that my contacts know I appreciate them as a friend, not just as a source of information. I make a point of inviting each club member I meet to my house to meet my wife and kids. I make my place open to them if they ever feel the need to drop in for a chat, which they occasionally do.

There are some clubs I don't know as well. Some are secretive. Some are just plain hard to meet or get along with, such as the Bandidos and the Black Uhlans. The Bandidos' notoriety stems from their shoot-out with the Comancheros in the Sydney suburb of Milperra in 1984, in which seven people died. What became known as the Father's Day massacre is acknowledged as a turning point in Australian motorcycle club history, something all clubs have had to counter since. I'll look at this case in detail in chapter 10.

While I've dealt with a number of clubs, I find that I need to deal with each individually. Such is the politics of the clubs scene that I can't deal with a number of clubs at the same time, as each would regard me with great suspicion. Therefore, when I'm dealing with the Rebels, I don't have any contact with the Hell's Angels, and vice versa. It can make the process slow, but is necessary.

Respect is everything in dealing with the clubs. As long as you respect them, they'll respect you. That's why this book is a major issue for me. I don't want to abuse the trust of my friends. Many of the club members I associate with know of this book. I've discussed it freely with them. However, they may find some surprises among these pages. Likewise, I may find some surprises next time I see them. I hope not.

There is a feeling among some clubs and club members that I'm out to exploit them, to use them for my own personal goals. I'm sure those members will feel the same about this book. Yet, a lot of members are happy for the book to be written. They've offered to help, and in many cases I've gladly accepted. They've been invaluable in straightening out some of the details, such as the rules of clubs, and giving personal interviews. I haven't been asked to exclude or gloss over any issues, nor would I grant anyone that wish. That, in itself, is a major thing for the clubs. To reveal anything about the club usually means instant expulsion.

This book has been written by an observer who has nothing to gain from either the clubs or police. I hope it will demystify the 'demonic' bikie image and reveal the true picture of the outlaw motorcycle clubs – the 1 percenters.

CHAPTER TWO 1% OF HISTORY

We've all seen them. Scruffy, loud and mean, with strange images and words covering their clothes. Yet, not many people know them. In a world of few secrets, the outlaw motorcycle clubs are perhaps one of the last secret groups to exist in our society. Where did they come from and why are they like that?

Let's take a little history lesson.

The motorcycle roared into life in 1884, with the three-wheeled variety the first to hit the road, followed by its two-wheeled cousin, a motorised bicycle, the following year. To begin with, the motorised tricycle was the dominant motorcycle until people realised, to their surprise, that the two-wheelers were actually more stable and handled better.

It wasn't until 1901 that the modern form of what we commonly call the motorcycle made its debut, when a model with the engine located underneath the seat was introduced.

By 1903, a significant number of motorcycle producers had been set up, including Griffon, Buchet, Norton, Triumph, Sarolea and Adler. A new manufacturer also produced its first motorcycle that year, called the Silent Grey Fellow – a fantastic name for a motorcycle. With a single cylinder 25 cubic inch engine capable of three horsepower, it was the first product of a company that was to become synonymous with bikers and outlaw motorcycle clubs – Harley-Davidson.

The two-wheeler gained its bad reputation almost immediately. By 1909 motorcyclists already had the image of being non-conformists. A *Harper's Weekly* magazine article of the time headlined 'The rise of the motorcycle' stated:

> They [motorcyclists] would ride in city or open country with their mufflers cut out, or in numerous cases absolutely devoid of muffling attachments. In some instances it was the rider's desire for noise, or to bring attention to the fact that he owned a motorcycle; in other instances it was the owner's desire for more power; but, whichever the case, this offence in principle and in conjunction with that of unsuitable attire has done more to retard the advancement of motorcycling in general than all other arguments combined.

The popularity of the motorcycle boomed, due mainly to the role they played during World War I in carrying important dispatch information.

Many motorcycle manufacturers, such as Norton and Triumph, were actually subsidised during the war, so important were the motorcycles to the war effort. Some manufacturers were even funded by governments who saw the motorcycle as an important communication device. British Small Armaments, more commonly known as BSA, was one such company. Harley-Davidsons were also mass-produced for large US Defence Department contracts for use in the war.

From 1910 to 1929, the motorcycle industry boomed, due

mainly to young men discovering that there was nothing more exciting than getting on a motorcycle and riding as fast as possible.

With the onset of the Depression in 1929, motorcycle sales dropped dramatically in Western countries. However, this adversity actually created the first motorcycle clubs. These clubs, called Gypsy Motorcyclists in Australia, often consisted of unemployed men who rode their motorcycles across countries in a gypsy-like fashion, committing petty crimes and taking menial labouring jobs to subsidise their nomadic lifestyle. The clubs rejected mainstream society values, a trait they share with modern clubs.

> Well, they [motorcycle rallies] were sort of like they are today. But the people that you met in the towns and the country were much more friendly. I can remember breaking down on the way to a rally and me and my girlfriend were pushing the bike when a cocky [farmer] came by. We loaded the old Norton on his truck and took it to his place [to repair]. We ended up staying for three days with that bloke and his wife and I kept in contact with them for almost 20 years.

> The rallies themselves were not much different. Meeting lots of old friends, camping out in the outdoors; there were no helmet laws then so it was real freedom feeling on the road. Occasionally some larrikin would throw gelignite down a toilet or do some other ridiculous thing but we always repaired any damage and made sure we were welcome back.

> It wasn't unusual for police to come along and have a few drinks with us and there was no tension between the police and the clubs in those days. A lot of the clubs were just guys who were from the same workplace or same

neighbourhood who started riding together on the weekend and holidays. These are really the guys who became known as Gypsy riders. I guess I was one of them for 10 years until I got settled down.

Old Timer Gypsy Rider

By 1939, when World War II began, motorcycle production rose again, as it had during World War I. Small cars had taken over many of the duties performed by motorcycles in World War I, but motorcycles were still widely used for reconnaissance and communications.

In fact, this has led to a superstition among modern bikers that green Harley-Davidson motorcycles are bad luck. The most common military motorcycle carrying important papers on the front line in World War II was the Harley-Davidson, decked out in military green paint. The riders were sitting ducks, so many riders today consider riding a green Harley will bring a similar fate.

The war not only gave bikers some of their most endearing bikes, it also provided one of the most famous names in the biker world – Hell's Angels. The term 'Hell's Angels' has actually been around military circles since World War I when evidence suggests a fighter squadron coined the name. In the 1920s there is believed to have been an American Motorcycle Association-affiliated club in Detroit called the Hell's Angels. However, it has no association with the modern club.

In 1930 millionaire Howard Hughes produced a war movie called *Hell's Angels*, while in World War II there were several military groups called the Hell's Angels, including the US Air force 358th Bomber Squadron and a US navy torpedo squadron. The now infamous Hell's Angels death's head emblem wearing a leather helmet, which has been patented by the Hell's Angels Motorcycle Club, originally appeared on the fuselage of the 358th Bomber Squadron.

In the Korean War during the 1950s, the 188th Airborne Paratroopers also called themselves the Hell's Angels and used the same emblem. When some of the 358th Bomber Squadron servicemen left the force they started a motorcycle club, emblazoning the emblem on the backs of their riding jackets.

World War II also produced a significant grudge against Japanese bikes among the hardcore biker groups. Even today, the outlaw clubs often refer to Yamaha, Honda and Suzuki motorcycles as Jap crap. Harley-Davidson, seemingly keen to play on the military theme went so far as to name one of its models the Fat Boy, an amalgam of Fat Man and Little Boy, the names of the two atomic bombs dropped by the Allies on Japan in 1945.

After the war, the motorcycle's popularity soared, prompted by the thousands of motorcycles sold off by the armed services.

Unfortunately Australia missed out on many of the war bikes, due to an amazing bureaucratic decision. When the Americans left Australia after World War II they grabbed all the Harleys in armed service around Australia, dug big ditches and buried them. Hundreds of old knuckleheads were sent to an abrupt end in unmarked graves across the land. The equivalent bikes would fetch up to $30 000 apiece in mint condition today. Don't tell me there hasn't been a tear shed by the bikies when they hear that story. Because of this and Harley-Davidson's lack of interest in expanding into foreign markets after the war, there were very few Harleys in Australia prior to the 1970s.

In the US veterans returned home from the war, looking for ways to spend their final army pay and let off some steam after years of military discipline. Many joined the motorcycle clubs of the American Motorcycle Association. However, many soon grew restless of that scene. Veterans who'd buried their comrades in Europe and the Pacific Islands found the rallies and runs offered by the clubs just didn't offer the same excitement. James Jones sums it up well in his book *WWII*:

About the last thing to go was the sense of esprit. That was the hardest thing to let go of, because there was nothing in civilian life that could replace it ... the love and understanding of men for men in dangerous times, and places and situations. Just as there was nothing in civilian life that could replace the heavy daily excitement of danger. Families and other civilian types would never understand that sense of esprit any more than they would understand the excitement of danger.

Many realised they just didn't fit back into society. It was natural that many of them joined together to capture that esprit with equally restless mates.

After being discharged [from the army] I used my payout to buy a motorcycle. I guess I did it because a few of my old army mates had done the same and encouraged me to come on rides with them; but the bike was cheap and the girls liked the bikes. It's funny but the bikes seemed to be something that kept the friendships going that had been made in the army. I've still got the old BSA in the shed.
Ex-serviceman

You may have noticed I haven't referred to bikies so far in my short history piece. That's because the outlaw motorcycle clubs and the bikies didn't really exist at that point. It was on 4 July 1947 that the bikie was officially born.

On that day the town of Hollister in California, about 100 kilometres south-east of San Francisco and not far from Monterey, played host to an American Motorcycling Association event called the Gypsy Tour.

There were an estimated 2500 AMA-affiliated riders, plus another 500 riders from patch clubs. They were called this due to the patches the riders wore proclaiming their allegiance to their small club, which was not affiliated with the national motorcycling organisation.

There are claims that after police arrested a patch-club member for disorderly conduct up to 2000 motorcyclists went to the police station to demand his release. The club member is believed to have been a member of either the Pissed Off Bastards From Berdoo or the Booze Fighters, two renegade patch clubs at the day. According to media accounts, there was a full-scale riot. Other accounts simply suggested that the 'boys got a little too drunk last night'.

It was undeniably a pretty wild occasion. Motorcycles were ridden in bars and restaurants, bottles were thrown from multi-storey buildings, and bikers rode through red lights, urinated in public and generally caused mayhem. However, according to one interview in *Easyrider* magazine, the only serious crime problem was the attempted jail breakout of Wino Willie Faulkner, the arrested biker.

The media made it a landmark event for the outlaw motorcycle clubs. The *San Francisco Chronicle* of 7 July 1947 described the event as 'The 40 hours that shook Hollister'. As the town lies directly on the notorious San Andreas Fault, which is famous for its earthquakes, this was also a very bad pun.

Life magazine also picked up the story. The American Motorcycle Association attempted to distance itself from what had happened, blaming the unaffiliated clubs. Presumably to defend the good name of motorcyclists, the president of the AMA released a dramatic press statement describing the motorcycling community as being comprised of 99 per cent law abiding citizens and 1 per cent outlaws. This 1 per cent statement referred to the patch clubs.

The patch clubs responded to the rejection by embracing the 1 per cent tag. It was soon worn as a badge on the riding gear of at least one club. These clubs soon became known as the 1 percenters or, as it's now represented on patches, the 1%ers.

One patch club was so annoyed by what had happened it decided to change its name. On 17 March 1948, the Pissed Off Bastards From Berdoo became the Hell's Angels Motorcycle Club. There were many other renegade clubs across the United States at the time, including the Booze Fighters, however this first chapter of the Hell's Angels in San Bernardino, California, is regarded as the first outlaw motorcycle club to have a formal organisational structure and constitution with by-laws.

The fallout from Hollister meant the Hell's Angels were now placed firmly in the spotlight as being a renegade outlaw club. The notoriety served to attract new members; members who leant more to the outlaw aspect of the club. The ex-servicemen who had formed the Pissed Off Bastards From Berdoo in order to capture the feeling of camaraderie in the services suddenly found the focus of the club being changed by the new members.

A few years after Hollister came yet another milestone in the development of the modern outlaw clubs. The movie *The Wild One* was Hollywood's version of Hollister, and was pivotal in defining the image of outlaw clubs. Marlon Brando played the leader of the Black Rebels Motorcycle Club and Lee Marvin played the leader of the Beetles Motorcycle Club. Besides setting the fashion for motorcyclists for years to come, the movie inspired a new generation of young American rebels to gravitate to motorcycle clubs.

The Wild One also reinforced the image of outlaw motorcyclists in the United States as it moved into the 1950s McCarthy era, a time when the public was deeply suspicious of any threat to American life. Outside the US, *The Wild One* had an enormous social impact. Motorcyclists across the Western world saw the Hollywood version of an outlaw motorcycle club rebel – the attitude, the clothes, the disrespect for society, the power of the rebels, and the way they treated women. Almost instantly, motorcycle clubs in England, Australia, South Africa, New Zealand, Germany, Denmark and Italy were mimicking the dress and swagger of the characters in the film. The clubs in these countries were not outlaw clubs, as they didn't have the 1%er badges and office bearers, yet they all emulated the characters in the film. Interestingly, such was the impact of the film, the Beatles pop group took its name from one of the bikie clubs it portrayed.

The UK scene was also bustling along, with the Mods and Rockers on their scooters very much representing the outlaw alternative lifestyle. Their fashion and bad-boy attitude was the initial influence on the Australian bikie scene.

Yes, I was a rocker, a hippie, then a bikie.
Angels MC president

The earliest Australian bikies followed the rocker trend of wearing brass plates denoting club affiliation on their jackets, before the introduction of the US-style patches and colours. The fashion was also closely aligned with the Rockers. For instance, jeans were tucked inside the boots, as it was done on the streets of London.

These earliest bikies quickly adopted the rocker-style tattoos to demonstrate their rejection of the straight world. Even in the early 1960s there were long-haired bikers sporting tattoos of swastikas. They belonged to clubs such as the Angels (not the Hell's Angels). Australia has acquired an odd reputation as being a country with one of the highest rates of tattooing among the European-descendent countries. No one is quite sure why, but it still appears to be a strong phenomenon among young people today.

Australia's first US-style outlaw club is believed to be the Gladiators, which proclaimed itself a 1 percenter club in 1963. That was two years after the first documented US-based outlaw motorcycle club opened a chapter outside the US, the Auckland chapter of the Hell's Angels in New Zealand, formed on 1 July 1961. However, it wasn't until the late 1960s and early 1970s that the outlaw bikie clubs hit Australia in any significant numbers. The first Australian Hell's Angels chapters were officially inaugurated in Melbourne and Sydney on 23 August 1973.

Following the Vietnam War there was a mini-explosion in numbers of people joining outlaw motorcycle clubs across the world. Again, war was the catalyst. Unlike the hero's welcome given to servicemen after World War II, returning Vietnam War servicemen were shunned, due to widespread opposition to the war. The returning servicemen felt let down by the system and abandoned by politicians and leaders who had sent them to fight a war that, in retrospect, seemed meaningless. Many also felt they'd missed a lot of the counterculture of the '60s – the free love and drugs – while fighting an unpopular war. Joining a motorcycle club enabled many to catch up on that part of their lives.

CHAPTER THREE THE LURE OF THE BIKE

Why ride a motorcycle? Many a wife or mother has pondered that question as they've watched their otherwise sane husband or son jump on a 'death machine'. 'Why not?,' he might well yell over his shoulder if he could hear her thoughts, before opening the throttle for his blast of weekend freedom.

Motorcycle riders know the risks, how the odds are stacked against the bike, that they carry very little and can be cold, wet and cause the body to ache uncontrollably after hours in the saddle. But they love it.

Sure, they're economical, can accelerate like a rocket to incredible speeds and have fantastic manoeuvrability. But there's more – that nearly indescribable element that brings the motorcyclist back each time, a mixture of adrenalin and danger.

I must admit the bug really hasn't bitten me. Sure, I've ridden bikes and had my licence for many years, but it was my first experience on a bike that made me decide they weren't really for me. I owned a Vespa scooter for $2^{1}/_{2}$ years in my late teens, when a friend of mine scored an old BSA 500. Because I could work the gears and knew where the brakes were, he let me have a ride. He gave me a quick lesson on what was where and off I went. I gave the throttle a nudge on a straight bit of road and felt the adrenalin pumping. I gave it a little more, then a little more. Shit man, I was hanging on for life. I looked down at the speedo, which read 95 miles per hour! I almost freaked out and started to back off the throttle but I wanted to push it that little bit closer to the edge. Bingo – 100 miles per hour. I looked down. The road was screaming past only six inches from my feet and tears were flowing from my eyes. Still, I wanted to go faster. Then I thought to myself, shit man, this is crazy, and jammed on the brakes. I slowly turned the machine around and sedately rode back to my friend. I was shaking, completely pumped up and hyped for days afterwards. I knew I'd kill myself if I ever got a road motorcycle.

I've ridden bikes since, but my centre of gravity means I invariably fall off the bastards. My riding nowadays is restricted to an ag (agricultural) bike and a four-wheeler that I use on the few acres I own, and the occasional ride as a pillion passenger.

That first ride is pivotal in determining whether people will embrace bikes or not. Rarely is it an acquired taste. Either you love or you hate it based on that first experience. Equally important is how that first ride comes about. My surveys and interviews reveal that a staggering 80 per cent of motorcyclists have their first ride because they simply knew someone else who rode.

> Dad had a Harley. We lived on a farm and the only vehicle we had other than the Harley was a ute [light utility truck]. So we were always pestering Dad to take us for a ride. I guess that was pretty well how it started. After the first ride, that was it. I can remember getting the bike into neutral and riding it down from the barn straight into a shed without getting it running. It was a real buzz and Dad loved it too.
> **Ex-club rider**

Bikes were always there. Mum and Dad used to go on rallies and take my sister and I with them in their sidecar. Some of my earliest memories are of camping at a rally with the family. Riding was just natural in that way ... I mean, that is how you travelled.
Independent Rider

My cousin bought an old Trumpy [Triumph] and took me on a ride. It was fantastic. I knew straight away that I needed to get a bike.
Club rider

For many it was a bit like a drug, with that one ride enough to hook them forever.

The first ride, man, was stunning. To be in control of this incredibly responsive machine was stunning. [It was] ... loud, powerful, wind hitting you in the face, all the natural elements that you don't get in a car. It was that experience that committed me to bike-riding from then on.
Club rider

It was the sense of power and freedom. The bike had so much more raw power than any car I'd been in. The road was alive with sensations. You could hear, see and feel the road and the speed. Steering was done with your body, not like in cages [cars].
Lone rider

Many riders actually draw an analogy with drugs when they talk about their riding experiences.

I can remember times after riding hard for a few hours where my mates and I just couldn't move for a least a half an hour. We'd be shaking and not able to function because we'd been so close to the edge. A fellow biker would bring you a coffee and just leave you alone until you'd come down.

Hell's Angel

Somebody once said that the buzz from a hard ride is a hell of a lot better than sex or drugs. It may be because I'm older, but I'd have to agree. There's nothing like the buzz you get from riding. I'm too old now to push it to the limit; but you still get the buzz. Like when you're not fully concentrating coming into a corner and your front wheel goes onto the shoulder. The experience of coming so close to serious injury, if not death, makes you feel that much more alive.

Club rider

The one word I come across over and over in my discussions with riders is *freedom*. For many, it's why they adopt the biker lifestyle. The sense of freedom in riding like there's no tomorrow on the open road, the wind in your face, handling a powerful and responsive machine – you can't get that in a car. In fact, most bikers say their real personality comes out when they're on the bike. Part of that may come from the demands on the rider. It takes a hell of a lot of concentration to ride a bike fast. For many, that's where the freedom lies. They can shut out the stress of office politics, shit jobs and bad relationships.

If it's a good ride, there's nothing like it ... you and the machine become one. The machine requires your total commitment, even if you are a very cautious rider. If you

are a little more aggressive rider, like the younger ones, the concentration necessary becomes unbelievable. The smallest road hazard becomes a major threat to life. It gets to the point on the edge of a hard ride where there is a balance between taking your machine further and a fear of dying. Managing that space is real freedom.
Lone Wolf MC member

Freedom for many of the more committed riders comes from jumping on the bike any time and just riding. Sometimes they'll go for days, even weeks, perhaps ending up on the other side of the country. If a job or a relationship goes by the wayside, so be it. For them, that's the freedom of the bike.

It's like a complete different world. One time, when I was living in Brisbane, I told my then wife I was going to the shop for a packet of smokes. I didn't stop until I was in Sydney. I felt great but I knew I'd be in the shits with the ol' lady. Still, that's what it's like. You start riding and there is nothing but you and the machine and the road. Fuck-all matters other than that when you're into it.
Ex club rider

You can see it. When I stop in from a long ride at a mate's place, he's totally envious. It's the freedom to just get on the machine and go as far and as fast as I want. Invariably, his missus is giving me shitty looks because she knows what me telling him about the freedom of travel is doing to him.
Coffin Cheater

There's no such thing as your typical biker. Everyone is different, with each having their own reasons for getting into bikes. However, you can generally divide bikers into a number of categories.

CHOOK CHASERS

I never cease to be amazed by Australians' need to give slang names to everything. They'll call tomato sauce 'dead horse' or a red-headed mate 'blue'. Mention 'Reg Grundies' and everyone knows you're talking about underwear. So it is in the motorcycle community. Chook chasers are off-road bikes. The name comes from their evolution as bikes used by farmers. The term now covers all off-road bikes, such as trail or scramble race bikes. Basically, anything with a knobbly tyre for off-road riding is a chook chaser.

The Australian biker community actually has strong rural roots, with many young boys learning to ride on a chook chaser. In the United States and Europe, most first-time riding experiences are on scooters in town, with their small wheels and low power.

Riding a chook chaser doesn't, technically, make someone a biker. However, many bikers not only learn to ride on these machines, but keep a chook chaser in the back shed for a blast now and then.

COMMUTERS

Commuters ride their motorcycles to and from work almost exclusively. For them, the bike is simply a means of transport, so they don't engage in biker events or politics. Until recently, commuters were likely to ride Japanese-made machines – 'rice burners' or 'Jap crap' – as they were cheap and reliable. However, the rise of the 'yuppie commuter', with more money in their pocket, has changed that. Now, commuters often ride Harley-Davidsons, Ducatis and BMWs. Commuters are also increasingly riding a new generation of powerful scooters produced by companies such as Motoguzzi. These are a hybrid of the motorcycle and the old-fashioned scooter. Even so, these new scooters are not regarded as motorcycles because they still have a low power-to-weight ratio and step-through seating.

TOURERS

Tourers are into riding for the social side of motorcycling. They ride long distances for fun, usually as part of a club, such as the Triumph Club of Victoria. In this case, club members would own a Triumph motorcycle and go on scheduled rides, or runs, over weekends. Tourers generally have the highest income and most prestigious occupations of all the motorcycling groups. Many tourers are high status professionals such as politicians and businessmen.

Tourers use their motorcycles for fun, yet are attracted to the camaraderie of the bike through events such as rallies. Tourers who are not part of a formal club will usually have friends with whom they ride. The tourer is at the fringes of the Australian biker subculture. They don't have an identity as a biker, even though their motorcycle and biking associates are important elements in their lives.

BIKERS

The previous groups are single-use categories. That is, they use the bikes for one primary activity, be it commuting, touring or churning up some dirt. Bikers use their motorcycles for all these and more. Their main interest in life is motorcycles and motorcycling. They read the biker magazines, attend rallies, ride on runs, and attend meetings on issues such as helmet reform laws. It's a gradual process, with individuals being drawn more and more towards the biker lifestyle until it becomes something others define that person by. The biker wears the clothes of the bike world – the emblems and paraphernalia on their riding gear that identify them as being apart from mainstream society. They'll generally have a customised bike; this also separates them from the weekend rider. Bikers generally distrust the police, who they believe take particular pleasure in booking motorcyclists for traffic infringements that other road users get away with.

However, it's the notion of freedom that ultimately defines the biker and separates biker culture from the rest of society. It's not uncommon for a biker to meet a fellow biker in a pub or rally and spend two weeks riding and touring together. Bikers generally believe conventional society is jealous of their freedom to just take off. This jealousy, they believe, causes the discrimination and animosity of the dominant car culture.

CLUB RIDERS

While tourers are often members of clubs, they're not bikers. Their primary identity is not that of a biker. Club riders hold those biker values. The riders in this category are not classed as outlaw motorcycle club members. Clubs are usually loose collections of bikers who meet for biker events. The Valley and Districts Motorcycle Club in the Latrobe Valley region of Victoria was a good example. Until it disbanded in 1997 it had about 30 members, was affiliated with the Motorcycle Riders Association of Australia, had a political agenda to promote motorcycling and enjoyed a good party. It had no gender, age or bike restrictions for members. Club members didn't wear patches. The MRA affiliation meant it wasn't an outlaw motorcycle club. Most motorcycle clubs and club riders fall into this category. The motorcycles ridden by club riders are often stock bikes, rarely modified into the fully-fledged choppers of the outlaw clubs. The Christian motorcycle clubs and returned services motorcycle clubs belong in this category, although both hang around the fringes of the outlaw clubs.

LONE RIDERS

This is where we enter the world of the outlaw biker. Lone riders are bikers who adopt the values of the biker culture but choose not to ride with a club. They're sometimes referred to as loners, lone wolves or free riders. Often, they'll ride with a few select 'road hogs' who are friends or acquaintances made on the road. The image of the lone rider biker is that of the American cowboy – independent, tough and free. Being on their own, they usually have a pretty good knowledge of how a motorcycle is put together. The bike will always be a Harley-Davidson, and likely to be heavily modified. The modification is a statement of the committed biker's identity. The lone rider looks like an outlaw motorcycle club member, attracting the sort of police heat club members receive.

As lone riders adopt the values of the outlaw motorcycle clubs they often mix with outlaw motorcycle club members. However, they're not actually privy to outlaw motorcycle clubs' inner workings nor do they enjoy any privileges of membership.

OUTLAW MOTORCYCLE CLUBS

Finally, there are the outlaw motorcycle clubs. These are what are known in Australia, New Zealand, the UK, South Africa and parts of Europe as bikies. In North America and Europe they are called bikers. A simple way to look at it is that an outlaw biker is a bikie.

These clubs are characterised by having a constitution, a rigid organisational structure and heavy levels of commitment to ensure their survival. They exist in their own world, cut off from mainstream society through a rigid system of rules and inherent belief system. Because of this, I've always considered them a subculture, and my studies reflect this.

The most obvious outside sign of the outlaw motorcycle clubs is the patches worn on their riding leathers. Members wear their patches proudly as a sign to society – *I'm a bikie. Don't fuck with me.*

For the clubs, there's nothing more sacred than the club colours or patches, for they are the symbols of the clubs. Respect for the colours both within the club and from other clubs is paramount.

The patches include the club name, logo, chapter location, and any other badge for service to the club. Importantly, for some clubs it also includes the 1% badge.

While there's no requirement to actually wear the 1% patch to be considered a 1% club, there's plenty of controversy among the clubs over who deserves to wear it. The Hell's Angels claim it's the only club that can wear the 1% patch, as it was the first. However, most of the 1% clubs wear it, including the Gypsy Jokers, Bandidos, Rebels, Odin's Warriors, Descendants, and Coffin Cheaters.

The other distinctive feature of an outlaw club is its territory, or turf. Territory is simply the geographical and social area in which a club can display its patches exclusively. That's very important to a club, to know it has an area in which it can do what it wants without being hassled by other clubs. That's why there are such fierce wars to restrict entry and passage of other clubs wearing patches.

The biker who goes on to join an outlaw motorcycle club is a pretty unique man (membership to these clubs is almost exclusively male). He must value the camaraderie of a close knit group of men, be able to navigate club politics, be willing to cope with extreme police harassment and have a family structure that allows him to be absent from the home for many nights each week. He must also be at least tolerant of crime and criminal activities. As we'll discover, it's not easy being a bikie.

CHAPTER FOUR FROM BIKER TO BIKIE

Robbo was a pretty normal kid, a bit of a little man from the moment he could walk. You know, masculine, hanging around with dad and playing with cars and trucks. Dad and Mum were good Catholic parents, even if his father was a bit slack when it came to church. Dad also liked a drink. When he drank he got violent, often dishing out beatings to Robbo and his two brothers. It'd be fair to say those beatings shaped Robbo's attitude towards authority as he grew up.

He was gregarious and social by the time he hit school. Yet, he knew school wasn't for him. It wasn't as though Robbo was unintelligent, just that he considered the street a better classroom.

At school and on the streets Robbo didn't back away from a scrap, even if the odds were against him. This attitude, that he could take on anyone, made him a bit of a hard case even before he'd entered his teen years. He was uncompromising, seeing the world in a competitive sense with only winners and losers. Others thought he was a bully. Yet in his mind he never picked a fight. 'Trouble seemed to come my way.'

Robbo liked to do risky things, and was regarded by his mates as a bit of a daredevil. He liked the thrill of living at the edge of injury and danger, forever jumping and skidding about on his bicycle. He felt more alive when he was on his bike, fully concentrating on performing feats his mates wouldn't dare attempt.

At the age of 12 a significant event occurred. Together with his 15-year-old brother, the boys succeeded in beating up their father after another savage attempt to discipline the pair. The old man never bothered the boys much again.

By the time he was 14 Robbo had left school and was working part-time jobs, all the time dreaming of getting his driver's licence and a car. It was all he could think about – when he wasn't thinking of girls. At 15, while furiously saving for a car, he discovered to his delight that he could get a motor scooter licence within six months. It was the answer to his prayers. While the scooter didn't have the class of a Ford or Holden, it'd get him around for the time being and provide him with the independence he so desperately craved. On a promise and some cash, he bought a second-hand scooter.

It was love at first ride. It couldn't do the stunts of his bicycle but it was able to do much more – it introduced him to the open road, where he could feel the wind in his face, albeit a gentle breeze even at the scooter's top speed. Robbo couldn't understand why only a few of his mates bought scooters while they waited to get their car licence.

At 16 he was accepted as an apprentice paint-sprayer, which gave the car-saving plan a boost. He soon bought an old Ford, which he lovingly restored and then 'hotted-up'. Working on cars was more a social occasion for Robbo and his mates. There was always plenty of music and grog on hand while they tinkered away.

While he and his mates and brothers were heavily into cars, Robbo felt a strong affinity to motorcycles. His friends liked riding yet they didn't have the desire to ride that he had. The pull was so strong that at the age of 19 he bought a 250cc Kawasaki motorcycle so he could get his full licence. Even this little 250 provided unbelievably better performance and delivered more thrills than his car. Sure, the big V8 sounded great but the Kawasaki would put the car to shame from a standing start. Then there was the agility and the fact that traffic was virtually never a problem on a bike because you could blast away from the cars at the lights.

Robbo also found the people who rode the bikes more interesting than his rev-head mates. While his mates were passionate about their machines, it didn't extend to embracing their passion as a way of life, as Robbo's fellow bike riders did.

In 1976, when Robbo was 21, he and a friend rode from Melbourne to the Bathurst motorcycle races. The ride was fantastic. By that stage, Robbo had upgraded to a 750cc bike, which would blow any car 'into the weeds'. Robbo only had to squeeze the throttle on the open roads and he'd easily hit 200 km/h. At this speed the adrenaline high was unbelievable. He'd become cocooned into a world where there was only the rider and the machine, where the slightest error meant instant pain.

The races themselves meant very little to Robbo. In fact, at the end of the weekend he had no idea who had won the main race. It was really about partying. The highlight for him was the almost annual fight with police. His strict father and the constant trouble he had found himself in at school had given Robbo a strong dislike for authority, so watching the bikies having a punch up with the coppers was his idea of fun.

Over that weekend he met many characters, some of whom became an integral part of his life as a biker. However, the ones he didn't meet, that he had been warned to stay well clear of by his friends, were the blokes in the small groups referred to as the 'outlaw clubs'. They kept to themselves and were pretty unremarkable. However, they appeared to have a fair bit of status among the other bikers, almost as if they were an elite crowd.

The races were a dream come true for Robbo. Those around him got up to the sort of daredevil stuff he loved as a kid. What could possibly beat dragging a car bonnet around behind a motorcycle at breakneck speed while someone stood on it, holding on for their lives? Or seeing how many people could fit on a motorcycle while passing a marijuana joint around? The three days of partying opened his eyes to a new world – the world of the biker. On the ride home he actually realised what had happened to him that weekend. He'd arrived at Bathurst as someone who liked to ride bikes; he'd left as a biker.

It wasn't something he announced when he got home. It was more subtle. Plus, he knew his mates would think he had gone over the top if he ever referred to himself as a biker.

Robbo began to use his bike more and more, attending rallies and making more friends in the biker world. His appearance began to change. He let his hair grow longer, wore his riding gear to venues where he'd previously dressed 'straight', got some rings and a tattoo. His behaviour changed. He had always been a bit of a lad, but dressed as he was these days, he felt he had a licence to be even more outlandish, shocking his friends from the straight world.

However, he still wasn't completely submerged in the bike world. He still had his mates who didn't ride bikes. He was a qualified spray painter with a steady job. He was also involved in a relatively stable relationship with a girl from a fairly conservative family. He was a biker but he was also still part of mainstream society.

In 1980, at the age of 25, Robbo was riding his motorcycle on a freeway in the early hours of the morning when, for no apparent reason, a car approached him from behind, just centimetres from his rear plates. Robbo hit the throttle and put what seemed a kilometre between him and the car in a few seconds. However, the car slowly edged up, signalling to pass him. When the car was level with Robbo's rear wheel, it swerved into Robbo's lane. Robbo pulled the bike violently to avoid the car and lost control. The bike went down. He rolled along the road, sustaining only a few bumps and bruises. The bike, however, was unrideable. Even if he wanted to chase the car, he couldn't. The front mudguard was twisted, and the rear wheel buckled out of shape. When he reported what had happened to the police they gave every impression of not caring. It proved to be a watershed event for Robbo. He realised that all the stories he had heard about car drivers and straight society discriminating against bikers were true.

Like many others before him, Robbo decided the best defence was to ride with others. He couldn't trust car drivers and cops. He also decided to become the most fearsome-looking motorcycle rider possible so car drivers wouldn't dare run him off the road. Likewise, the police would have to be bloody serious to stop him. He started to dress and look even more unconventional than he had prior to the crash.

He ditched the Japanese bike he'd been riding and replaced it with a Harley-Davidson, a loud fierce machine that reflected his new outlook on the world.

He also found himself drawn more and more into hanging out with a local outlaw club, Satan's Cavalry, which contained some of the fiercest looking bikies in Melbourne. However, he chose not to become a member when the club was patched over by the Coffin Cheaters. His values began to change from biking as a lifestyle choice within straight society to living life as a bikie and rejecting and simply not caring about the straight world. It was at that point that Robbo stepped into the world of the 1 percenters. He changed from being a biker to a bikie.

If you look at Robbo's life it seems he was always destined to become a bikie. Former US Hell's Angels president Sonny Barger once defined a Hell's Angel as:

> ... being born and not made ... He is the kid in the classroom that doesn't quite fit in. He is the thrill seeker

who tries to do tricks and jumps with his bike. He is often in fights, even though he doesn't look for them.

After years of research, I'd have to agree with him. Here are some of the responses from my discussions.

I can't say exactly when I knew I was different. I know my mother says that I always was. A bit rougher ... loved to try the dangerous things ... you know, swimming upstream. I had my share of friends and that but I gotta say that I knew I was different, didn't really fit in, you know. Being so big didn't help either ... the army was good but I hated all the orders. I worked as a car mechanic for years and couldn't take the boss. Finding the club was the best thing that ever happened to me.
Hell's Angel

From the start, man. From the start ... I can't remember feeling like I fitted in to the citizens' scene. I tried though. It just seemed like I had this voice in the back of my head saying 'this is bullshit' about the whole fucking school thing. But even before that, I could find a few good mates who had a similar view to me, and we got into all kinds of shit.
Bandido

Look. I did very well in school and university. I hold down a good job as a [professional]. I've got a great marriage and good kids. I'm making it in the straight world OK. It's just that I felt the need to have a more enriched life than what's offered by the straight world. That's the lure of the club.
Rebel

Very few bikers become outlaw club members. The 1% tag given to the renegades in the Hollister incident more than 50 years ago still holds. If anything, it'd be significantly less, there being only about 50 000 outlaw motorcycle club members worldwide, with about 3000 to 4000 in Australia. These are rough estimates, as the figures given by the clubs and the police fluctuate wildly. The police overestimate the numbers to make it seem there are bikies everywhere, while the bikies play down the numbers to back up their argument that they are no threat to society. The truth is somewhere in the middle.

A biker cannot simply become a bikie. He must take the steps from being a social rider to a committed biker, then make the move to outlaw club member.

Those who become outlaw club members do so for many reasons. One of them is image. When talk turns to bikes and bikies, who hasn't had the image of a Hell's Angel or a Coffin Cheater come to mind? The rugged renegade taking on the law at any chance, thumbing his nose at society. The clubs are happy for this image to be fostered, even if it may be a little askew of reality. I mean, you can't go around being nasty 24 hours a day.

For many bikies the menacing image gives them some protection, whether real or perceived. As in Robbo's case, bikies and bikers strongly believe car drivers are out to harm them. They're likely to grab anything that affords them some protection.

It's easy to see where the persecuted minority feeling comes from. In Australia, motorcycles account for about 2 per cent of all vehicle registrations yet motorcycles account for 7 per cent of all road fatalities. The proportion of motorcycle accidents caused by cars is consistently 60 per cent. By far the most common excuse by the car driver at fault is 'I didn't see him.' Bikers get pretty sick of this one because they can clearly see bikes when they're driving cars. Couple that with a strong feeling that punishment meted out to car drivers responsible for accidents with bikers is weak and you have the ingredients for a major grievance across all sectors of the biker community.

Many seasoned riders have tales of cars intentionally forcing their bike off the road.

> I was riding my Harley along the Hume Highway one night, cruising at 110 [kilometres per hour] when two yobbos in a red Ford Falcon pulled up alongside me. They were looking at me and I looked back at them. All of a sudden, they simply pulled over straight into my lane at a bend. I had no choice but to go onto the shoulder of the road. I don't know how long I kept the bike up, but I did for some time. Then I lost it. I went sliding straight along the shoulder, thank God. I stopped and tried to collect myself as the car sped off. I was too shaky to do anything.
> **Club rider**

The biker magazines are full of similar stories. In many cases the feeling of being in a minority has forced riders to ride in groups, generating the brotherhood of the clubs. It also prompts many to take on a heavier, more road warrior look to scare car drivers.

> I was getting pissed off. Within two months I had two near misses with car drivers who didn't see me and an experience where a car just seemed to run up my rear in an attempt to literally kill me. For a while, I was thinking about giving up riding. Then I got back on the bike for a short run and knew that I couldn't do that. So I decided to only run in a group. But that wasn't really practical either. My solution was to start to look heavy. Like if you fucked with me, you were in the shits. I still carry a

spanner on my bike that I can throw through a car driver's window if one tries to run me off the road again. But that is why I dress the way I do. The tats, earrings, leathers and colours are all saying 'You fuck with me and you are in deep shit'.
Lone rider

If the antics of certain car drivers don't turn a person away from a biker lifestyle, there's another road hazard that might – the police. While outlaw motorcycle clubs are most likely to be subject to police scrutiny or harassment, the average biker also feels targeted by police. It's particularly true of bikers who have modified or chopped their machines.

There I was getting booked for going 113 in a 110 [kilometre] zone. The Volvos and Mercedes were ripping by us going well in excess of what I was doing. In fact, the cop pulled me over as a vehicle was overtaking me. I then spent the next hour being thoroughly searched and checked, as well as being asked questions about my residence, affiliations, who I knew in the bike scene. I don't know what it is, but the cops are just like that, man.
Lone rider

Police hassles seem to be concentrated on the committed Harley-Davidson bikers although the rice burners describe similar problems in the biker magazines. As bikers graduate from riding the first scooter or chook chaser, to a rice burner, then a Harley-Davidson and finally a modified or chopped Harley, they find the police become an increasingly larger problem. Most outlaw motorcycle club members find that two to three hours of police interrogation is not unusual when the heat is on. Such was the case with the Gypsy Jokers in South Australia in early 2001 when they tackled the seven road blocks manned by 100 police as they travelled to their clubhouse in Adelaide.

The bikers believe police are more likely to protect car drivers over bike riders. As Daniel Wolf wrote:

> A biker who has been victimised easily develops a hostile attitude towards other 'assholes who drive cages'... In five years I was run off the road three times. I managed to catch up to the cars twice. The second time, the driver pulled alongside a police car when he realised I was following him. The police listened to his version of events, so I was searched and warned, while he chuckled and drove off.

It's not easy becoming an outlaw motorcycle club member. Most clubs have a long, arduous process of admission and members must adhere to strict rules to maintain their membership. To become an outlaw motorcyclist can require years of scrutiny by fellow club members, impeccable credentials as a biker and, in certain circumstances, even a requirement to commit an illegal act.

The first criterion in becoming an outlaw motorcycle club member is to become associated with a biking lifestyle. The person must then develop into what the American bikers call a 'righteous biker' – committed to the biker lifestyle.

Once a biker is deemed by outlaw motorcycle club members to be a committed biker he's then invited to 'hang around' with the club as a friend of the club or an associate. He's not a member so he's not allowed to vote, attend club meetings or become involved in club business. He is, however, invited to parties at the clubhouse and to rides or runs where initiations and other club business are not on the agenda. They can hang around only if the entire club agrees. If a club member rejects the presence of a non-club member at a club function they must leave immediately.

Hanging around the club is always by invitation only. The member who invites an outsider to a function or even sits with them at a hotel for a drink is responsible for the behaviour of the non-club member.

Usually associates want to become members, so hanging around with the club is a time when friendships between the club and prospective members are forged. This is vital as the associate must be nominated by a full member in order to move onto the next stage – that of the nominee.

However, some associates don't want to join the clubs. Take Terry, for example. He's been in and around the outlaw motorcycle club scene since the 1970s. He has a lot of mates in the club, but has never applied to become a member, nor is he privy to club business. Equally, the editor of one of Australia's top motorcycle magazines is a former member of the Hell's Angels and has maintained good contacts and friends within the club even after quitting it. He's a friend of the club, but a very unusual one, as he'd be one of the relatively few ex-members still accepted by the club after departing.

An associate who wants to join a club would be expected to attend as many functions open to them as possible, to prove they were fair dinkum. Enthusiasm is one of the key elements clubs look for in associates. It is, however, only one of several qualities. Loyalty, masculinity, discipline, independence and courage are the principles of brotherhood. If someone doesn't demonstrate these qualities they're not going to be admitted. If they do, they'll be invited to apply and will be sponsored by a full member.

I know of one bloke who was very keen on joining the Satan's Cavalry. While JD had good biker credentials, he wasn't well respected by everyone in the club. He was the kind of guy you either liked or hated. Certain members of the Satan's Cavalry were pretty ambivalent about him, to say the least. Nevertheless, JD didn't pick up on the fact he should kick back and let others warm to his courage, bravado and up-front ways, rather than be threatened by him. Consequently, one night he got very upset after a lengthy drinking session at the clubhouse. He'd been hanging around for a while and thought he'd done enough to warrant an invitation to join the club. So he stood up and put the question outright to the club. 'Let me in,' he demanded, 'Tiny [not his real name] has agreed to be my sponsor, so I want to be a nominee.'

If he had any hope of joining it disappeared at that moment. The outburst was seen as a sign of disrespect and proof that he wasn't a suitable candidate. Not long after, when he finally realised membership wasn't going to be offered to him, he judiciously decided to leave and never return.

However, this is a rare case. Very few of those invited to join get knocked back. The process of slow assimilation into the club means that any person who isn't likely to make the grade simply won't be asked to apply nor will they be able to find a sponsor. Of those who do get knocked back there's a certain amount of shame associated with the rejection. I've found they're usually unwilling to talk about their experiences. The repercussions for the club member who sponsors someone who is knocked back are also severe. Rejecting someone who's gone through the process of applying is, in a sense, a rejection of the sponsor, and even the sponsor's faction of the club.

No one really knows what proportion of people invited to befriend an outlaw motorcycle club actually end up joining the club. It would vary widely between the clubs. The more established, larger clubs would have many friends who'd never be considered as membership prospects or offer themselves for club membership, while smaller clubs looking to expand would be more likely to offer an invitation.

If a friend of the club is acceptable to the majority of members and wishes to become a member, he moves to the next stage. The

Hell's Angels call this the prospect stage, while most other clubs call it the nominee stage. An applicant must present an argument, if asked to do so, on why he'd make a good member. The club must approve his application with a unanimous vote. For major clubs with a number of chapters the application goes to the full membership. The vote in favour has to be at least 51 per cent before he becomes a nominee.

The nominee stage is a time to test the prospective member. It's different from the associate stage when the emphasis is mainly social. It's now a case of the nominee proving he can be a worthy member of the club. He must demonstrate that he's willing to be part of a brotherhood and be disciplined enough to follow club orders. Nominees are usually required to perform mundane tasks to prove their commitment. If the nominee doesn't perform well or refuses a request, he's unlikely to receive the vote for full membership.

Sometimes the club will set a serious test to see how the nominee reacts. The now defunct Satan's Cavalry used to force nominees into a situation to see how they would react when called on to defend a fellow member. It usually involved a full member taking the nominee out drinking. The member would start a fight and intentionally start to lose. If the nominee jumped in and helped his mate, he passed the test. If he tried to resolve the dispute peacefully, or worse still, failed to get involved, he'd be kicked out of the club. He'd probably also receive a thumping into the bargain.

The set-up fight is disappearing as a testing tactic because it put too much heat onto the clubs to pick fights in pubs.

Another test is to see if a nominee will break the club rules. It's been known for clubs to set up prospective members by tempting them to violate club rules such as injecting speed or heroin or stealing from a club member. If he succumbs to temptation he's out. The nominee soon learns the club rules are sacrosanct.

Amid the consideration of character there's a more practical requirement of a prospective member – he must have a motorcycle or be in the process of getting one. Needless to say, they must be able to ride the bloody thing as well. No Jap crap is allowed. The motorcycle must be a Harley-Davidson. The major clubs stipulate the bike must be modified, although there is a trend towards letting stock Harleys into the clubs.

It used to be a relatively informal process to become a nominee, a stage that lasted about three months. After gaining public enemy status, the nominee period lengthened to up to four years, and the process to become a full member became much tougher. To weed out police infiltrators, some clubs in the US now require a nominee to commit a crime to gain membership. Luckily, it hasn't got to that stage in Australia.

Law enforcement agencies admit it's become almost impossible to send undercover police into the clubs with such odious and lengthy entry requirements. The bigger clubs will also conduct a thorough background check of each nominee, sometimes by a private investigator. I know at least one Australian club that has used voice stress testers when interviewing nominees. The checks are non-negotiable hurdles for the nominee. If he fails a background check or stress test, or any other information is brought to the club's attention, the application is immediately rejected.

A nominee is permitted to wear the bottom rocker on the back of his riding coat, normally a sleeveless denim or leather vest. This bottom rocker reveals the club name and the location of his chapter. It would say Rebels MC, Sydney, Australia; Gypsy Jokers MC, San Francisco, California; Hell's Angels MC, South Africa.

On the front of the jacket will be a patch to indicate that the member is a nominee or prospect, depending on the club.

However, the patches on the jacket are not complete. Only with full membership does one receive the full colours, which includes the club logo, such as the Hell's Angels winged death's head or the Bandidos' fat bandito wearing an oversize sombrero and brandishing weapons. The colours remain the property of the club, so members generally pay a nominal sum for their use. The full member is also permitted to wear the 1% patch, if the club wears that patch.

Receiving the bottom rocker means the nominee must become submerged in club politics. They must participate in weekly general meetings, or 'church', pay dues and attend any event they're told to. To hear a burly bikie talking about going to church is a bit incongruous. However, it's a common term for the weekly meeting, usually held on Wednesday evening. It has no religious meaning, merely that it is a weekly observance everyone is required to attend.

The nominee has limited membership privileges, but is not yet allowed to vote, hold office, be privy to committee meetings, or earn certain badges.

Part of the commitment required of the nominee is to attend runs. For clubs that require a unanimous vote of members to admit a new member, runs and meets are extremely important events for members of other chapters to meet the nominee.

The nominee process varies from club to club. Some clubs, such as the Hell's Angels and the Gypsy Jokers, require members to have a full-on commitment to their lifestyle. These clubs go to great lengths to ensure a nominee is made of the 'right stuff' before they hold a final vote of the national governing body. The vote must be unanimous before the nominee can become a full member. Other clubs may require the vote of the state membership. Smaller clubs may only require the vote of the chapter. The nominee must get more than half the vote to achieve full membership. Anything less, and the application is immediately terminated. The rejected nominee can try again in about six months, either with the same chapter, or with another chapter of the club.

In some of the major clubs the nominee is not granted full membership until they have completed a probationary period as well. For instance, the Bandidos have a 12-month probationary period. Though able to almost fully participate in the club, the probationary member's standing means his votes at club meetings and contributions to decision-making are regarded as less important or meaningful than full members.

Another piece of the membership jigsaw puzzle is the tattoo. The full member is permitted to have the club logo and motto tattooed on their body – for example, 'God forgives; Outlaws don't' for the Outlaws, or 'We are the people that our parents warned us about' for the Bandidos.

The tattoo would usually include the date they were admitted. Like the colours, the tattoo remains the property of the club. This can cause a problem when a member leaves. Three things can happen. If the member leaves on good terms he can have the exit date inserted and continue to bear the logo. If things are not so amiable the club will usually demand it be covered with another tattoo. If the split is downright ugly, the club can tell the ex-member it wants the tattoo removed – now! There has been the rare case of a tattoo being violently removed. I'll spare you the details.

In most clubs, a full member is expected to acquire a club tattoo within a year of joining the club.

The final step in the admission process is the initiation ceremony. All outlaw clubs have an initiation rite or ceremony. It's the degree of extremes and the form of the rites that are hotly debated. One US police training document titled *An Inside Look at Outlaw Motorcycle Gangs* states:

> Rituals range from stopping a woman in public and demanding she take off her underpants and hand them to you, to laying on the ground face down while your

fellow bikers urinate, defecate and vomit on your original colors. Some clubs just pour grease and oil over you while others may require you to submit to the sexual pleasures of the club mascot, which in most cases is a dog.

From my experience this seems a pretty far-fetched notion, put out by an organisation keen to portray outlaw motorcycle clubs as demonic groups.

I haven't noticed any club members I've dealt with in recent years smelling as though they'd been vomited, shat or urinated upon. This includes relatively new members who would have been through such alleged initiation rites. You can usually tell a new member by their clean colours, indicating they're unlikely to have been soiled through an initiation ceremony. Of course, they may have been stripped of their clothes for the rites, as the club would hardly want to desecrate the colours.

Daniel Wolf, who rode with the Rebels in Canada so he could write about the club, was present at an initiation ceremony where the nominees were stripped of their clothes and staked out, spread-eagled on the ground. The club members then smothered the nominees with sump oil, axle grease and other foul substances. To top it off, they poured beer on the victims, urinated on them, and then threw them into the river.

As far as I know, there's been no reported incident of a woman being asked to remove her underpants and hand them over to members of outlaw motorcycle clubs in Australia, New Zealand, South Africa, Denmark, Germany or Canada. Perhaps this is peculiar to the United States. With most major clubs having some connection with the United States, I find it highly unlikely that the mother chapter would allow these initiation rites to occur in one country but not another.

As for having sex with the club mascot, no self-respecting outlaw motorcycle club member would vote such a person into membership of their club. The idea is totally ludicrous. The central goal of the club is to develop a brotherhood with whom you can identify and rely upon for support and backup. Having sex with dogs may be some club members' idea of acceptable behaviour but I've yet to meet them. In my experience, having sex with a dog would be grounds not only for expulsion from the club but also to receive a beating.

The source of many of the myths about the initiation ceremonies is the clubs themselves. Although they say they don't care what mainstream society thinks of them, it's actually a fundamental part of the bikie value system to cause outrage or, as they put it, 'show class'. What better way to show class than to create a distorted image of an initiation run?

The initiation ceremony is the final stage in the membership process. Once that's out of the way, the new member can run for office, and take responsibility for organising runs and other activities. He's an equal among equals in the club.

Of course, the flow from biker to outlaw bikie is not always seamless. Many people who hang around the club choose not to become members, while many nominees opt out of the process before they get to the voting stage. There is even a sizeable drop-out rate of full members when many realise the scope of the commitment needed to be a member of an outlaw motorcycle club.

Some prospective members shy away after being exposed to alleged criminal involvement of the clubs and their members. They wanted the rebel lifestyle without the law breaking. They either shift their sights back to a biker lifestyle or head for a non-outlaw club.

One of the reasons I gave up riding is that some of the group I knocked around with at the time were starting to party extra hard, read 'smack', and in doing so started to play around with the likes of the Coffin Cheaters. All a bit

heavy duty for me. After all we were into alligator boots and smart leather – not the outlaw look or game.
Former social rider

If this is called riding motorbikes and having fun, it was too much fun for me.
Former club rider

However, the person attracted to the outlaw clubs in the first place has a pretty good idea of what they are letting themselves in for.

CHAPTER FIVE THE CLUBS

There are only two causes I'd die for – my family
and my club.
Fink

So, who are the outlaw motorcycle clubs? How's this for a sample: Accretes, Aesthetes, Anderson Confederates, Annihilators, Apollos, Arms, Avengers, Axeman, Backdoormen, Barons, Bad Bones, Bandidos, Barbarians, Bikers United, Black Uhlans, Blagards, Blonks, Blue Angels, Boanerges, Booze Fighters, Branded Few, Bravados, Breakaways, Broke Brothers, Bro's, Brotherhood of Grey Ghost, Brothers, Brothers Fast, Brothers Regime, Brothers Rising, Brothers Speed, Celtic Brothers, Chosen Few, Chosen Ones, Circle of Pride, Club Deroes, Cobras, Coffin Cheaters, Comancheros, Confederates, Cossacks, Coven, Crossroads, Custom Riders, Dead Men, Derelicts, Descendants, Devil's Breed, Devil's Disciples, Devil's Henchmen, Diablos, Dirty Dozen, Donald Ducks, Drifters, Drivers, Epitaph Riders, Evil Ones, Fates Assembly, Fifth Chapter, Finks, Flaming Knight, Foolish Few,

Forbidden Wheels, Fourth Reich, Freedom Riders, Freedom Seekers, Free Souls, Free Spirits, Free Wheelers, Free Wheelin' Souls, F-Troop, Galloping Gooses, Ghetto Riders, Ghost Riders, Gladiators, God's Garbage, Grave Diggers, Grim Reapers, Gypsy Jokers, Hangmen, Heathens, Heaven's Angels, Hell's Angels, Hell's Henchmen, Hells Outcast, Helter Skelter, Henchmen, Highwaymen, Huns, Immortals, Iron Axe Men, Iron Coffins, Iron Cross, Iron Horsemen, Iron Riders, Iron Wings, Iroquois, Kingsmen, Knights, Last Chance, Life and Death, Limited Few, Lobos, Loners, Lone Wolves, Lords of Iron, Lucifer's Legion, Mad Dogs, Mandamas, Matadors, Mercenaries, Misfits, Mob Shitters, Mongols, Mongrels, Monks, Mother Fuckers, New Breed, Night Riders, Nomads, Nordic Henchmen, Nordic Knights, Odin's Wrath, Odin's Warriors, Outcasts, Outlaws, Outsiders, Pagan's, Pharaohs Poor Boys, Pranksters, Psychos, Queensmen, Rare Breed, Ravens, Reapers, Rebels (California), Rebels (Australia), Red Devils, Remaining Few, Renegades, Restless Few, Resurrection, Righteous Brothers, Righteous Ones, Road Angels, Road Barons, Road Saints, Road Pirates, Road Toads, Rock Machine (an odd name that has always struck me as "new-age"), Rogues, Rude Brothers, Rum Pot Rustlers, Saddle Tramps, Sadists, Sarasons, Satan's Cavalry, Satan's Choice, Satan's Riders, Satan's Serpents, Satan's Sinners Satan's Slaves, Satan's Soldiers, Satan's Tramps, Scorpions, Shifters, Sidewinders, Sindicate, Spartans, Smokin' Skulls, Sons of Odin, Sons of Satan, Sons of Silence, Statesmen, Steel Stallions, Storm Riders, Strangers, Suns of Darkness, Swords of Justice, The Men, Thugs, Thunderguards, Tramps, Tribes, Tribesmen, Tyrants, Undertakers, Vagabonds, Vendettas, Vermins, Vigilantes, Vikings, Violaters, Warlocks and Warlords, War Pigs, Wheelmen, Wheels of Soul, Wind Tramps, Windwalkers, Wingmen, Zbeers, Zudmen and Zulus. Many of these clubs are found in Australia, and this list is by no means complete. Some of them are defunct, as clubs are set up and disappear all the time.

These clubs are 1% clubs, although not all of them wear the 1% badge.

There are also a number of clubs that hang around the edges of the 1% clubs – the Christian clubs and the 10% clubs. These clubs are also considered patch clubs. To the outsider, these clubs appear to be hardcore bikies with the colours, but they lack the intensity and commitment of the 1% clubs. They're also a bit less naughty. The Christian clubs in Australia are the Ambassadors, Brotherhood, God Squad, Holy Ghost Riders and Longriders. The 10% clubs include the Vietnam Vets Motorcycle Club, and the Veterans Motorcycle Club, which is open to serving and ex-armed service people. As the Veterans Motorcycle Club website says:

> We aren't about territory; never have been, never will be. We are not a 1% MC. Nor are we about drugs. We pose no threat to any other club. But be assured that we do take our colours very seriously.

The Ulysses club is another 10% club, with its fantastic slogan 'Grow old disgracefully'. Junior membership is available for those over 40 years of age, with full membership granted to those over 50 years of age. Most of the Harley women's groups would also fall into the 10% category, although there were a few 1% women's clubs in Australia.

There are about 30 to 40 1% clubs in Australia. Taking into account those large clubs with multiple chapters, there'd be about 250 to 300 chapters of 1% clubs. There are another 60 or so 10% clubs. There are many more clubs on the fringe of the scene such as the Shed Six, Angels Motorcycle Club and BLF, named after the famous Australian union, the Builders' Labourers Federation. These clubs do not display patches.

While NSW has the greatest number of outlaw clubs, Western Australia takes the prize for having the greatest concentration of bikies. It must be something about the isolation of Perth, but there are more bikies per head of population in Western Australia than anywhere else. Over the last few years, much of the club violence and inter-club warring has taken place in that state.

Clubs guard their memberships figures with fierce secrecy. They're absolutely paranoid about the police and other clubs knowing how many members they have. However, I estimate there are about 3000 to 4000 outlaw club members in Australia. That's down from about 8000 in 1980, although the clubs maintain that membership is not a problem. I find it pretty ridiculous that they guard their membership figures so tightly. It's easy to work out, as each chapter has between 10 and 25 members. They can't sustain any more. There are about 800 outlaw motorcycle clubs across the globe, with about 50 000 outlaw motorcycle club members worldwide.

Internationally, there are four major outlaw clubs – Hell's Angels, Bandidos, Pagans and Outlaws. The Hell's Angels have more than 10 000 members throughout the world. The others are harder to pin down, as they're constantly taking over small clubs. The last proper attempt to count their members internationally was in 1989, when it was found the Outlaws had 850 members, the Pagans 320 members and the Bandidos 300 members. To get today's figures, my guess is that you could multiply the Bandidos' membership by 10 to get about 3000, and boost the others to at least a few thousand each.

These clubs may be getting bigger but that's generally because they are taking over small clubs. The overall international bikie population is now fairly stable after declining in the last decade, when outlaw motorcycle clubs across the world underwent an incredible round of forced amalgamations and territorial wars, which reduced both the number of clubs and the number of club members.

The amalgamations reached fever pitch in the late 1990s due to the much-vaunted Pact 2000. The pact first reared its head in a 1995 FBI report. This report said:

> In 1993–94 in Sydney, Australia, following worldwide expansion and consolidation of a small number of gangs to take over the motorcycle gang networks, there was a meeting between the main gangs of Australia where it was decided by the main Australian gangs, that by the year 2000 there would be six main gangs in Australia.

It's been said the six clubs were the Hell's Angels, Outlaws, Bandidos, Rebels, Black Uhlans, and Nomads. This was despite the fact that the Outlaws did not have a presence in Australia at the time.

The report made its way to Australia through former New Zealand politician Mike Rann, who is now South Australian Premier. It finally ended up in the Prime Minister's office. When Rann went to the US the FBI asked him for a briefing. It was a bit like playing pass the message. The further it went on, the more real the existence of a pact became.

The date came and went and still many clubs remained, although during those years a hell of a lot of clubs disappeared, often patched over by one of the big six clubs. The Bandidos and Rebels, in particular, experienced rapid growth during the late 1990s.

There is now a period of stability among the clubs, with few small clubs left that can be easily taken over.

You may notice I use the word 'club' rather than 'gang'. It may seem like semantics, but despite the widespread use of the term 'bikie gangs', they are in fact clubs. It's a huge issue with the clubs who feel they're branded as gangs to imply something sinister.

The word 'gang' automatically conjures up images of a group up to no good. The police freely refer to them as gangs, as do the media. It pisses the clubs off no end.

> It's a law enforcement term. It's used to try to make us worse than what we are. Once a club becomes a gang, then the police can get all the support from the citizens they need.
> **Hell's Angel**

So, what's the difference between a club and a gang? The *New Oxford Dictionary* of English defines a gang as: 'An organised group of criminals. A group of young people involved in petty crime or violence.' That same dictionary defines a club as: 'A formal voluntary organisation or society which is convened to explore mutual interests and activities.'

Age, activity and motivation seem to be the differences. The motorcycle clubs argue that, unlike the apparent crime orientation of modern street gangs, they have a legitimate purpose – to pursue an alternative lifestyle through motorcycles. Yet, the bikie clubs can't deny crime that occurs within the clubs. The argument is whether it's done as a club or by individual club members; something I'll explore in a later chapter. The outlaw motorcycle clubs are also quick to point out they don't allow members under the age of 18. It's rare for someone to be admitted to an outlaw motorcycle club before they are 25. The average age of motorcycle club members is mid 30s.

Yet, perhaps their strongest argument is when they point to the letters MC on their patches. It stands for motorcycle club. If it's part of their official title, how could anyone argue the point, they ask? Many MRA-affiliated motorcycle clubs are more than happy to see the outlaw clubs referred to as gangs, to clearly distinguish between themselves and the outlaw clubs.

I refer to them as clubs, although I find the only real bodies they can be compared to are gangs such as street gangs. Many police reports start out referring to gangs and then revert to the term 'clubs' a few pages in. It's probably a moot point to outsiders, but it's something that really concerns the clubs.

The other thing that needs to be clarified is the difference between the words 'club' and 'chapter'. It's easy to get tripped up. Simply, the club is the organisation – Hell's Angels, Coffin Cheaters, Gypsy Jokers. If the club is large enough to have what you might call branch offices these are called chapters of the club – the Gypsy Jokers Adelaide chapter, for instance.

It's unclear why the clubs chose the word 'chapter'. It does have academic and religious connotations but I don't believe these have had any influence. I'd have thought that a more military term, such as regiment, would be used, considering the military background of many of the clubs. I suspect chapter was just the appropriate word that someone started to use in the early days. The US Hell's Angels sometimes refer to 'charters', a notion that appears to be catching on with some of the Australian chapters, who now refer to themselves as such.

The clubs are also known to engage in a bit of semantics, with some Australian Hell's Angels chapters no longer referring to their 'clubhouse', due to its legal implications. The argument is that if a club has a clubhouse, it has assets. If the police want to seize a club's assets the club can deny they have a clubhouse. The chapters refer to it as the 'usual place we gather'. It's part of the strange world the clubs exist in. It's hard to believe, yet it's just one of the anomalies that attract men to the outlaw clubs.

To my mind, the major outlaw motorcycle clubs in Australia are the Hell's Angels, Bandidos, Rebels, Coffin Cheaters and Gypsy Jokers.

The most well known club, and the biggest internationally, is the Hell's Angels. The club is sometimes referred to as the Big

Red Machine, and in the US it is increasingly referred to as the Hell's Angels Motorcycle Corporation, a reflection of its size, internationalisation and commercial activities.

The origin of the Hell's Angels Motorcycle Club, as we know it today, is a bit shaky. The man who should know, Sonny Barger, the former US national president, says that in 1957 a club he was riding with in Oakland adopted the death's head logo and called itself the Hell's Angels. The club later discovered there were two other clubs in California with the same logo also using the Hell's Angels name. One of these, in San Bernardino, was formerly the Pissed Off Bastards, which changed its name after Hollister, becoming the Hell's Angels in 1948. This chapter is generally acknowledged as the first Hell's Angels chapter.

The club was incorporated in 1966: 'Dedicated to the promotion and advancement of motorcycle riding, motorcycle clubs, motorcycle highway safety and all phases of motorcycling and motorcycle driving.' The death's head logo was patented in 1972 and the name turned into a trademark in the 1980s.

Worldwide, the Hell's Angels have about 100 chapters – 65 in North America and 35 in other countries. Their reputation probably precedes them locally. There are only seven chapters in Australia with a total of about 150 members nationally. There is one chapter in Darwin, Brisbane and Sydney and two chapters in each of Adelaide and Melbourne. There are unsubstantiated rumours that there is a second Hell's Angel chapter in Sydney. The figures are pretty small considering it's the club the public most associates with bikies. In Melbourne, where the club is most active, there would be 40 Hell's Angels sprinkled among three million people. It's not a high ratio.

There is some confusion as to when the club started in Australia. A group was given a charter to start a Hell's Angel chapter in Sydney in 1967. However, the US Hell's Angels claim not to know anything about it, and there is little local reference to it. It has been claimed that the formation of the Gypsy Jokers' club was helped by a club calling itself the Hell's Angels in 1969, complete with the death's head logo and 1% patch. This was at least three years before the first Australian Hell's Angels chapters were officially inaugurated in Melbourne and Sydney on 23 August 1973.

The Hell's Angels are always keen to separate themselves from the other clubs, to show they are the leaders. In recent years they've started to move away from wearing the 1% badge because they believe too many clubs are wearing it. In line with this attitude, there has also been a trend towards wearing loud Hawaiian shirts to again get away from the stereotypical bikie image set by Marvin and Brando in *The Wild One*. It's long been possible to find some Queensland Hell's Angels getting about in these shirts.

Any profile of the Hell's Angels must include Sonny Barger. He's the most influential bikie of his time, making the Hell's Angels as we know the club today. Along the way he made a name for himself as a tough, unrelenting leader. Born in Oakland in 1938 to a German-Dutch father and an Italian mother, he was nicknamed 'Sonny', according to the tradition for a first-born Italian son. He was abandoned by his mother when he was only four months old, when she ran off with a bus driver leaving Sonny with an alcoholic father unable to hold down a steady job.

It was a terrible start to life, as is often the case with the most hardened club members. Sonny and his sisters found themselves shunted from his grandmother's house in East Oakland to various motels and hotels on California's highways where his father worked as an asphalt layer, and then back to his grandmother's. She died when he was only eight years old and, with his father never home, it was left to an older sister to raise Sonny. His father eventually remarried, bringing a stepmother into Sonny's life, but this only made his life more miserable as he now received regular beatings.

Things were no better at school, with Sonny in at least one fight a week in both primary and junior high school. He actually enjoyed a fight. In the neighbourhood where his family lived fighting was considered a pretty normal way of life. Sonny managed to get himself expelled from high school for attacking his teachers.

His father and stepmother kicked him out of home when he was 16, so he forged his birthdate on his birth certificate and joined the army.

The army was a godsend for Sonny. He'd finally found a family, with the discipline he'd been missing throughout his life. He found men bound together by a true sense of brotherhood. Fourteen months after he enlisted, Sonny's birth certificate forgery was discovered. He was given an honourable discharge and sent back to Oakland. But before this happened he had made another major discovery. Following basic training, he was stationed in Honolulu where he came into contact with some hard partying veterans who were into motorcycling in a big way. Sonny liked what he saw.

Upon his discharge, he held a succession of manual unskilled jobs, but he found himself wondering how he could recapture the experience of belonging that he had felt in the army. He even tried to re-enlist but was rejected by a psychiatrist who felt his tattoos and attitude indicated potential aggression problems.

He turned to a local motorcycle club, the Oakland Panthers. He was no stranger to gangs or motorcycles. He'd bought his first scooter when he was 13 and had formed at least one street gang by the time he was 14. It was called the Earth Angels and comprised friends from his neighbourhood. Local gangs of this sort were common in the working class and underclass of US cities at the time.

He dropped out of the Oakland Panthers when he found it didn't hold the brotherhood attitudes he was looking for in a club. He started riding with a loose-knit group of mates in Oakland. One of them came across a patch from a defunct North Sacramento Club with the now infamous World War II Hell's Angels death's head logo. Sonny and his mates thought the emblem was 'really cool' so they named their group the Hell's Angels.

The Hell's Angels gave Sonny what he was looking for – a sense of belonging and meaning, just like he had experienced in the army. It became a family as he understood a family to be.

Unbeknownst to Sonny and his club, there were already other Hell's Angels' motorcycle clubs on the scene, including the former Pissed Off Bastards in San Bernardino. After some conflict, the various clubs amalgamated, each becoming chapters of the Hell's Angels Motorcycle Club.

By 1958 Sonny Barger was president of the Oakland Chapter of the Hell's Angels.

The early years of the club were marked by turmoil between the various chapters. In particular, there was a major dispute between the San Francisco and Oakland chapters over who was going to call the shots. Through Sonny's leadership, power shifted to the Oakland base.

The early club was a far cry from the modern Hell's Angels. For a start, women were allowed to be full members; there were even some female office bearers. It was a time when the Hell's Angels were mainly interested in partying, building their motorcycles and riding them.

Recreational drug use soon became a feature of the club. As it was the early years of the drug culture people had a different view of things. At that time, marijuana, cocaine and heroin were illegal but LSD and designer drugs such as Peyote and methamphetamines were legal.

Weapons, fighting with other clubs and petty crime to support relatively nomadic lifestyles soon became part of the Hell's

Angels' life. Along with that came the drug overdoses, injuries from bike-riding and conflicts with other clubs, arrests and hassles with the law.

Sonny's first encounter with the law came with his arrest and conviction in 1957 for drink-driving. The charge landed him in prison for three years. As a Hell's Angel, his charge sheet grew with predictable speed. On 13 November 1963 he was arrested for possession of narcotics. On 30 April 1964 he was arrested for possession of marijuana and spent six months in prison. On 13 February 1965 he was arrested for assault with a deadly weapon and convicted of assault to commit murder. Later that year, he was charged with assault with a deadly weapon but the charge was withdrawn. On 10 March 1966 he was charged again with assault with a deadly weapon and scored six months in prison. So the story continued, with 10 more formal scrapes with the law until 1973, when he was arrested and convicted on a variety of charges including kidnapping and narcotic distribution charges. By this time he was hopelessly addicted to cocaine. He successfully plea-bargained for a sentence of 15 years to life. Through technicalities and appeals Sonny was released in 1977. All that time he had maintained his leadership of the Hell's Angels. In the outlaw clubs, time spent in jail is not considered time out of action.

By 1978, the Hell's Angels had grown to be undoubtedly the biggest outlaw motorcycle club in the world. It had changed from being an ad hoc club of society misfits to a finely tuned multinational organisation. As national president, Sonny was the pivotal character in its growth and management. He was blessed with excellent organisational skills and leadership abilities that would have served him well in the straight business world.

As the club grew so too did the attention of the police. By the late 1970s the authorities had defined the club as an organisation whose primary purpose was to commit crime. In 1979 the Hell's

Angels became the first organisation to be prosecuted under the *Racketeer Influenced and Criminal Organization Act*. With Sonny orchestrating the Hell's Angels' defence, the jury found that the Hell's Angels' *raison d'être* was not to commit crime. Clubs repeat Sonny's mantra from that case to this day – members commit crime, not the club.

Sonny soon had to switch his attention to his health. In 1982 he contracted throat cancer, prompting the removal of his larynx. He now speaks through a mechanical voice box. But that didn't keep him from the spotlight. In 1987 he was convicted of conspiracy to bomb a rival outlaw motorcycle club and sent to prison for five years. He had finally purged his cocaine addiction by the time he was released.

Sonny served his final prison years in Arizona, falling in love with the climate and wide open spaces. When a Hell's Angels chapter was formed in Arizona in 1995 he packed up and headed for the desert. He found his third wife, Noel, in Arizona. She raises horses and he rides motorcycles and runs a motorcycle shop. These days he's considered an elder statesman for the Hell's Angels Motorcycle Club.

I fleetingly met Sonny in a restaurant in Oakland years and years ago, before he'd made a name for himself. He looked like a rough customer to me, although he had some sort of charisma about him. I'd love to catch up with him again.

The Bandidos are an extensive global outlaw motorcycle club, opening their first Australian chapter in Sydney in about 1984. The Bandidos started out in Houston, Texas in 1966 as a social club consisting mainly of wharf workers who wanted to ride as an outlaw club. They took their name from a television commercial at the time for Frito Bandido.

They've gained national prominence in Australia in a relatively short time, with multiple chapters in all states and a total of about 250 members Australia-wide. It's more active in New

South Wales, with chapters in Sydney, the Hunter Valley, the mid-north coast, central NSW and the oddly-named chapter called Racing Club, which is based in Sydney but floats all around the place. As its name suggests, it has a racing bent – mainly dirt racing.

There are three chapters in Victoria – Ballarat, Geelong and north-east Victoria – and three in Queensland in Brisbane, Cairns and the Sunshine Coast. Adelaide also has a chapter.

The Bandidos club is sometimes referred to as the Bandido Nation. It comes from its origins in Texas, where the street gangs often put nation after their title to indicate that they'd moved beyond being a mere gang, into something much bigger and more complex. There has also been police speculation that the Bandidos adopted it as some sort of Ku Klux Klan affiliation, although this has never been proven. In a similar vein, the Outlaws also often refer to themselves as the Outlaw Nation. The Outlaws are a relatively new club in Australia. They have established 11 chapters in recent years, including the rapid expansion of seven chapters in the second half of 2001. Outlaws chapter locations include Brisbane, Mackay, Hobart, Launceston, Devonport, Melbourne, Pakenham, Shepparton and Sydney.

The Rebels is Australia's largest club in terms of membership. It's also a home-grown club, originating in Sydney in 1969. The Rebels and the Hell's Angels waged a war in the 1970s, prompting the Australian Rebels to affiliate with the now-defunct New York-based Rebels MC.

The Rebels have made rapid inroads into the Australian outlaw motorcycle club scene since the late 1990s. They're the most successful of the new-age outlaw motorcycle clubs with 63 chapters across Australia and about 1200 members. According to other clubs, the Rebels' rapid growth has meant lower membership requirements than other outlaw clubs. Other clubs I've spoken to claim many of these new members have little real commitment to the bikie lifestyle. While it could take years to become a full member of a hardcore club such as the Hell's Angels or Gypsy Jokers, it could take as little as 3 to 6 months for an applicant to join the Rebels. These sources say if the Rebels take over a club, they invariably grant full membership immediately.

Interestingly, the same accusation is being levelled at the Hell's Angels in Canada, which has six chapters in the Toronto region. It's extremely unusual to have that many Hell's Angels chapters in such a small area, prompting accusations from other clubs that the Hell's Angels have 'gone slumming' in a chase for members. The Canadian bike scene is extremely volatile, with a number of clubs in a constant territorial war, so the club may have taken over other clubs as part of the war, or was looking to boost numbers to strengthen themselves against rival clubs.

Some of the hardcore clubs also believe the Rebels and, to a degree, the Bandidos, don't respect other clubs and their colours. Respect, however, is rarely shown to them. I often hear other clubs refer to the Rebels and Bandidos as the Rabble and the Band Aids, respectively. It's that sort of sniping between the clubs that leads to many of the violent confrontations and turf wars.

The Coffin Cheaters is another major Australian outlaw motorcycle club. The club is a home-grown Australian club with about 200 members. There's a reference to the Coffin Cheaters in Hunter S. Thompson's book, *Hell's Angels*. That was in about 1964. I haven't been able to find any more recent references to a US club of the same name.

The Coffin Cheaters have chapters in all Australian states except South Australia and the Northern Territory. Their biggest presence is in Perth where there are three chapters, followed by Victoria with two chapters – Melbourne and eastern Victoria – and two chapters in each of New South Wales and Queensland – Sydney, Brisbane, Cairns and the NSW south coast.

Australian police believe the Coffin Cheaters are affiliated with the Outlaws. It's never been proven and the club certainly won't say. If they are hooked up with the Coffin Cheaters it's unclear what this will do to club politics.

The Gypsy Jokers is another local club, although a few years after it was formed it became an affiliate of the US club of the same name. The club has chapters in Perth, Adelaide, Wodonga, Mount Gambier and Sydney, with about 120 full members in Australia. The Gypsy Jokers have the highest profile in South Australia and Western Australia, and a number of violent incidents have occurred in both states, including shootings and clashes with police, putting them under the spotlight.

The most notorious of these was the death of former Perth policeman Don Hancock and another man in a car bomb in September 2001. The finger of suspicion was immediately pointed at the Jokers, with clubhouses and homes of members raided. It was alleged the bombings might have been linked to the death of a Gypsy Joker in the WA mining town of Boulder in early 2001 only hours after being ejected from Hancock's Hotel. At least two members of the Gypsy Jokers were charged with the murders, with one of those charged turning informant in return for a lighter sentence.

The club was formed in 1969 with the help of the then Sydney chapter of the Hell's Angels. I doubt you'd find that spirit of co-operation between any outlaw clubs today.

The clubs shared many things, including their constitution. The Gypsy Jokers' rules today remain identical to the Hell's Angels' rules of the day. The Hell's Angels even took the extraordinary step of giving the fledgling club permission to wear the red and white 1% badge that was part of the Hell's Angels' colours to demonstrate the Gypsy Jokers had approval from the Hell's Angels to fly colours in their territory.

The friendship between the clubs was not to last. A Hell's

Angel prospect who'd helped start the club opted to leave and become a fully-fledged Gypsy Joker afer the Hell's Angels told the Jokers they wanted them to disband and become the West Sydney chapter of the Hell's Angels. After all, the Hell's Angels argued, the Jokers had used one of their members to set up the club, were using the Hell's Angel's constitution, and were even using their red and white colours on the front badge of their coats. The Gypsy Jokers flatly refused. It split the clubs so badly they became sworn enemies. The animosity lasts to this day. Some Gypsy Jokers still defiantly wear the red and white 1% badge that the Hell's Angels gave them.

The Gypsy Jokers have been instrumental in the formation of a couple of other outlaw clubs. One new club, the Fourth Reich, shared colours with the Gypsy Jokers as a sign of solidarity and comradeship.

Not long after the Fourth Reich was established in Wollongong in the early 1970s, 10 of its members were accused of raping a woman. The 10 men fled to Queensland, forming a club called the Black Uhlans. No charges were ever laid over the rape.

The Fourth Reich and Black Uhlans used the Hell's Angels' rules and organisational structure passed on by the Gypsy Jokers. Again, the Black Uhlans' patch colours were the same – gold, black and red – a symbol of the brotherhood between the clubs.

The Gypsy Jokers soon began to spread, with chapters established in Mount Gambier and Adelaide. The Adelaide chapter was the result of a friendly patch-over of a local club, The Mandamas. This club was having trouble with the Hell's Angels because it carried the same colours on its patch – red and white. It decided to join a larger club to stand up to the Hell's Angels.

In 1976 the eastern club learned of the existence of another club in Perth calling itself the Gypsy Jokers. The clubs realised they couldn't have two independent clubs with different patches, both calling themselves by the same name, so they decided to become one club. The WA chapter took on the patch of the eastern club – a triangle representing the idea that one went places in life but always returned to the same spot, surrounding a picture of an Asian with a fractured skull and a tear in his eye. It is believed that this represented the Vietnamese from the war. It has now been changed to a skull of indeterminate race. The thirteenth tooth of the skull is missing. This stands for the thirteenth letter of the alphabet – M for marijuana. The crack in the skull stands for violence and the earring for a gypsy.

Following the consolidation of the club, the next step was to handle relations with the US Gypsy Jokers, which had become aware of the Australian club. Representatives of each Australian chapter – Sydney, Adelaide, Perth, Newcastle and Mount Gambier – were invited to the US Gypsy Jokers' Seattle headquarters. The Australians were well looked after by their American counterparts, supplied with motorcycles and invited to a succession of parties. The parties were sometimes designed to test the mettle of the Australians. Invariably they ended in a planned fight to see how the visitors handled themselves.

They passed the test with flying colours and after three weeks the US Gypsy Jokers invited the Australian club to become official affiliates of the club.

There is a substantial number of other home-grown Australian clubs with chapters nationally. These clubs, which include the Black Uhlans and Odin's Warriors and, arguably, the Comancheros, are strong clubs and unlikely to join or affiliate with the larger clubs.

The Comancheros, known to many people for their involvement in the Father's Day massacre in Sydney in 1984 (explained in detail in chapter 10), have three chapters – two in Sydney and one in Brisbane. However, the club has a more complex structure than most, with a set of 'sub' or feeder clubs which hang around them. It's from these clubs that the

Comanchero members are chosen. They prove their worth in the lesser club, so to speak. There are about 80 full Comanchero members.

The Black Uhlans are hard nuts to get any information on. I just can't seem to crack it for a discussion with any of them. The club is based in Queensland with chapters in Brisbane, Maroochydore, Townsville and Cairns, as well as chapters in Sydney, Dubbo and Darwin. There are now 70–90 members nationally. The club is reputed to have the finest clubhouse in Australia, in Brisbane; however, other sources tell me the Coffin Cheaters in Perth have the best digs.

The Finks are another pretty secretive club. They're a national club with four chapters, in Sydney, south-east Queensland, Adelaide and Wodonga. There are about 80–100 members nationally, with the majority in Queensland. The Finks is quite an odd club because it has not had a president for many years. It has a secretary and treasurer in each chapter, although there is some debate as to whether each chapter has a sergeant-at-arms. Unlike other clubs, office bearers don't wear badges denoting their position, so it's hard to tell who is who.

I've only recently been able to make any meaningful contact with the Finks, as they like to stick to themselves. As well, they've had a very public war with the Hell's Angels dating back to the Sydney Bike Show of 1980, which caused strained relations between the clubs for almost 20 years. Since I had a fair bit of contact with the Hell's Angels the Finks regarded me with some suspicion.

The Finks started in Sydney in 1969. According to them, they grew out of an unnamed motorcycle social club in the western suburbs. However, the Hell's Angels claim the Finks are one of its offshoots. Both are adamant that theirs is the correct version, so who knows.

The Finks' name was proposed after a week of trying to think of one. It came from the Wizard of Id cartoon strip, where the main character, Bung, gets around calling out 'the king is a Fink'. The founders thought it was a pretty good name for a club.

However, about half the members refused to ride with a club named the Finks and left the meeting, most never to return. According to one of the club's founders, the dissident group preferred a more 'hard core name, like the Outlaws'.

The Finks' attendance rules for weekly meetings, or 'church' and the normally strict outlaw club codes of behaviour are much more relaxed than other clubs. The Finks have no desire to associate with international clubs or create chapters internationally. The war with the Hell's Angels made the club pretty introspective. They didn't recruit any new members for 10 years. However, by the late 1980s, the club began taking on members and now has a balance of young and old. It's by far the most multicultural club in Australia with several Aboriginal and Muslim members. They even had an American Indian as a member for many years. The club also seems to run on family lines, with a surprisingly high number of brothers joining. It also has servicemen as members, including two SAS divers.

The Odin's Warriors is another secretive club. I believe it has two chapters in Queensland and another one in Melbourne. It doesn't appear to be aligned with any other club. I haven't been able to penetrate them, so information is hard to come by. However, I really respect their name as it shows such flair for an outlaw club. Odin was the ancient Nordic God of War.

Then there are the single chapter clubs that successfully survive patch-over threats from the larger clubs; these include the Fourth Reich and the Descendants.

There is one question I get asked more than others – which is the baddest, meanest outlaw motorcycle club in Australia? It's not an easy question to answer. The Gypsy Jokers, Black Uhlans, Hell's Angels and the Finks are all what I call hardcore clubs. The Finks has been described as 'the most disorganised but most violent' of the Australian bike clubs, with their calling card once saying 'I have been visited, onioned, bashed, or robbed by a Fink.' These clubs are focussed, well-armed, heavily committed to their survival and relatively cohesive, demanding high levels of commitment by members. These are the bad arses that often find themselves accused of violence and crime. Simply, while most clubs scare the straight community, these few scare the other clubs. Under this group would be the Coffin Cheaters and the Bandidos. Below them would be the Rebels. However, all outlaw motorcycle clubs are hard units. Some are just harder than others.

There really is no *most* notorious club in Australia. You could say the most notorious club is the one getting the media coverage, which varies from year to year. The Nomads were a real force and a notorious club in the early 1980s. By 1984 the Bandidos and Comancheros were on the scene as the baddest boys. However, the Gypsy Jokers have really been in the spotlight in recent years, and have probably earned the mantle.

From a personal point of view, I consider the Black Uhlans club to be notorious, purely because it's virtually a secret society. It's reputedly the wealthiest club in Australia, allegedly owning a significant number of retirement units in inner Melbourne.

While being shown this supposed stretch of real estate by a rival club member one day, I asked him how I could get to talk to the Black Uhlans.

'You don't,' he replied sternly. 'You leave them alone.'

Why are they so secretive? Why are they so wealthy, if in fact they are? One can only wonder. All I know is they want nothing to do with me and my research.

Internationally, as with the Australian scene, there is no most notorious club, as the scene continually changes depending upon the events of the day. If I was pushed on the issue, I'd have to give the nod to the biggest club, the Hell's Angels, by virtue of its size, the police pressure it experiences and the amount of consistent media coverage it receives. For many in the straight world, when the word bikie is mentioned, the name Hell's Angels immediately springs to mind.

Prior to the arrival of clubs such as the Hell's Angels the Australian clubs were basically individuals riding together with little or no restriction on membership. 'The club was only just the club,' said the founding president of one club at the time.

On Friday we got together, Saturday we partied and on Sunday we went back to work. It was a little social thing. We were just hell bent on having a good time and not doing any harm to anybody.
Former Iriquois' president

Then the large American clubs moved in, taking over the small clubs. The clubs call it an amalgamation, or the much more romantic term 'patch-over'. To patch over means the club literally puts its patch over another club's patch. You can't get a much more definite act than that, particularly when they hold a party and burn the conquered club's patches. The club that has been patched over not only loses its patch, but also its territory. The intention of the patch-over is usually to absorb the smaller club's members. The small club could even become a chapter of the more powerful club. The clubs that get into patch-overs feel they must amalgamate with other clubs in order to defend themselves against other predatory clubs who will confiscate their patch – eat or be eaten.

To have a large hardcore club roll up on the doorstep and declare they're taking over a territory is very frightening for many smaller clubs that are basically social clubs. The small club usually has no choice. If they refuse, they have to expect the larger club to launch a violent takeover, which many small clubs cannot sustain. However, some small Australian clubs, such as the Fourth Reich in

Melbourne, with about 25 members, and the Descendants, based in Adelaide, with only eight members, have both successfully defended their patch against the big clubs. These clubs, however, contain some of the hardest bastards you'll ever meet.

Other clubs, such as the Gypsy Jokers don't patch-over other clubs and make little effort to recruit. It's one hard mother of a club to get into, so it's not in the business of taking over small clubs.

When a club is taken over, members have two choices – get out or join the new club. Of course, in any small club members will leap at the chance to join a stronger club like the Hell's Angels or Bandidos. The members of the small club must go through the joining and probation process.

Patch-overs are not the exclusive domain of the big US clubs. Australian clubs are not averse to throwing their weight around when it comes to forced amalgamations. Satan's Cavalry, a small club in country Victoria, faced a dilemma a few years ago when members were told it was to become a chapter of the Coffin Cheaters or be disbanded. They had no choice. The Coffin Cheaters took their patches and the small club effectively disappeared.

Another interesting case, notwithstanding the acronym of one of the clubs involved, was the takeover of the Central Upper Northern Tourers at Roxby Downs in South Australia, by the Rebels.

Three mates, who worked in the uranium mines at Roxby Downs, started a motorcycle-touring club called the Rum Runners in 1986. The club grew to about 15 members by 1996, when it became the CUNTs. The new name was a reflection of the attitude of the club at the time. Remember, this was, and still is, a pretty hard town. It wasn't a 1% club, as members didn't wear patches and were only distinguishable by a badge on the front of their riding vests.

In 1997 the club held a bike show to raise funds for the club. Five minutes before the show, three local Rebel nominees arrived at the show and informed the CUNTs they were taking the profits of the show. It turned out these three had a charter to start a Rebels chapter within a 300 km radius of Roxby Downs. Soon after, 30 fully-fledged Rebel members showed up in town to support the nominees. The CUNTs were told they didn't have permission to ride as a club in Roxby Downs. That was the end of the club. Just like that!

'We were fuckin' stunned,' said Gypsy, the CUNTs' president at the time. 'But there was shit we could do about it.'

However, they did fight back. Gypsy and his members played the local mine politics. The three Rebels were portrayed as being a risk to the company that ran the uranium mine. I suspect it was made very clear to the company and union that an outlaw motor-cycle club was not a good thing for the town. The CUNTs' members also threatened to resign if the three Rebels nominees, who also worked in the mine, were not dealt with. I believe the company decided it was easier to get rid of three relatively junior employees as opposed to 15 more senior and established employees.

Two years after they took over the CUNTs, the Rebels pulled out of the town. It was a rare victory for a small club. As soon as the Rebels left, the CUNTs got together and had a huge party. They are still happily riding together to this day. I've asked the Rebels for their version of events in this patch-over, but they have failed to respond to any of my requests.

Patch-overs are not always violent. Many small clubs are keen to become a chapter of a large club such as the Hell's Angels. In these cases, the Angels can take their time to see if a club is worthy of wearing the death's head. Prospective members from the smaller club still have to undergo a trial period with the mother chapter. However, they have a lot more freedom than if they had been patched over against their will.

Usually only one chapter can fly the colours of the mother club in a town, which can cause a bit of friction with other local clubs who want to become chapters of the larger clubs. There can also be strife when two small clubs in an area each want to become part of rival clubs. As dominance of territory is a condition of joining the mother club it can trigger a territorial war.

A club that wants to enter the territory of a larger club has three options – ask the dominant club for permission to wear their colours in the territory; cover their patches while they're in another club's territory, or run the risk of having the shit beaten out of them by entering a territory wearing rival patches.

CHAPTER SIX RULES, BLOODY RULES

God only gave us 10 rules. How many does a bike club need?

Former Comanchero

There's a saying, by whom I'm not sure, that if there was complete freedom there'd be no freedom at all. Think about it. If society had no rules our lives would be in disarray. Anyone could do what he or she wanted without fear of punishment.

It's apt I introduce a chapter on outlaw motorcycle club rules with this notion. The outlaw motorcycle clubs consider themselves to be among the last bastions of free people, free from the straight world. Yet, even they need rules to survive. While the clubs try to keep the rules to a minimum, they loom large over everything the club does. There are rules for most things – how to become a member, the amount of time to devote to the club, conduct at the club and on runs, treatment of fellow members, drugs and weapons, women, how to leave the club and even how to deal with the outside world.

These rules are sacrosanct. For example, not having your motorcycle in running condition for one month of the riding season is considered grounds for expulsion from some clubs. Most clubs have a rule that no members are to talk to the media unless authorised by their executive. Even to deny something is considered an interview, and is grounds for instant dismissal. The former president of one club had an interesting view of this rule: 'You can say anything you want as long as the cops already know about it.'

It's the greatest anomaly of the clubs. Many club members see themselves as modern cowboys, the outlaw heroes of the Wild West. Yet they require the structure and co-ordination of the group to achieve that individual lifestyle. With that comes the politics inherent in any structured gathering of people. It's the fundamental paradigm or conundrum that I face with the clubs. I keep hearing the terms *individuality* and *freedom of expression* when bikies describe their way of life, but invariably their conversations are full of rules, politics, and drama. These are completely opposite. It's irreconcilable.

Protocol can dictate basic issues, such as how and where to ride to a certain location. One major club's rules state that if members are together they must ride as a group. No member can ride alone. One day a group of members decided they needed some supplies for the clubhouse, so they jumped on their bikes as a group and went to the supermarket. Upon returning, one of the group realised he'd forgotten his smokes. The rules prevented him scooting down himself. Everyone had to get suited up again, fire up the Harleys and escort him to the local shop for the cigarettes. I'm not sure why someone couldn't spare him a smoke. (It wasn't the Outlaws – they have a no-smoking rule in their clubhouse).

The outlaw motorcycle club is a participatory democracy, which means all business is subject to group decisions. The outlaw motorcycle clubs may like to think they're cohesive units but when it comes to club business they're just like any organisation, with everyone putting in their two bob's worth. It can make club meetings drawn out complex affairs, with heated debates about anything and everything.

The club meetings are generally held once a week during the active 'riding season' and once every second week during the off-season. The agenda is usually set by informal discussions among members around the club or at social gatherings.

The meeting, or church, is a formal affair, guided by Roberts' Rules of meeting procedures – motions, in favour, for and against, etc. However, it's also guided by a very simple philosophy – everyone gets their say but not necessarily their way. The meeting format is pretty much standard across all clubs and chapters. They start about 8 p.m., usually on a Wednesday. The president calls the meeting to order and a formal roll call is taken. Only full members are allowed to attend church. The club meetings are an important part of the outlaw lifestyle, so missing three meetings in a row is generally grounds for expulsion from the club. Thus, apologies are important, as are acceptance of the apologies. Following the rollcall, the minutes of the previous meeting are voted upon as acceptable or not. Then, any unfinished business from the previous meeting is dealt with. This is generally followed by a report from the executive committee that acts as a kind of brains trust for the club. The executive is comprised of office bearers and two or three other full members. Following the executive report and discussion of the report, there is then a beer break, where issues are informally discussed. The meeting is again called to order and new business is discussed.

It differs a bit from a normal meeting in that drinking is allowed. However, intoxication at church is a finable offence, usually about $20. If a member is too pissed they usually get kicked out of the meeting and cop the fine.

Given the raucous and assertive nature of both biker and bikie culture it's often difficult to make out whether the rules are in operation at meetings or not. However, consensus is the key, and as long as everyone has their say, it seems to work fine.

The notion of everyone having their say means chapters cannot be too big. Chapter memberships are usually kept below 25. This not only ensures meetings run smoothly, but also allows the bond between members to remain strong, and prevents fracturing of the club through factions. Any bigger and the decision-making process would become unworkable. Once a chapter reaches 25, a new chapter will generally be created.

You must remember, this number refers to full members. The FBI estimates there are 10 associates for every member of an outlaw motorcycle club. A club with as few as 10 members can still be a pretty busy place, with many friends and associates hanging around at any one time.

The smallness of clubs means most members must be active in the club's political life. In a club or chapter of 15 members, possibly five of those would hold an executive position. For instance, each club would have a president, vice-president, secretary, treasurer and sergeant-at-arms. Smaller clubs may have only a couple of office bearers. One such club is the Descendants, which has only eight members. Its office bearers are reduced to a president, treasurer and sergeant-at-arms. The major clubs, which stretch across the globe, would have these positions at each level. Clubs such as the Bandidos and Hell's Angels have international office bearers, national office bearers and chapter office bearers.

These large clubs have monthly executive meetings and yearly conventions, called world runs, that are attended by bikies from all countries in which the clubs have a presence. Those clubs with a national charter will also have a national run, which is where most of the national business takes place. Each chapter must elect a member to represent them at the national or international level.

NATIONAL ORGANISATIONAL STRUCTURE

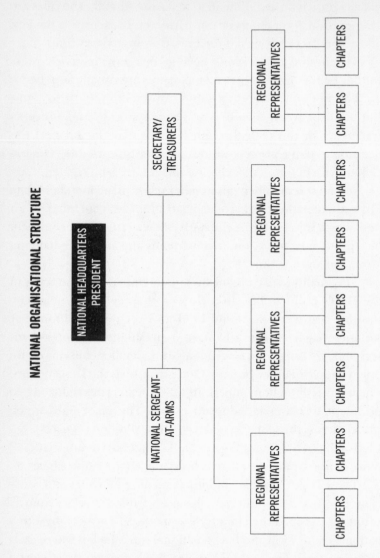

CHAPTERS ORGANISATIONAL STRUCTURE

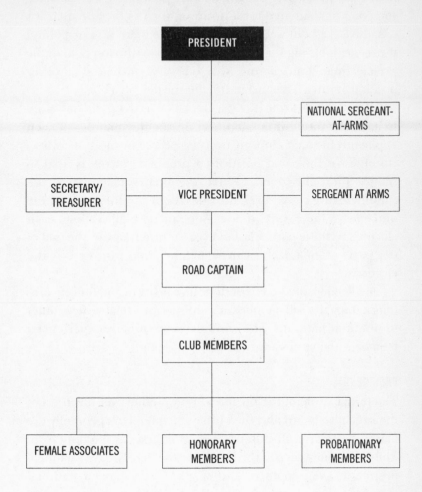

All positions are democratically elected. Elections are usually held annually for national and chapter positions. It's unusual for someone to challenge for a position, such as president, as it's usually worked out well in advance. While there is some behind the scenes lobbying for positions, the person who loses out in the pre-election manoeuvring will often be promised another position, or they'll be next in line for the top job.

If it comes to a vote it's by secret ballot, with candidates asked to leave the room while members debate the qualities of each applicant. In some clubs, if there are three or more members running for the same position, a preliminary vote is held to reduce the field to two. Once the final vote is taken, the candidates are called back into the room and informed of the outcome. A huge party to clear the air normally follows each election. As these parties last at least for three days, by the end of the party often no one can remember who won or lost the elections.

While there are no restrictions on who can stand for office, as long as they're a full member, it's unusual for a relative newcomer to put their hand up. The candidates are usually experienced members who've already held minor positions.

PRESIDENT

The primary role of the president is to preside over meetings of the executive board and the club or chapter. He's generally the liaison person for all club business and serves as spokesperson. The larger clubs, such as the Bandidos and Rebels, have a national president. Even some of the smaller clubs have a national president. The Comancheros, with only three chapters, has a national president, its founder Jock Ross. However, that's probably due more to Jock's particularly autocratic style than any need to have an overriding executive. The same is true of Red, the Odin's Warriors' president who has been in the position for many years.

In most clubs the president's role is to execute the decisions of the club, not to autocratically rule the club. He'll make minor decisions and resolve inconsequential debates among members, but the heavy stuff has to be decided by the entire group. This restriction on the president's powers reflects the fact that, by and large, the clubs are extremely participatory democracies that require members to be involved in governing the club. The president does, however, have the right to tell everyone to shut up and put the matter to a vote.

The president has a very stressful role. Constantly liaising with police, the weight of having to refer virtually everything back to the members and the overall leadership role can place a lot of strain on an individual. I've seen people who have accepted the president's role being forced to step down after a few months in office because of the stress of the role.

I remember one former president of a Hell's Angels chapter who had to resign when the pressure of the presidency got too much for him. I saw him at Broadford not long ago, and he seemed a different man. He was obviously still a member as he was hanging around backstage, but he no longer appeared to be carrying the weight of the world that comes with a club presidency. Conversely, some thrive on the pressure. These are generally the presidents who rule the club with an iron fist, such as Jock Ross. He's been president since the Comancheros was formed in the early 1970s, even while serving time in prison for the Milperra murders. Mick, the president of the Hell's Angels South Australian chapter has been at it for about 12 years. However, he's not autocratic like Jock, and takes the occasional year off to relax from the pressure.

Some presidents seem to be born to the position, such is their leadership skill.

Two such club presidents are Alex Vella of the Rebels Australia and Sonny Barger of the Hell's Angels in the US. This pair has led large national clubs with hundreds of members. Barger was president when the Hell's Angels grew from three chapters in the US to more than 110 chapters internationally. Considering that the Hell's Angels is a voluntary organisation with a turnover of about 75 per cent of their members every 10 years, that's no mean feat.

Alex Vella has been called Australia's answer to Sonny Barger. He'll never say it, because of the club rivalry, but he'd feel good reading it. He's a unique creature, a leader of men, but head of a club that is universally disliked and disrespected in the hardcore bike world. That's because of Vella's achievment in creating Australia's largest motorcycle club, and the Rolls Royce cars and battalion of Harleys in his garage. A former champion boxer, he's now a millionaire through making wise investments. He was actually able to force the New South Wales police to give back seized property as he had an impeccable paper trail to prove it had been bought legitimately.

One former club president told me that often the leadership is hoisted on the most 'problematic' people in the club, in an attempt to make them responsible for their actions. 'Self-discipline is instilled by the responsibility of leadership,' he said. It really is a case of making the man. It's the led or be led principle, which says: 'If a member can neither lead or be led, they should be expelled.' The Gypsy Joker charged over the assault of a policeman in early 2001 was later actually elected president. It was a case of seeing how well he would perform as the leader of the club.

However, if presidents chosen in such circumstances fail to prove their worth, it's been known for them to be thumped and dumped from the position, or even black marked and kicked out of the club if he really mucks up. Generally though, the president is at least the leader of a major faction of the club, and moves to expel him would cause a very serious split within the club.

VICE-PRESIDENT

As in government, the role of vice-president carries little power or responsibility apart from the times when the president is absent. If the police are on the club's case, that may be more often than not. Often the vice president's most important function is to quell factional conflict within the club. The leader of a faction is often appointed vice-president to keep the peace. Or simply, as in politics, the vice-president is someone who aspires to become president.

SECRETARY

The club secretary fulfils the standard functions of any club secretary – recording and maintaining meeting minutes and policy changes; keeping an eye on meeting procedure and corresponding with outsiders on behalf of the club.

It's no easy task. Imagine trying to take minutes for a club meeting with everyone ignoring the rules of the meeting, strongly arguing their point of view, or going off on a tangent. The secretary must endeavour to capture the essence of what's happening to record the minutes. For an outlaw motorcycle club, these minutes are highly confidential so it's the secretary's responsibility to ensure they are kept in a safe place.

TREASURER

The treasurer's functions include collecting the dues and fines and monitoring income and expenditure. Again, the role is no different from any other club or society. The position holds little power and certainly no budgetary authority. The highly democratic nature of clubs ensures financial decisions are closely scrutinised.

SERGEANT-AT-ARMS

This is perhaps the most peculiar and interesting of all the positions in a club. It's also one of the most influential. Every Australian outlaw motorcycle club has a sergeant-at-arms.

It's believed the grand title was actually pinched from the Freemasons, while another theory has its origin in the Tower Guards in London. One of the few places to find a sergeant-at-arms is in the Westminster system of government. While nowadays largely ceremonial, it once served the same role as the bikie sergeant-at-arms – to keep the peace.

The police often refer to this position as the 'enforcer' – the person who ensures the rules of the club are observed. Sometimes the sergeant-at-arms will have to 'enforce' the rules when members step out of line, but usually he'll act as a 'quality controller'. That is, he's responsible for maintaining the standards of the club or chapter. He'll levy fines and make sure colours are returned. His duties even extend to ensuring tattoos are end-dated if a member is expelled.

He often has his work cut out. He's expected to enforce rules for a bunch of fiercely independent people bent on rebelling against society norms. That sometimes means they rebel against club rules. An example of the sergeant-at-arms' duties would be during meetings when discussion gets heated and the procedures start to falter. The president might signal to the sergeant-at-arms to restore silence and order. He's the only club member allowed to use violence towards another member in meetings, but that's pretty rare. The sergeant-at-arms will usually be chosen because he's the sort of bloke who can diffuse a situation before it gets to that. He'll have a forceful personality, sober habits, and have his wits about him. He's usually a communicator and a thinker. Yet at the end of the day he has only one vote like everyone else.

It's common for the sergeant-at-arms to be a relatively long-term position at the club, with terms of 5 to 8 years. The stable personality of these people allows them to stay in the job longer than the type of personality required for the high-pressure role of president.

THE RULES

It's easy to overstate the organisational aspects of the clubs. Most run without a lot of the procedural bullshit. However, what cannot be overstated are the rules. Without rules the clubs couldn't function. However, some rules are more important than others. All clubs have rules set down in the form of a constitution. The clubs closely guard these constitutions. Their reasoning is that the rules are no-one else's business. Fair enough, I suppose. Only a few club constitutions have made it into the open, including the two that follow. They're both from US clubs and are a few years old. The fines, for instance, would be considerably higher nowadays. Most Australian clubs adopted the Hell's Angels' rules outlined, and these remain largely unchanged to this day.

Satan's Angels Motorcycle Club
Rules and regulations

The rules of the club will be strictly enforced. If anyone breaks them they will be dealt with by an appointed committee made up of the five original members. There will be a special group of rules and if broken will require immediate dismissal. There will also be general rules. If these are broken, it could mean either dismissal or suspension, whatever the committee sees fit.

Breaking any of the following rules will be reason for immediate dismissal:

1   Failure to pay his dues in accordance to the section dealing with the paying of dues.
2   If a group or individual attacks any member, the whole club shall stand behind him and fight if

necessary. If, however, the member is drunk and aggressive and purposely starts an argument, the rest of the members will escort him away, or step between before trouble starts.

3   No member will disgrace the club by being yellow. (The above rule will be put forward to applicants. If they feel they cannot abide by these rules and are not in favour of them, they will be denied membership to the club.)

4   No member will destroy club property purposely.

5   No member will take the attitude that he doesn't have to help other members and other members don't have to help him.

6   No member will go against anything the club has voted for and passed. Meaning if we decide to have a ride and when we reach there we will sleep out in sleeping bags, no one will go off by himself and rent a room for the night unless he is sick with a cold or that sleeping out would be impossible for some reason. The people in charge of the ride will decide if he has a legitimate reason.

7   No members will get together on their own and plan something for themselves on club rides. It will be brought up to the whole club and the whole club will participate in anything that is decided upon.

8   The club will always stay together on rides, field meets, etc, and will not fraternize with rival clubs. The only way a member will be permitted to leave the main group will be to notify the president or whoever is in charge. When the time comes that the majority feel it's time to leave, we will all leave together. Anyone staying behind for a good reason will do so at his own risk and can expect no help.

9   Members will have good attendance. Must have good reason for not attending meetings or rides, such as working, sickness, no transportation, bike not running.

Dues

Dues will be $2 per month, payable every meeting or every second meeting. Upon failure of paying dues within two weeks, members shall be suspended and turn in his crest [sic]. If within two months dues still aren't paid, the crest will be forfeited to pay them and member will no longer be considered a member. The only exception to this shall be if a member is in jail, or out of town for a period of time. If he is in jail, dues won't be expected, but if he is out of town dues will be paid when he returns.

Applications

Anyone wanting to become a member must go through a two month waiting period or more. Upon voting him in, the voting of members will only be taken as an opinion. The five original members will decide whether he is in or not. To be voted in, an applicant will fill in a form and a fee of $5 is charged. If at the end of two months it's decided he will not make a good member, he is refused membership and his application fee is not returned to him.

   Whether he is voted in or not will be based upon:

1   Participation in club affairs, rides, meetings, etc.
2   Must have a running bike worth $50 or over.
3   Show a sincere interest in club and bikes.
4   Will stand behind club and members.
5   Will go along with what the majority of club decides.
6   Interested in road club. Road rides come before competition events.

7   His opinion on rule numbers two and three.

8   Is on the road with bike equipped for the road.

General rules

1   No girlfriends taken on weekend rides unless decided upon by membership.

2   If club calls a ride all members will attend. If a member is working, sick, bike not running, he will be excused. If a member turns up at a ride and has no bike, someone who isn't packing can pack him [riding pillion] unless he is already packing or if his bike isn't in good enough shape to pack or if packing a rider will in some way do harm to the bike.

3   On weekend rides, a member should be able to take the time off work to attend. If, for some reason, it's impossible and there are over four members who can't leave 'til the following day, the rest of the club will wait for them.

4   Meetings will be closed except for prospective members and anyone there on business. Or, the meeting before a weekend ride, anyone wishing to attend the ride will be allowed at the meeting. Any non-member attending one of our rides will follow our rules. This goes for any other club attending our rides. If they break our riding rules, we stop and let them continue by themselves.

5   Anyone who has been kicked out will return his crest and will receive only half of what he paid for it.

6   During a meeting there will be no talking among members until they get the floor through the president. A sergeant-at-arms will be appointed and anyone not abiding by the above will be evicted.

7   No-one shall pass the road captain or whoever is in charge of the ride.

8   Where we go on our rides will be voted upon by the entire membership.

9   The treasurer shall keep a clear record of all money paid in and out during the week and will balance it out before every meeting. The books will be gone over once a week.

10 Everyone will attend the meeting on his bike if it's favourable weather, unless his bike is broken down or not running at the time.

11 If, for some reason, such as a licence suspension, a member can't ride on the road, or if his bike is not running for a long period of time, or if he is without a bike for a short time, he will turn in his crest, and upon getting back on the road, the crest will be returned.

12 Everyone must have a bike. Consideration will be given to any member who is in between bikes but he must sincerely intend to get another bike in the near future.

13 It is recommended to members to have their crests fitted to their jackets with snap buttons so they can be removed without damage.

14 No-one shall lend his crest or T-shirt to any non-member unless it is someone who is being packed. Once off the bike, the non-member must return the crest.

15 Around town, no members will purposely cause trouble wearing a crest, such as causing a disturbance at the clubhouse in such a way as to have cops brought in.

16 Everyone wears his crests in rides – only crests, no club jackets.

17 Anyone leaving town for period longer than six months turns in crest and is no longer a member. Can submit application when he returns.

18 Anyone missing meetings, even if at work, gets fined $1 except for guys in hospital or jail or out of town for a period of time. Two weeks' holidays not included, including applicants [nominees].

Hell's Angels
By-laws

1 All patches will be the same on the back, nothing will show on the back except the HELL'S ANGELS patch. City patch is optional for each charter. One patch and one membership card per member. Member may keep original patch if made into a banner. Prospects will wear California rocker on back and prospect left front where top of pocket is on a Levi jacket. FINE: $100 for breaking above by-law.

2 No hypes. No use of heroin in any form. Anyone using a needle for any reason other than having a doctor use it on you will be considered a hype. FINE: Automatic kick-out from club.

3 No explosives of any kind will be thrown into the fire where there is one or more HELL'S ANGELS in the area. FINE: Ass-whipping and/or subject to California President's decision.

4 Guns on California runs will not be displayed after 6 p.m. They will be fired from dawn 'til 6 p.m. in a predetermined area only. Rule does not apply to anyone with a gun in a shoulder holster or belt that is seen by another member if it is not being shot or displayed. FINE: $100 for breaking above by-law.

5 Brothers shall not fight each other with weapons;

when any HELL'S ANGEL fights another HELL'S ANGEL it is one on one, prospects same as members. If members are from different charters, fine goes to California Treasurer. FINE: $100 for breaking above by-law or possible loss of patch.

6   No narcotic burns. When making deals, person gets what they are promised or the deal is called off. FINE: Automatic kick-out from club.

7   All HELL'S ANGELS fines will be paid within 30 days. Fines will be paid to that charter's treasurer to be held for the next California run.

8   One vote per chapter at California officers meetings. For California votes, two no votes instead of a majority, two no votes to kill a new charter and if a charter goes below six they must freeze or dissolve on the decision of California officers meeting.

9   If kicked out, must stay out one year then back to original charter. HELL'S ANGELS tattoo will have an in-date and out-date when the member quits. If kicked out, HELL'S ANGELS tattoo will be completely covered or a 1/2 inch X through the tattoo. Of which of these is left to the discretion of the charter.

10 Runs are on the holidays; Three mandatory runs are Memorial Day, July 4, Labor Day.

11 No leave period except hospital, medical or jail.

As you can see, there are major rules that result in expulsion if broken, and minor rules that attract a fine. However, break enough of the minor rules and it turns into a major issue. It's based on the concept of the black mark. Members are allowed five black marks in three years. Any more and they must hand in their colours and/or resign from the club. The colours are usually put in the club safe and the ex-member given time to prove he can obey club rules, so he's not cut off completely.

Black marks are usually given for serious misdemeanours, such as using stronger drugs than alcohol at church or bringing police heat onto a club. I expect the Bandido who put forward membership for two undercover policemen who infiltrated the club would be a good example of the sort of behaviour that would earn a black mark.

It can be a battle being a club member. The time and social commitments place enormous strains on personal and professional lives. The commitment expected of a club member would make a high-powered executive wince. The club is expected to take precedence over family, work and friends. For the hardcore clubs, members are expected to put the club above all else.

It's not a weekend thing, or social matter. It defines that person, perhaps for the rest of their life. I've often heard someone referred to as a former bikie or former Hell's Angel long after his association with the club has ceased.

It's a life. Being a true club member is a whole lifestyle. You can't really have another life.
Former club president

The responsibility of when you decide to wear a patch, it's a way of life.
Former club president

Outsiders don't understand the commitment, leading to the bikie becoming cocooned into the world of the clubs, away from mainstream society.

I guess I was about six months into being a full member when I noticed that I really didn't have friends from outside the club any more. I'd really only maintained one friend and he lived a fair way away. It's like the club takes on complete ownership over your time and life. In some ways, that's great but in other ways, when I'm with my ol' lady, we talk about old friends and associates and wish we could find the time to see them now. But you can't. If you do go to see them, they just want to talk about the club anyway, and we are not supposed to speak about club business with 'cits' [citizens].

Bandido

I could see it. The more I participated in club activities, the less I had in common with my old set of friends. It got down to the point where I just couldn't be bothered seeing anyone outside the club. On occasions, I'd run into people who I knew. In these cases the people were either shit scared of talking with me or so intimidated about what I was wearing on my back that there was just nothing really to talk about except what had happened to so and so and trivial shit like that. No, the club is my life now and I've accepted it.

Hell's Angel

Under some clubs' constitutions, missing major meetings or runs for family reasons is not tolerated. Being in hospital or prison may be a valid excuse, yet a child's illness is not considered significant enough to prevent a member from being fined or expelled. Some members accept that sort of discipline as necessary for the club to survive. Others soon decide the commitment is just too much.

I didn't obey all the rules. In particular, I associated with members of other clubs. First and foremost I was a bikie.

Then I was a club member. This wasn't acceptable to Jock
[Ross, the president].
Former Comanchero

The commitment places an incredible strain on families.
Wives and steady girlfriends also find they're cut off from old
friends, sucked into the world of the club, where the only social
occasion is a trip to the clubhouse or a night out with other club
wives or girlfriends. Some accept it, while others soon let their
man know that he must decide – it's either her or the club. It's why
you find many club members actually end up with partners who
have some association with the clubs – a sister of another member,
or someone who has grown up in a club family. Even from this
background it takes understanding women to be partners.

It's a real pain. Sometimes he'd be gone for days and I'd
worry about him like crazy. And the club, God, did they
expect their pound of flesh … like maybe half his non-work
time was devoted to club events. It was worse when he was
president. At that point he was gone at least five nights a
week and working during the day. It got to the point where
our youngest child called him 'uncle daddy' one night and
it brought the whole thing to a head. After a lot of crying
and my carrying on, he agreed to quit the president's job.
Later, he decided to quit the club. We still enjoy going out
riding together but all the hassle and absences are just gone.
Wife of former Bandido

It's one of my greatest fascinations with the bikie clubs. The
incredible discipline imposed by the clubs on their members is at
such odds with the public image of the clubs. It's also completely
at odds with the reasons bikers become immersed in motorcycle
culture – the freedom of it all.

Many bikers opt not to become club members because of the politics.

Yeah, I was a prospect for the Rebels. I just couldn't hack the politics. All the rules, all the factions, all the bullshit ... I finally took off the rocker and handed it back to Alex and told him I didn't want the fuckin' thing.
Former Rebel prospect

However, there's a view that those who opt out because of the rules were never cut out for the bikie lifestyle in the first place.

Look, the rules are important. They tell you in no bullshit terms what the bottom lines of the club are. Some of the blokes in the club need this kind of clear picture of the world, you know?
Club member

There's a much stronger code of decency in the clubs than in the outside world. The simple reason is the punishment comes harder, and no technicality will get you off. If you fuck up, it's pretty well known before you do it. Don't go crying that you didn't see the sign or didn't realise what would happen. You wouldn't have got past being a prospect if you didn't know. The rules are there. There are very few but they are administered very strongly.
Former club president

Which brings me to my old mate Rudi, who was responsible for broadening my research.

Rudi chose not to join a club due to his dislike of their rules and politics.

I first met Rudi in 1985 when I moved to the Latrobe Valley in eastern Victoria. He was enrolled in a Diploma of Welfare Studies course I was teaching at Gippsland Institute of Advanced Education and stood out like dogs' balls. He'd show up to class in the most disgustingly tattered and stained full-length wool army coat. With his long reddish brown hair and beard he looked a sight. He proudly wore his biker rings and I had a strong suspicion there were an assortment of tattoos under the multiple layers of biker T-shirts and paraphernalia. Physically, he stood about 180 cm or 5 foot 11 inches with a stocky build.

My first encounters with Rudi were challenging. Whenever I'd use a biker-related example in my class on deviance he'd become aggressive and sometimes truculent. I found it easier to let him tell the biker stuff, then I'd try to integrate the information into an academic context. We soon started working on a few biker-related projects. At the time he was still a bit slow, as he'd taken up study after crashing his bike. He had plates and screws in his legs and shoulders, which forced him to walk with a pronounced limp.

He never fully recovered from the crash when, as he put it, a 'stupid bitch' drove her car into the side of him when she did a right hand turn as he was going through a green light. 'The cow couldn't see a big black bike on a sunny day.'

Nevertheless, he proved invaluable, for he was a biker through and through, with a keen, analytic and inquisitive mind that made him extremely useful for biker research.

Rudi was one of those classic bikers who became a hardcore biker after they felt persecuted by society. In his case, it was the unfairness of the punishment meted out to the car driver who seriously injured him.

The accident left him in a pretty bad way. He broke his legs and ribs and all his teeth and was actually given the last rites at the scene. At the subsequent court hearing two police sat next to him as the verdict was read out – an $80 fine for the driver. Rudi went berserk. The police, who obviously expected him to react, grabbed him and settled him down, explaining later that an $80 fine was a good result. Car drivers usually got off lighter in these cases. Rudi couldn't believe the injustice. He was paying more on speeding fines. 'My idea of fair play disappeared.'

Not only did he take on the appearance of the hardened biker after that, finally buying himself a Harley, he also became passionate about biker politics and what he believed was a government attack on his lifestyle. He was one of the founding members of the Helmet Law Reform Organisation, a coalition of riders that wanted to eliminate the laws that made wearing a motorcycle helmet compulsory. They campaigned for a probationary period where helmets would be compulsory, followed by optional use after that. They never succeeded.

In about 1984 he became a key member of the local biker club, the Valley and Districts Motorcycle Club. It was mainly a social club, yet also had a political edge, soon finding itself in conflict with the Motorcycle Riders Association. While the VDMC and the MRA both supported issues such as no hard wiring of lights and elimination of man-made motorcycle hazards on major roads, they couldn't agree on how to achieve these goals. The MRA was devoted to 'working within the system', while the VDMC believed in pressure and action. Rudi thought the MRA were 'pussyfooting about and not rebellious enough'. Rudi actually joined the local MRA under the leadership of Dave Hornsby because they were a bit more radical and forceful. The MRA Gippsland was eventually expelled from the mother body due to the differences in the groups.

Rudi's passion for the VDMC and the biking lifestyle found a focus in the work he and I did in reforming the policing of motorcycle events. He passionately believed self-policing was the best way for motorcyclists to gain respect. We attended countless events reporting to various authorities and compiling data on what the Hell's Angels term 'self regulating'.

Yet he never wanted to actually join a 1% club. Like so many, he was turned off by the rules of the clubs and the commitment required.

Well, the guys in the clubs having to do this and having to do that ... all the commitment to the club just turned me off. The one club I would have joined would have been the [Hell's] Angels. I ran into the Satan's Cavalry but had run-ins with some that took me back to my school days. You know, some wannabe acting like he is shit-hot because he's got a nominee rocker on his coat.

All told, I didn't like riding with people. If you were with a group or club, then you had to bow to consensus. That wasn't for me.

Rudi's attitude reflects that of many members who decide to opt out of the clubs. They can't actually cope with the demands and structure of a group, so it tears them apart to be members. They don't want to be worried about having to do everything as a group. They want to recapture the impetuousness of biking. In many cases the most respected members are those who actually leave the clubs. They may not have the patches, yet they actually live the lifestyle they want to live, free from the rules and the commitment that, together, form the greatest enigma of the outlaw bikie world.

CHAPTER SEVEN WORK AND PLAY

Everybody has friends who piss in the pool. My friends
just do it from the high dive board.
Club member

Bikie life can be pretty hard, with a huge commitment required by
even the most junior members. However, I don't want to present
too harsh a picture. It's not all rules and commitment. If it were,
the clubs wouldn't survive. Members are drawn to the clubs to
associate with like-minded people who enjoy a laugh, a party and
offer some camaraderie. Outlaw biking is actually built around
four tenets – riding, brotherhood, territorial defence and
partying. Of the four, territorial defence is considered a necessary
evil, which I'll look at in Chapter 10. The others are really what
the clubs are all about.

Take brotherhood, for instance. Brotherhood is no fanciful
notion for the clubs. If you look at the rules in the previous
chapter you'll notice many of them are based on doing things
together and standing up for fellow members. However,

brotherhood can't be manufactured by rules. Members must be genuinely committed to each other. It's hard for outsiders to understand that there is a notion of family among the clubs when all they see is an unruly and violent image. When members call each other 'brother' they actually mean it. For many, the club becomes their family, particularly if they've come from dysfunctional homes.

> ... it was shithouse. Me and my sisters were split up and sent to different foster families. By the time I was eight, we were all sent to an orphanage when it got to be too much for Dad. He was a total piss pot by that point and couldn't look after us... the club is excellent. A bunch of guys that has a 'real' family feel to it...[you] know straight away what the rules are and you got brothers there to help you.
> **Coffin Cheater**

> He was brutal [the father]. Bashed the shit out of me and the family till I was big enough to stand up to him. I was 15 and I took a baseball bat to him that first time and stopped the bashings but it made the house pretty tense. The club seems much more relaxed and homey than that place ever did.
> **Club member**

Then there's the bond of real family ties. Most Australian outlaw clubs have multiple members from the one family. Many join because an older brother is a member. It stands to reason, as that's why many people are introduced to motorcycles in the first place. In the street gangs of New Zealand, India and the United States, there are cases of gang membership spanning many generations. In Australia, where the outlaw motorcycle club phenomenon is less than 50 years old, the intergenerational associations are not so obvious. Nevertheless, it's not unusual for a son to want to follow in his father's footsteps or for younger brothers to want to follow older brothers and join an outlaw motorcycle club.

> When I was little, I wanted to know what was so good at the clubhouse that Dad wanted to be there rather than home with us. I couldn't wait to join up to find out.
> **Hell's Angel**

The Bandidos had three brothers from the same family who were founding members of the club in Australia. There were also three brothers in the Hell's Angels in Melbourne in the mid-1980s and currently the Finks have a number of brothers. Conversely, I've also heard of a case where one biker joined a club because he didn't want to associate with his brother, who was a member of a rival club.

But most members are not looking for a substitute for their families. They're after the traditional camaraderie of any club.

> I can't speak for others but I joined the club because I like riding motorcycles, tattoos, nice women and the company of my mates.
> **Hell's Angel**

> The club's a bit like a working man's Masons or Foresters. It gives you a sense of identity and the camaraderie of like-minded blokes.
> **Finks Associate**

> The club really helps us out. You know you've got blokes backing you up in any situation.
> **Coffin Cheater**

As well as this notion of brotherhood, there is, incredibly, the concept of community good within the clubs. It sounds hard to believe when we only ever hear about bikies when they've been arrested for violence or drugs. But there's good inside there somewhere.

The Finks, for instance, donate any profit from their fundraising to charities at the end of each financial year. Last year it went to a charity supporting leukaemia sufferers. The women's club Dykes on Bikes has held runs with money raised donated to breast cancer research.

However, unlike the street gangs of the US and their push for minority rights, outlaw motorcycle clubs fail to include any social goals in their constitution, charter or by-laws. There's reference to social interests, self-advancement interests and motorcycling sports and politics promotion, but nothing about community work.

There's a strong outlaw motorcycle club presence in all aspects of motorcycle political life. For example, I was surprised to once find a senior member of the Hell's Angels folding leaflets and stuffing envelopes for the Motorcycle Rider's Association during a campaign to scuttle a plan to put small yellow bricks on major Melbourne roads to separate cars from trams. It was feared they'd only serve to separate bikes from riders.

The bikies sometimes get involved in charity events such as Christmas toy runs and blood donation drives. Others do that little bit more. One US Hell's Angel actually carried the Olympic Torch in the lead-up to the 1984 Los Angeles Olympics. He was chosen for his community work, although I believe it was done outside any club involvement. That's how most community work is carried out, as an individual, not as a club.

The clubs want to be out of straight society so they're not inclined to become involved. A few years ago I was chatting to a senior office bearer of the Hell's Angels' Melbourne Nomad chapter at his home when there was a knock on the door. It was around about the time of night when every loony seems to want to sell something, so I was looking forward to seeing what would unfold. Franko (not his real name) opened the door and this bloke introduced himself as the local 'Neighbourhood Watch' coordinator. He then asked Franko if he was interested in joining the local Neighbourhood Watch Association. Franko, totally deadpan, replied: 'Nah, man. It's not in my interest.' Imagine if the Neighbourhood Watch man realised that behind the door was a Hell's Angel. What if Franko had said yes and a Hell's Angel joined the committee? It'd make the neighbourhood patrols pretty interesting.

However, it's not to say the clubs aren't neighbourly. There's one story of a club member who suspected a house across the road was dealing drugs. He started to get sick of cars turning up at all hours, so he decided to tackle the issue. One evening a car full of blokes was sitting outside for longer than he thought necessary so, armed with a baseball bat, he headed outside to prompt them to move on. Imagine his surprise, and that of the car's occupants, when it was discovered they were police casing the place suspected of dealing the drugs.

The clubs are not averse to a bit of vigilantism. One club got sick of a group of skinheads hassling a Jewish business down the road from the clubhouse. The bikies eventually went to the shop one day when the skinheads were up to their antics and promptly beat the shit out of them.

But the clubs don't only get their kicks from beating up skinheads. They love a good laugh, even if the humour is pretty gross. Try this for size. The Finks were on a run to meet another club a few years back. A member of the Finks, aptly known as Bluey the Grot, came across a dead fox. Despite it being decayed and gangrenous, he threw it in his pack. I believe the club they were meeting was called the Savages, which was led by a bloke called Filthy Fred. When Bluey met Filthy Fred, he was alleged to have said: 'So, you're Filthy Fred, let's see how filthy you are.' Bluey grabbed the decaying fox by the tail and stuck a toothbrush up its arse. He pulled it out covered in rancid goo, and proceeded to brush his teeth with the toothbrush. He then handed the brush to Filthy Fred and said: 'Now, it's your turn.' Fred may have been filthy, but he had the good sense to decline.

Another time, the Finks rented a bus to drive from Adelaide to Brisbane for a bike show. To save time on toilet stops, they cut a hole in the bottom of the bus. Needless to say, the rental company didn't return their deposit.

As you can see, bikie humour is raucous and raw. It's part of the nominee process that potential bikers have to 'get' jokes. If they don't, they're not going to survive for long. Here's a sample.

Q: What turns a nine stone weakling into a 16-stone man of steel?
A: Polio

Q: Why don't blind people go parachuting?
A: Because it scares the hell out of their guide dogs.

This bloke breaks down in the middle of nowhere and gets down to look at his bike. A voice just behind him says, 'It's the spark plug'. He looks around but there are only two horses standing in the paddock near the road. He stares at the horses when one of them appears to move its mouth and say, 'It's the spark plug, mate'. This can't be happening, the bloke thinks, and continues to work on his bike.

Sure enough, the problem is the spark plug. He fixes it and heads into the nearest town for a beer.

In town, he tells the barman what happened. The

barman looks at him and asks: 'Were there two horses in the paddock?'

'Yeah', the bloke replies. 'A brown one and a white one.'

'Was the brown one near the fence?' the barman asks.

'Yeah,' the bloke replies. 'Why?'

'You're pretty lucky,' says the barman, 'the white one doesn't know anything about bikes'.

A biker was making love to his girlfriend by the side of the road when a cop car pulls up.

'Just what do you think you are doing?' asks the cop.

The biker looks up at the cop and says, 'I'm screwing my girlfriend.'

'Great' says the cop, 'I'm next then!'

'Sounds good to me,' says the biker, 'I've never screwed a cop before.'

Q: What's the difference between a porcupine and a carload of cops?
A: The porcupine has pricks on the outside.

Q: What's the difference between your wife and your job?
A: Your job still sucks after five years.

Q: What's the difference between a pair of women's knickers and a cop car?
A: The knickers only hold one cunt.

Hang around a clubhouse long enough and you'll hear worse than these. The clubhouse is a central part of bikie life. Like any headquarters, it's where the heart of a club lies, even if the club's philosophy is based on riding motorcycles.

As you'd imagine, the clubhouse is a major investment for a club, both financially and in terms of administration. Yet, having a clubhouse is vital to the life of the club. Most clubs start out meeting at members' houses and garages. After a couple of years, if the club looks like continuing, it's time to establish a clubhouse. Most rent before they can afford to buy. The landlord would have to be pretty tolerant, for most clubs would want to modify the property to bring it up to 'bunker status'. This means reinforcing it to protect against unwelcome guests, such as the police or other clubs.

Of course, once the locals see what's going on there's usually a hell of a ballyhoo and objections lodged with the local council.

Australian local government has little power to prevent the sort of changes the clubs makes, such as concrete reinforced walls, security cameras, reinforced doors, perimeter fencing and even dogs to patrol the perimeter. I'm not quite sure what a council would make of the Loners in Canada, who had a 220 kg lion patrolling its clubhouse. The club was taken to court by the local council for breaking a bylaw on keeping exotic animals. It makes the mind boggle.

It's a common theme across the world. The City of Montreal was powerless to stop a Bandidos' bunker being built in its city at the same time an Adelaide council was being asked to explain why the Gypsy Jokers and Rebels were able to build fortress clubhouses. There were actually calls from the State Opposition in early 2001 to raze the Rebels clubhouse after violent flare-ups between the club and police.

I visited the Gypsy Jokers clubhouse in late 2001 to see what all the fuss was about. It's located in an industrial area of Adelaide, not far from the Hell's Angels' and Finks' clubhouses. Adelaide is a tightly knit scene; members from the different clubs know each other pretty well and occasionally socialise together.

The first thing I noticed was the size of the block. It's about a half an acre in the old measure, or about a quarter of a hectare. Surrounding the perimeter was an almighty wall, about 3 metres high and built out of railway line and sleepers. It certainly wasn't built for its looks. The only break in the wall was for two large electric gates at the front of the clubhouse. It's incredible how tight the security is. The gates and perimeter fence are under constant video surveillance. On the gate is a keypad. Members punch in the code and the gates swing open. Visitors, such as me, push the call button and wait for an answer. You have to say who you are and why you are visiting. Only when you're deemed acceptable do you get the go ahead to enter.

Despite the tight security, there were no guard dogs, only a super-friendly cattle dog. You must remember, these places may look sinister but they're places for social gatherings, so four-legged storm-troopers are not very practical.

A Bikie clubhouse certainly gives the appearance of being party central. There'll be pool tables, video equipment, fridges, stove, couches, chairs, bars, tables and beds for members who need to crash. The Gypsy Jokers, for instance, had a large entertainment area beside the clubhouse, with another large area reserved for members to work on their bikes. Part of the reason they're found in industrial sites is not only because councils don't want them anywhere near residential areas, but so they can have their noisy parties without disturbing anyone.

It's expensive to establish and run a clubhouse, costing about $30 000–$50 000 annually to keep a chapter going. The clubs need to get income from somewhere. On top of the basics, such as keeping the lights and gas on, there are strange little things clubs must have, such as security cameras and radio scanners to alert them to nearby police. There has to be a safe, which costs a few bob, and a back-up generator in case something funny happens to the mains power supplies.

There are also hidden costs, such as bail money. The coffers of the clubs will generally pay a retainer for lawyers and bail bondsmen, although bail is not paid lightly. Members are expected to remain in prison to await their trial rather than waste funds on bail money. You need a pretty good reason for the club to pay your bail.

The bulk of a club's income comes from the sale of alcohol. Beer and bike parts are sold to members at prices slightly below retail. Members must also pay for patches and other paraphernalia such as cards and club stickers.

There are, of course, membership dues but they count for little. A full member pays dues of about $500 a year. However, with a maximum of 25 full members, that doesn't go far. Club fines do their bit, with an average $50 fine for violations of club rules, such as being late for a run. The club treasurer is always hoping for a few undisciplined members.

Some of the well-organised clubs have financial investments in legitimate businesses that supply income, such as the case of the Black Uhlans and its alleged retirement homes in Melbourne. Some clubs have invested in tattoo parlours and brothels, while other investments are a bit more down to earth. It is said the Melbourne Hell's Angel chapter specialised in making fish ponds, so it started a gardening business, using nominees for labour. The money was subsequently invested in property and a tattoo parlour.

Many clubs own their own clubhouse, with some of the large clubs owning extra holdings. The Melbourne Hell's Angels own a 15-hectare beachside property at Eden in southern NSW, which is used by club members for holidays, and also rented out to campers to generate income. The chapter also owns the 25-hectare Broadford property where it stages its annual concert.

The clubs also hold fund-raising parties. The largest and most well-known bikie fundraiser in Australia is the Hell's Angels concert held in Broadford each December. In its heyday it would attract up to 9000 people. The last few years have been a struggle, with crowds falling to below 4000, so I wouldn't be surprised if we've seen the end of Broadford. The large events seem to have run their course, with Australia's second largest outlaw club concert, Ponde, near Adelaide, having wound up in 2001.

Each club usually holds a couple of fund-raising parties a year that are open to outsiders. Most members don't like these parties, with a lot of citizens asking about club business. However, the members have to grin and bear it as they're required to attend, usually as 'bouncers' to keep the peace. I suppose if someone is asking too many questions they can throw them out. Another fundraiser is the field day, where strippers and the bike competitions feature. The clubs approach the field days with a lot more enthusiasm than the open parties as they generally attract only fellow bikers.

The clubs also have open nights at the clubhouse, where the club bar is opened up to anyone who wants to come along – except the police, of course. They're advertised through bike shops, swap meets and word of mouth.

Another opportunity for outsiders to socialise with the clubs is at swap meets. These are generally where motorcycle parts are bought or traded, but they are also an occasion for a huge party, and are held close to a pub so the clubs can kick on afterwards. In recent years the swap meets have been less prominent. I'm not sure why, although I suspect it may have something to do with amalgamation pressures.

The biggest and most anticipated social events are the runs. These are get-togethers out of the city to either celebrate an occasion, such as an anniversary, or just to party. The runs are for members only as there is usually a fair amount of club business at these events. It's a chance for chapters to get together and thrash out some politics and make inter-chapter decisions.

The runs are full-on parties, with plenty of grog, dope-smoking and strippers. A similar event is the biker rally, which is open to the general biker community, which would also include a gymkhana with prizes for the best and worst bike. The rallies, however, lack the intensity of the runs. The outlaw clubs like to go that step further. Instead of a wet T-shirt competition they'll have a stripper, and usually a double act to boot. They'll party harder and longer than the biker rallies, and often do so under police surveillance.

There are some great stories about the runs. The Finks pride themselves on their toughness. For several years on their runs they had a boxing ring where the top rope was actually barbed wire. Folklore has it that the wire had to be removed and replaced by a conventional rope after too many sets of boxing gloves were getting ripped on the barbs. However, I believe there were a few injuries involved as well.

Another popular run that has become a major fundraiser for some clubs is the poker run. It's similar to the run, but usually done in town and is open to outsiders. Members ride from pub to pub, collecting cards along the way. At the end of the run the person with the best poker hand wins. Interestingly, prizes are offered by some corporate heavyweights – major breweries, spirit manufacturers and motorbike companies. These companies recognise the bikies as valuable customers, and don't mind being associated with them. The Hell's Angels poker run in Adelaide attracts up to 400 people.

Many of the pubs visited on a poker run would generally be classed as biker pubs. These hotels are known to be friendly to all bikers. A few hotels are hangouts for particular clubs, which can make them targets in territory wars. It's common for these clubs to have an unspoken agreement with the pub that while it may have its own security staff the club will be responsible for its own club members and look after bike-related disturbances at the pub.

These pubs are like any other pub except the conversations usually focus on biker traditions, good rides, mechanical advice, good repair shops, and the names and addresses of friendly mechanics. Of course, a stripper or two is not uncommon.

Pubs on major highways that welcome bikers and bikies are highly valued. They can do good business out of being known as a place to stop. One such pub was the Genoa Hotel on the Victoria–NSW border in eastern Victoria. Genoa hosted a major bike rally from 1984 to 1987, which I spent some time observing. The focus of the rally was, naturally enough, the pub. The first year the Motorcycle Riders of Australia rally attracted about 1200 people. Clubs soon saw the pub as a convenient place to either stop between Sydney and Melbourne, or a place for a weekend visit. Notably, the Hell's Angels frequented the hotel as a standard watering stop on runs to their property in Eden. The Ducati club used it as a destination for runs from Sydney and the BMW club used the hotel as a stopover on their runs from Melbourne.

Unfortunately, when the owners of the time left, the subsequent owners didn't have the same view of bikers, and the hotel lost its place as a biker hotel.

Another question I'm commonly asked is how the hell do the members support themselves, considering they must devote so much time to the clubs. In some cases it seems as if they spend most of their time down the club, making it difficult to hold down a meaningful job. With office bearers not being paid, they still must find time for work.

While bike riders in general come from a broad spectrum of society, the world of the bikie is much narrower. There are, however, a few professionals and middle-class men in the clubs. A Coffin Cheater from Perth, Eddie Withnal, has a Masters degree in literature, is taking a PhD in sociology and runs his own public relations company; a Gypsy Joker has a senior management position in a major Australian company; while I've heard of a Brazilian Hell's Angel who's an accountant and a Canadian Hell's Angel who plays the first trumpet with the Toronto orchestra.

However, these men are exceptions, with the clubs almost exclusively working class. Blue-collar bikies would be an apt tag.

The only detailed study of bikie occupations was done in Canada, within the Rebels' Alberta chapter. It found most members had blue-collar jobs or were tradespeople. You'd find this would be the case across the world. The analysis of the Alberta members' jobs was:

Ken	Part-owner of motorcycle shop	Full-time
Caveman	Truck driver	Seasonal
Steve	Part-owner of motorcycle shop	Full-time
Blues	Machinist (Plastic/Metal)	Seasonal
Larry	Labourer (auto body shop)	Full-time
Raunch	Welder	Seasonal
Gerry	Foreman in house construction	Full-time
Mike	Truck driver	Seasonal
Whimpy	Motorcycle mechanic	Seasonal
Clayton	Carpenter	Seasonal
Snake	Labourer, oil rigs	Seasonal
Dale	Butcher	Full-time
Jim	Auto body repairman	Full-time
Onion	Labourer, oil rigs	Seasonal
Saint	Mechanic/ tech student	Full-time
Danny	Electrician	Seasonal
Yesnoski	Machinist	Seasonal
Voodoo	Truck driver	Seasonal
Armand	Labourer, oil refinery	Seasonal
Killer	Labourer, construction	Seasonal
Crash	Labourer, oil rigs	Seasonal
Terrible Tom	Heavy equipment operator	Full-time
Wee Albert	Pipe fitter	Full-time
Ed	IBM technician/bouncer	Full-time
Indian	Truck driver/bouncer	Full-time

Popular occupations of Australian bikies tend to be in the areas of bike maintenance and tattoo industries. In recent years, many bikies have also become involved in hydroponic businesses. While perfectly legitimate, these businesses are blatantly aimed at those wanting to grow dope indoors.

The other interesting aspect of the above list is the nicknames. Nicknames are an important part of biker life, with nearly everyone attracting some sort of moniker. It's rare to find someone called by their real name. They're dished out based on personality (Rowdy for the quiet type), physique (Tiny is common for the biggest blokes), or an adaptation of their real name, such as the good old Davo or Robbo. Some great old nicknames from the '70s Adelaide club scene include Metho Tom, Blacktown Harley, Robbie Roadrunner, Terry the Tramp, Lucky Keiser and Barry Bullshit. It's pretty important to be given a nickname, as it means the club has accepted you.

Remember that you will be judged by the horse you rode in on.
Biker saying

Riding, as one of the tenets of bikie life, means a bikie must not only have a bike, but a bike he can be proud of. It can prove a financial burden for some members who hold down pretty basic paying jobs when a new standard Harley costs more than $25 000. With many clubs stipulating that the bike must be modified, the member is required to spend even more.

The process of heavily modifying a bike is known as 'chopping'. Chopping a bike involves stripping down a stock, or factory, motorcycle to its barest essentials and dramatically rebuilding it to the owner's personal specifications. Modifications include extending the front forks to change the angle of the forks and replacing the standard handlebars with 'ape-hangers' to compensate for the fork extension. Ape hangers get their name from their extra length, which gives the rider the appearance of an ape hanging his arms in the air.

The standard exhaust system is next to go, with new, less muffled pipes giving the Harley its distinctive trademark sound. The motor is then bored and stroked, giving the bike a greater power to weight ratio. The suspension is sometimes removed. This 'hard tail' gives the bike lower radical profile, but it can be a pain in the arse, literally, with most bikies deciding to leave the suspension alone. One long run on a bike with no suspension is usually enough to convince a bikie to forego looks for comfort. Finally, there's the paint, perhaps the most crucial issue when considering the image of not only the bike, but also its rider. The paint job must produce a machine the club is proud to be associated with.

Customising a motorcycle is more than just producing a special machine. The bike represents the bikie himself. The look and details of the bike sends a signal to other bikies as to the type of person who owns and rides it.

In the mid-1960s many US clubs, including the Gypsy Jokers, Satan's Slaves, Satan's Sinners and the Jokers Out of Hell, embraced the chopper, making it the only acceptable form of transport. However, times have changed, with many outlaw motorcycle clubs allowing stock Harley-Davidsons these days. It cuts the costs for members, but means a bit of the personalised nature of the bikes is lost.

However, not all club bikes are gleaming show ponies. There's a trophy given at every rally for the 'Rat Bike'; it's awarded to the roughest or rattiest machine at the rally. Bikers take great pleasure in keeping these mechanical and visual nightmares on the road. In the bikie world, it's class to have a rat bike. It's a testament to the bikie's mechanical abilities and skills to be able to keep it on the road. It's also a symbol of the loyalty and devotion the biker has for his machine. The Tasmanian club, the Donald Ducks, took particular pride in the shoddy appearance of their bikes.

The elements I've explained in this chapter are just some of the aspects of club life. It really only touches the surface. All clubs are different. Some run on the smell of an oily rag, others like the opulent lifestyle, with the flash bikes and smart headquarters. However, each adheres to those four basic tenets of outlaw club life – riding, brotherhood, territory and partying. Everything else plays second fiddle.

CHAPTER EIGHT GOD, SATAN AND OTHER MYTHS

The world of the bikie is as much about myth and fantasy as it is about bikes and territory.

The clubs do little to counter the legends that surround them. They provide the aura of invincibility that encourages many likely enemies to give them a wide berth. They create outrage among the straight citizens, something the clubs revel in as a sign they're no longer part of the normal world. However, I've found the legends also create problems for the clubs. The notion that the clubs are huge organised crime outfits is largely a myth for most clubs, yet it puts incredible pressure on them from the police. I know the clubs would love to rein in this myth, but once the myth has been established it's almost impossible to get rid of. The outrage stuff also makes life difficult for many members. They find themselves shunned by former friends, their family tarnished by the clubs' reputation and their job prospects diminished.

Yet some aspects of club life that may, at first glance, appear to be myths are in fact true.

Take God, for instance. Incredibly, religion plays a bigger part in club life than many realise. Perhaps even more so than the clubs themselves care to admit. It's an area I've been interested in for a long time, as the clubs are contradictory in so many ways. I was keen to find out if religion was in the same boat.

From 1986 to 1990 I conducted a survey on religious orientation among the Australian biker scene, with respondents from Motorcycle Riders' Association clubs and outlaw clubs. The majority claimed 'none' as their religion (78 per cent), 11 per cent claimed to be Satanists while a meagre 7 per cent nominated Christianity. None claimed to be agnostics. When I looked at outlaw club members only, 52 per cent said they had no religion, while 23 per cent claimed to be agnostics. Christians accounted for a respectable 20 per cent and the Satanists came in dead last at 5 per cent. The surveys were not exactly scientific, conducted mainly at runs and parties, but they give a reasonable snapshot of the place of religion in the biker world.

You would presume religion is a part of mainstream society the bikies would want to reject, yet religion is never far from the surface. One of the main reasons for this is the work of the Christian motorcycle clubs. They're such an anomaly, hanging around the fringe of the bikies.

The members of these clubs see themselves as having some sort of calling, yet they want to do it through motorcycles. They perform the role of traditional holy men in the biker world, officiating at marriages, christenings and funerals. They also see themselves as being able to act as counsellors for outlaw bikies. Many of them know their stuff. A former president of the God Squad, for instance, is a Baptist minister, while another member is a Jewish Talmudic scholar, so it's not as if they're rank amateurs.

I remember coming across the camps of the Christian motorcycle clubs at Broadford one year. They were no different from any other clubs, with signs out the front of the camp having the bikie-esque 'show us your tits' scrawled on them. They had a mountain of beer cans any outlaw club would be proud of. However, the camps offered 'chill out' zones for bikies who'd drunk or smoked too much, where they could get their shit together or stop getting into further trouble. Of course, many bikies steer clear of the Christian clubs because they fear having religion shoved in their face, as some Christian club members are prone to do. I've only heard of two outlaw bikies who have seen the light, so to speak, and jumped over to the Christian clubs.

In many ways, the Christian motorcycle clubs are identical to the outlaw clubs, with colours, tattoos and slogans. Of course, the tattoos and patches have Christian themes, not the usual Satanic images of the bikie clubs.

The chapters are also roughly the same size and they ride identical bikes. They attend church once a week, as the outlaw clubs do, and have fines for infringements such as not spending enough time on their bikes. They act like outlaw motorcycle clubs. They're relatively guarded and secretive about their colours, ride in similar formations and have outlaw organisational structures.

Admission as a club member involves roughly the same process as for an outlaw club. First, you must 'hang around the club'. Then someone from the club has to agree to be your sponsor in joining the club. There is then a vote to allow you to be an official prospect of the club. The prospect period is several years, due to concerns about the quality of applicants. You have to be dedicated to be a Christian biker. And you have to know your stuff. As part of the application to join the God Squad, prospects are required to complete a 24-page questionnaire and are subjected to oral exams on their religious beliefs. They also must know certain parts of the Bible.

Prospects are also required to keep a log of the kilometres ridden and the number of club functions attended. The patch can be taken back by the club for various offences.

The largest Christian club in Australia is the God Squad, which has four Australian chapters, in Melbourne, Sydney, Brisbane and Launceston, and two international chapters. At any one time it has up to 150 members. The Long Riders, with about 50 members, have chapters in Adelaide, Melbourne and Perth, while the Pilgrims, Ambassadors, Holy Ghost Riders and The Brotherhood are single chapter clubs. The Brotherhood has five to ten members . The average membership age across the clubs is late 30s to early 40s.

John Smith is the bikies' preacher. The current international president of the God Squad, he's been involved with outlaw motorcycle clubs for many years. He's in a unique position. His club is not actually a 1% club, but a 10% club, which puts him firmly on the edge of the outlaw clubs. I've known Smithy for many years and count him as one of my good friends from the biker world.

The last time I caught up with him was at a Coffin Cheaters' chapter party. It was magic. Smithy even went so far that night as to confer upon me the title of 'tribal elder'. I'm not sure what it means, but as a fellow tribal elder who is four years older than me, he can make all the decisions and shoulder whatever responsibility comes with the title. That night was an incredible reminder of the bizarre world the bikies exist in, with Smithy pointing out the background of some of the people at the party. Among the hardcore club members there were several God Squad members, some converted 1 percenters, a sprinkling of graduates from the staid and conservative University of Melbourne, some full-on preachers like Smithy, and there was even a Talmudic scholar!

Smithy and I bought reams of tickets for our grog and got down to the business of chatting about his life. Smithy was drinking two or three whiskies to my one beer or whisky. Our interview plan soon flew out the window as I got too pissed to string words together, let alone take notes. We did, however, have the sense to agree to sit down after a service he was holding the next day at the campground outside the Coffin Cheaters' clubhouse. Incidentally, the clubhouse had recently been re-zoned so the club could establish a brothel. Smithy didn't seem too phased about doing a sermon there. Something about going to the sinners ...

By the time he conducted the service the next day, I'd hauled my sick and sorry arse out of there. I was actually glad to get away after Smithy showed me something that shook me up. We were chatting about his place in the biker world when he pulled out a photograph. As I said, I'd known Smithy for many years, yet I was shocked when he showed me a picture of himself wearing a long Kentucky coat and holding a 357 Magnum pistol in one hand and a long barrel Colt 45 in the other. His arms were crossed over his body so the barrels of the guns rested at shoulder height. His greying beard and piercing eyes only added menace to the picture.

What shocked me more than the image were Smithy's words, that this was how he saw himself in the biker world. I think the shock that someone of such spirituality could be seduced by such a violent notion really jolted me. So much so that I stumbled down to the sausage sizzle to sober up before getting a mate to take me home.

John Smith was born in 1942 in the working class Melbourne suburb of Reservoir. His grandfather was a working man who underwent a religious conversion upon meeting his grand-mother. His grandfather quit his job and became an evangelist and missionary based in the suburb of Preston. His father was one of three children, becoming a fitter and turner with the railways until he also underwent a religious conversion and became a Methodist Minister when Smithy was 7 years of age.

Smithy was a sickly child, suffering a severe burn injury at a very young age that saw him spend more than a year in hospital. At the age of 11 he contracted rheumatic fever, which hospitalised him for another two years. These extended bouts of illness meant Smithy was a bit older than his peers at high school.

The age difference, coupled with the fundamentalist religious orientation of his upbringing, made high school 'possibly the worst experience of my life'. He had few friends to protect him from the cruel taunting of the other students. Unlike many in this position, Smithy chose not to lash out, instead turning to his religion and spiritual experience for strength. He also persevered with his studies, obtaining his Higher School Certificate.

Upon leaving school he wanted to get away from the unhappiness of his childhood. He headed to Kedron Teachers College in Queensland, where he met his wife, Glenna. It was, as Smithy says, 'love at first sight'. They were soon married, and remain happily married today.

After graduating with a Bachelor of Arts he moved back to Melbourne, enrolling at the Melbourne Bible College where he learnt the fundamental Methodist religious traditions. His family's approach to religion had made Smithy a very conservative young man. He even participated in right-wing political activities, including rallies in support of the US during the Vietnam War.

After graduating from Bible college, he got a job as a teacher at Wonthaggi High School in country Victoria. He also preached at the local Methodist church. It was here his life changed. Following a sermon where he denounced Martin Luther King as a 'womaniser and Communist', a parishioner confronted him with the question: 'Have you heard Martin Luther King preach?' Smithy was forced to admit he hadn't. She persisted. 'Have you read Martin Luther King?'. Again, he was forced to answer 'no'. At that point, the parishioner handed him a copy of the film Strength to Love, an account of King's life, which included the legendary 'I had a dream' speech. Smithy watched the film and was mesmerised by what he saw. His eyes were suddenly opened to what was going on around him.

That film changed his life. He began to question many of his conservative beliefs and attitudes. Almost immediately he saw the folly of his ways in supporting the war, and how he had taken an almost non-compassionate view of minorities. He realised he must devote himself to helping others, particularly those on the edge of society. The moment he came across the outlaw motorcycle clubs he knew what his calling was. He had, in his words, 'a Mother Teresa type of experience'. He suddenly saw his missionary path, having 'a calling from God'.

'I would devote my humble talents and abilities which God had given me, to work with these people who were outcasts and estranged from mainstream society,' he declared.

First of all he had to learn to ride, as he had little experience with bikes, or those who rode them. The club he first came across was a now defunct club called the Drifters, but he soon heard of the Hell's Angels, Gypsy Jokers and other clubs, and began moving in their circles.

In an attempt to immerse themselves into biker culture to carry out their missionary work, Smithy and a few of his colleagues formed a club called the Victorian Christian Motorcycle Association. One night the members of the association were sitting around watching television when The Mod Squad burst onto the screen. It was a revelation. What a great name – The God Squad.

However, before their excitement translated into actually adopting the name they learnt of another club in Sydney with the same name, formed a few years earlier. Ironically, this club had run out of steam and was in the final throes of disbanding. Smithy got in contact with them, initially to see about the Victorian Christian Motorcycle Association becoming its Melbourne chapter, but soon found himself being offered the club colours to take away so he could form the club himself.

Smithy knew the way clubs worked, particularly the importance of earning a patch. It seemed a bit hollow to be merely given a patch. So Smithy politely declined the offer but agreed to become a prospect for the club. The Sydney president was keen to see the club continue, so agreed to keep the club going for the 12 months of Smithy's prospect period, much to the annoyance of others on the Sydney executive who were keen to move on.

After serving his year Smithy became a full member. He could now say he had earned the right to wear the patch, rather than merely accept it as charity. He was voted in as a full member in 1973 and the Sydney chapter immediately folded. Smithy found himself national president with the charter to form the Victorian chapter of the God Squad. He then devoted himself to working with Australia's outlaw motorcycle clubs 'running a rescue shop just outside the gates of hell'.

His first challenge was to define a role for the club within the world of the outlaw motorcycle clubs. After all, what did a pack of devout Christians have to offer hardened bikies? The answers began to emerge after much work and sweat. At first, the serious outlaw clubs denigrated the patch-wearing Christian club. They believed that if a club wore a patch it was an opposition club. However, it soon became evident that the outlaw motorcycle clubs and bikers required certain legitimate ceremonies, such as marriages, baptisms and, most of all, funerals, to be carried out by an authorised person. For some clubs the God Squad was the group they turned to.

Another issue for the fledgling club was its missionary work. The club charter was to save souls and offer a helping hand to people who wished to find salvation. This was a particular challenge for Smithy, as his conversion to liberal politics put him at odds with the dominant conservative values of the outlaw clubs. Smithy and his colleagues devised a long-term strategy to overcome this problem. The club would socialise and party with the clubs. Its role was to be there in case anyone wanted to talk or make serious decisions about life. They'd be available for counselling if required.

The God Squad began to make inroads when the outlaw clubs realised they weren't a bunch of wowsers or snitches. They partied as hard as any club. Smithy and the God Squad also began to change, behaving more like an outlaw motorcycle club than traditional missionaries – hence the pile of empties outside the God Squad tent. Like any club, they soon had a clubhouse; a large warehouse in inner-city Fitzroy. It was part Salvation Army kitchen and part outlaw clubhouse, with dinner available at no cost to those bikers who couldn't afford a feed.

Under Smithy's leadership, the emphasis of the God Squad became strongly counterculture. Civil disobedience by members was not only encouraged, it was expected.

In the early 1990s the club split, and a breakaway club, the Longriders, was established. The break was partly ideological and partly personality driven. It was also due to the God Squad's Melbourne chapter exceeding 25 members; the upper limit a club can handle without becoming factionalised.

The Longriders moved west, establishing chapters in Adelaide and Perth, cities where the ruling outlaw clubs had never allowed the God Squad to establish themselves. The God Squad chapters remain along the Australian east coast at Melbourne, Sydney and Brisbane.

Smithy held the reigns of power in the club for 20 years until the mid-1990s when he was stricken with prostate cancer, forcing him to step down from the presidency.

Following recovery from the illness, Smithy enrolled in a seminary program in the US at the University of Kentucky. The picture of the guns that I mentioned earlier comes from this era. He's currently completing a PhD on the outlaw motorcycle club movement as a counterculture and is in the final stages of writing his dissertation.

The relationship between the outlaw motorcycle clubs and Christian motorcycle clubs can be pretty icy, with many outlaw clubs increasingly asking why the Christian clubs dress like outlaw clubs when clearly they're not. For this reason some clubs refuse to use the Christian clubs for marriages and funerals because they regard them as rival clubs.

The outlaw clubs can get particularly upset when a Christian club flies colours in their territory. In the early '80s a preacher wanted to establish a Christian motorcycle club in Sydney. However, he wanted to set it up in Comancheros' territory. The preacher called on Comanchero leader Jock Ross to request permission for the Christian club to fly their colours on Comanchero turf. Jock allegedly responded by sending out a club member to beat him up. After he recovered from the beating, the preacher returned to the Comanchero clubhouse to again request Jock's permission for his club to fly their colours. This time Jock was said to have emerged, along with a few other club members, and beat the preacher senseless. He woke up in hospital with a broken jaw and fractured ribs. Following several months of recovery, and much prayer, the preacher summoned up the strength to visit the clubhouse for a third time to again request permission for the Christian club to fly their colours. Even Jock had to acknowledge his persistence. Permission was finally granted, but not until Jock made the preacher sweat it out as the club debated whether or not to grant him his wish. The preacher proved it was possible, even in the meanest territory, to fly colours with the permission of the dominant group, although not many would have his determination to achieve it.

However, that's not to say there isn't respect among the outlaw clubs for the Christian clubs. I was at Broadford in 1987 when the master of ceremonies, a Hell's Angel, came on stage with a special announcement:

Whoever stole the camera from the God Squad had better return the fucker. No questions will be asked if it's brought to the backstage area in the next hour. If we have to find it, then it's going to be a different story.

I heard that the camera was returned.

The Saturday afternoon at Broadford is the annual baby christening for the outlaw clubs. It's a very moving event. Outlaw motorcycle club members, their wives and associates often agree to act as godparents to the children. What has always struck me about this is that the responsibility is not taken lightly. I was present at the christening of the children of one bikie, who I'll call Jacko. He was a committed lifetime bikie who hung around the fringes of the clubs, particularly the Hell's Angels. He was in his early 50s when he met and married his second wife, Gillian. She had excellent bikie credentials, coming from an outlaw motorcycle club family.

Jacko and Gillian went to Broadford in 1986 to have their eight-week-old daughter and 15-month-old son christened. They chose a lone rider and associate of the Hell's Angels as the godfather of the youngest child. They had some heavy hitters for the godfathers of the toddler – a Hell's Angels sergeant-at-arms and John Smith, God Squad president.

Four years later it was discovered that Jacko was allegedly bashing Gillian and their children – the club members' godchildren. In desperation, Gillian showed up on the doorstep of the Hell's Angels associate and his wife, who was also godmother to both children. The couple took Gillian and the kids in, eventually helping them find a job and a nice place to live. The Hell's Angel sergeant-at-arms was called to inform him of what had happened to his godson. He was very supportive and helpful in the situation.

While this was going on, Jacko disappeared. About two years

later he re-appeared, working for a motorcycle shop in rural Victoria. He refused to be interviewed about what had happened, saying he no longer associated with the Hell's Angels or any other outlaw motorcycle club. I always suspected he'd been seriously 'counselled' by the Hell's Angels, even though the sergeant-at-arms later told me that wasn't the case.

To me it shows club members take their role as godparents seriously. They may say they reject religion, but christenings mean something to the bikies, carrying the responsibilities of care and support as it would for any extended family.

Another major religious event is the funeral. It's not surprising, considering the relatively dangerous lifestyle bikies lead. Most biker funerals are Christian ceremonies, organised by family and conducted in a church. For the more committed biker or outlaw motorcycle club member the experience can be quite different.

Several clubs, such as the Bandidos, have entry clauses that give the clubs permission to bury their brother. The clubs organise the funeral, which can cause some awful conflict between the family and club. I attended a funeral for a bikie that was actually two services – a Christian service organised by the dead member's family and an atheist service organised by the club. Jimbo (not his real name) would have liked the conflict.

Depending on the club and the wishes of the deceased, the funeral ceremony tends to be a variation of a Christian ritual, although in recent years atheist funerals have come into vogue. There's also the occasional Satanic service. The Australian bikie movie *Stone* provided an excellent example of an old-time Satanic burial of a dead member. A deep hole was dug so he could be buried standing up. When the member was put in the hole, the speaker called upon Satan to accept the body and spirit of the fallen brother, explaining to Satan that he was being buried feet down so that he'd meet the devil standing in the afterworld. I've never heard of any actual coven worship or warlock activities at Satanic funerals.

In the Christian version, preachers or priests are involved in the ceremony, with a fairly prescribed set of readings and an occasional hymn. There's little difference when compared to a traditional Christian burial for a non-biker. In the agnostic and atheist burials, friends and associates appoint a member to put the dead to rest, without the usual ceremony that goes with the religious version.

The funeral is a major event for the clubs. Funerals are afforded the same status as a run, with all club members required to attend in their colours. The funeral runs are also open to other clubs, as long as there's not a turf war under way. There have been cases of temporary truces being declared among warring clubs so one club can attend the burial of its rival club's dead brother. After all, bikies share the same biker beliefs. They're only human.

The funeral run usually starts at the deceased member's clubhouse, with pick-up points for the various clubs along the way to the church or place of ceremony. After the service comes the standout feature of the bikie funeral – the procession of bikes that always follows behind the hearse. The hearse is sometimes a bike with a sidecar attached to carry the coffin, draped in the club colours. The riders immediately behind the hearse fly flags representing the different nations in which the club has chapters. In Australia, funeral runs can attract up to 500 riders. There's no more powerful and dramatic display of biker power and solidarity than the sight of 500 solemn bikers rumbling through the streets in a bikie funeral procession.

Once at the cemetery, if the bikie is to be buried, club members put various artefacts and tokens in the grave as a sign of respect. It's often a bottle of the member's favourite drop, or a particular run badge. As they're tossed into the grave atop the coffin, the bikies mumble a few final solemn words to their mate.

Then comes the wake. Christian, Satanic, agnostic, it makes no difference. The bikie wake is one big piss-up, with plenty of laughs and stories about the deceased. In a way, particularly if the bikie died violently, the wake is a sort of debriefing from an experience that may have rattled the club.

The issue of Satanic worship among the clubs has always dogged them. It's easy to see why. Imagine if the clubs carried no reference to Satanism. You could scrub the Hell's Angel's, Satan's Slaves, Devil's Disciples, Diablos, Warlocks, Pagans and Satan's Cavalry for a start. The truth is, the names mean nothing, and are chosen for their shock value more than anything. The Hell's Angels' name came from military circles and has nothing to do with being a warrior for Satan. The Angels laugh at any suggestion that they're connected with the occult.

However, a lot of bikies bear badges and tattoos reflecting Satan. Rings with the Devil's symbol 666 are prominent on the fingers of outlaw club members. It's not just the bikies. Many bikers wear them. I've interviewed bikers and club members about whether there's anything in the devil icons. They made it pretty clear it was all for show, to outrage or distance them from society.

That [Satanic worship and practices] is just bullshit. It's to put the wind up citizens. If somebody tried that shit on for real they'd get straightened out real quick.
Lone rider

I can only remember one brother who went weird with the Devil stuff. He ended up going nuts and leaving the club, his wife and everything.
Satan's Sinners

It's shit man. There is nothing there but showing class to citizens by having a righteous name for a club. I mean, what sort of name says that you are independent and FTW [Fuck the World]? When we started out in the States the club was called the Booze Fighters, for Christ's sake. That was changed straight away to what we are today ... Hell's Angels.

Hell's Angel

No undercover police who have infiltrated the outlaw motorcycle clubs have alleged to have witnessed or even inferred that the clubs are engaged in Satanic practices. Given the animosity between outlaw clubs and police we'd have heard about it pretty quickly if one of their moles saw anything.

The only reference to devil worshiping I've come across was from Greg Hirst, the leader of the Brotherhood Christian Motorcycle Club. In the early 1990s he said he was '... very concerned with the increasing Devil worship amongst the clubs in the Western Suburbs [of Sydney].'

However, when asked if he'd seen any evidence of rituals or other tangible evidence of Satanic practice he admitted he hadn't. It appears he was referring to the increasing number of clubs who had Satanic references in their names and on their patches. In recent years, Greg has agreed the Satanic influences of the outlaw motorcycle clubs 'have not grown significantly since 1990'.

Outlaw motorcycle clubs are also riddled with racist slogans, badges and symbols. Nearly as popular as the '666' and other Satanic signs that adorn the bikie patches is the swastika. It attracts more outrage than anything else because of its connection with Nazism. It's not something that's usually worn as mere decoration, so the wearer is presumed to have fascist beliefs. Not so, say the clubs.

'Class, man. Nothing but class,' is how one swastika-wearing club member described it to me, and that seems to be the general view. Wearing a swastika doesn't necessarily mean holding the beliefs of Nazism.

> ... this is because I'm a fucking fascist. [said pointing to the swastika tattooed on his arm]. You don't believe me, do you? Truth is, neither do I.
> **Club member**

> It's bullshit, man. Sonny [Barger] tried to get agreement not to wear the swastikas way back in the '70s but the issue of whether to wear one or not was still left up to the individual. It wasn't until the German chapters came on board that the wearing of swastikas was banned officially. Any club wanting to have a chapter in Germany fucking well better ban them because their legislation specifically prohibits the wearing of Nazi symbols.
> **Hell's Angel**

But are outlaw motorcycle clubs racist?

Since the days of the earliest clubs they have nearly all been regarded as having some sort of racist overtones. I've read a mountain of literature and heard all the police stories about outlaw motorcycle clubs being racist organisations. For instance, the FBI report, *Inside Outlaw Motorcycle Gangs*, states:

> Their feelings strongly parallel those of the Klu Klux Klan and the late Adolph Hitler's beliefs. This is seen by the tattoos, patches and pins worn by the members, such as Nazi Swastikas, White Power fists and pins that openly state, 'White Supremacy'.

Yet, I've never been sure, so I set out to find the answer. I found it in, of all places, the Hell's Angels clubhouse in Auckland.

In 1987 my wife and I went to New Zealand to meet the national president of the Hell's Angels. I didn't even know his name, only that I was to meet him at the Hell's Angel's clubhouse. I was excited about visiting the New Zealand chapter because it's historically important in the bikie world, as it was the first Hell's Angels chapter to be set up outside the US.

Liz and I were a little nervous as we took a taxi to the clubhouse in the early evening. The New Zealand club and gang scene is much more hostile than Australia's. Earlier that day there had been an alert on the radio for the public to be on the lookout for a member of the Mongrel Mob. The Mongrel Mob, along with its arch rival Black Power, an exclusively Maori club, are the two most well-organised and dominant street gangs in New Zealand. Even the bikie clubs regard them as bad bastards. The Mongrel Mob tried to open a chapter in Perth in the mid-80s, but was quickly run out of town by the Coffin Cheaters, Club Deroes and the Gypsy Jokers. The WA police were allegedly happy for the outlaw motorcycle clubs to prevent the Mongrel Mob from getting a foothold in a city which already had its fair share of racial problems.

The gang member who was subject to the public warning across NZ radio had killed two people in a camping ground and could be easily identified by the name of the club tattooed on his forehead. How's that for commitment to the club! The day before, we'd heard Black Power had trashed a hotel in Auckland.

All of this had happened after Liz and I met a few of the Maori Lone Rider bike riders earlier in the trip. They were the scariest bastards I'd ever come across. Not only were they physically enormous but they carried sawn-off baseball bats attached to their belts. Their faces were fully tattooed (called a moko in Maori) and they all rode heavily modified choppers. You can imagine our trepidation as we made our way to the Hell's Angels club house. Surely, we thought, the Hell's Angels would have to be pretty fierce to compete in such a hostile gang environment.

We were immediately caught off-guard when we arrived at the clubhouse. It was a beautiful place in an up-market residential Auckland suburb. To give you an idea of the suburb, the Prime Minister, Helen Clark, lives there. We were a bit early and only the large and imposing sergeant-at-arms and a few prospects were there. Nevertheless, we were greeted and invited in. On entering the clubhouse we were impressed by its neat appearance. The sergeant-at-arms appeared a bit perplexed as to why we were there, but graciously offered us a drink. We casually discussed the New Zealand club scene, while more members and associates showed up. The sergeant-at-arms and the vice-president kept us entertained after the president called to say he'd been delayed. I was pretty relaxed until a discussion about the Hell's Angels' experiences with the Mongrel Mob and Black Power became quite animated, with one heavy character getting excited about the 'nigger street gangs'.

Just as an uncomfortable silence fell on the conversation the national president walked through the door. You could have knocked me over with a feather. He was a strikingly handsome Maori accompanied by another Maori member and a white member. The national president was articulate, intelligent and sensitive. It turned out he was well travelled, worked as a law clerk, had a young family and was interested in migrating to Australia.

We were completely stunned as we'd read the police reports about the total white membership of the outlaw motorcycle clubs, seen the fascist emblems and tattoos, and read literature suggesting we were dealing with neo-fascists. Yet, here was the president of the New Zealand Hell's Angels, a person of colour. Not only that, we learned there were other Maori members. Remember, under Hell's Angels' bylaws, a nominee requires 100 per cent of the vote of the national club and the endorsement of the mother club to gain entry. I was forced to reconsider my views on clubs and racism at that point.

That reassessment was reinforced when I later came across the story of Big John. Big John was a full member of African descent with the Hell's Angels Windsor chapter in England. He'd even been an office bearer. He died tragically while in police custody in 1984. Again, the decision to admit Big John would have been made by the mother club, following a unanimous recommendation by the local club.

I've also come across an account of at least one African-American member of a Canadian chapter of the Hell's Angels, as well as many members of Polynesian, American Indian and Hispanic descent in US chapters, including presidents of several small US outlaw motorcycle clubs. The Wales chapter of the Hell's Angels had a prospect of African and Scandinavian descent.

There are plenty of all-African American clubs in the US, such as the Black Falcons Biker Club and United Riders and Imperial Bikers MC. Sonny Barger was said to have awarded a 25-year anniversary plaque by the Hell's Angels to the East Bay Dragons, an all-African American motorcycle club in Oakland. Closer to home, the Finks in Adelaide has a strong eastern European and European background, with a number of Muslim members, as I noted earlier. An Aboriginal was involved in the club when it began.

The New Zealand experience and subsequent research taught me an important lesson about racism in the outlaw motorcycle clubs. I realised I had to re-think stereotypes, and not assume that the hype is right. I've made it a point in all my interviews to ask club members about racism, and whether a coloured person could join their clubs. Invariably, race does not appear to be an issue.

Yeah. We'd let someone prospect, no matter what colour. He might start with a bit of a disadvantage as some [members] are prejudiced; but if he was a good bloke he could turn them around, easy.
Coffin Cheater

No worries. We've already had an Aboriginal member and one who is Chinese, I think. At least the guy is Asian, I'm not sure if he's Chinese.

Hell's Angel

We've already got many ethnic members. Even the president's a wog, for Christ's sake! I can't see why not.

Rebel

Let's put it to you this way. I'm not in favour of the old meaning of nigger. Today, it's not necessary to be black to be a nigger nor are all niggers black. We look at people for what they are and if they act in a niggardly [stingy, mean or cowardly] fashion, then we call them niggers whether they are black, white or in between. For our club, it's who you are that counts.

Hell's Angel

Another myth that bobs up is the number of clubs and club members. As I explained earlier, there are few bikies in Australia, about 3000 to 4000. However, in times of conflict between clubs and authorities, the public is led to believe bikies are everywhere. It's a common political ploy – play up the club numbers and their influence to justify the heavy-handedness and funding for the police.

It's more blatant in the US, where police officials are elected. Police estimates of the number of bikies often vary enormously depending on what suits the situation. When the election of the police chief is imminent the number of club members rises or drops depending the incumbent's agenda. If the police chief was elected on a promise of making the streets safe the figures are understated. However, if the chief wants to run a 'clean up the streets' campaign the number of club members will often be overstated.

The police are also pretty keen on myths surrounding many of the patches the bikies wear. In chapter 9 I'll look at the supposed wing patches that are meant to signify sexual achievement but another controversial and hotly debated badge is the Hell's Angels' 'Filthy Few' badge. Police believe the Filthy Few badge refers to someone who has murdered for the Hell's Angels. The club says this is bullshit. It says it comes from the early days of the Hell's Angels, when the bikies who were the first to arrive at a party and the last to leave called themselves the filthy few. After a few days partying they were a pretty rough sight. It has stuck, with the Filthy Few patch a highly treasured award for service within the club.

However, the police are not the only ones to do a bit of myth-making. The outlaw motorcycle clubs are adept at fostering a few of their own. It's no surprise that most of them centre on the police. The meaning the clubs put on any action by the police can be pretty over the top at times. There is never anything routine when it comes to the police. If a bikie is stopped and his bike checked it's victimisation. The clubs often fear they're being photographed by police at runs and public events, even funerals. You only have to read the websites devoted to biker news. Here's a sample from one major outlaw club site *Outsider's 1%er News* – 'FBI finds itself under scrutiny'; 'Suspected spy camera gone near biker club'; 'New Evidence Shows Whitewash of FBI Role at Waco'; 'Spy camera blamed for false arrest'; 'Surprisingly, police blame bikers for brawl' and one of my favourites: 'Sham FBI conference used as cover for party'. There's certainly no love lost between the clubs and the police. They also hold a similar view, as do many in society, of the media.

However, I'm not surprised the clubs take these views. They foster many myths about themselves, so it's only natural they indulge in a few with their enemies.

In many ways, the clubs are a myth. Without the aura they

have built around themselves they would fail to exist in the form we know them today. Some say they're living in a boys' fantasy world any way. The outlaw motorcycle clubs disagree, saying their world is very real and it's the outside world that is living the strange existence.

CHAPTER NINE THE WOMEN

What I am is nothing more
Than what you see down on the floor
I'm not a man, I'm not a mutt
I'm just the bitch you call your slut
You like to ride me hard at night
That's when the moon looks just right
'Say, have a seat and open wide'
These are the words you say with pride
I know the rules, I know the words
But no is something I've never heard
I know I'm here to keep him sane
That's why he calls me bitch by name
'By Name', Kimberly Manning

The treatment of women is one of the more controversial aspects of the bikie clubs, which tend to be almost exclusively male. Let's consider the mainly US labels used to describe women – ol' ladies, mamas, sheep, broads and party girls. Sound crude and sexist?

You're right, it is. That's the way it is in the bikie world, although I suspect you wouldn't hear that sort of language at the bikie's home. The Australian clubs are not as heavily into the labels, generally referring to their partners as girlfriends and wives, although you do hear men referring to their 'ol' lady' occasionally. The US clubs are more into verbalising and making a big song and dance about these sorts of things.

According to outsiders, particularly the police, the clubs treat the women as possessions, to be played with and to serve the men when required. In return they have no rights within the clubs, are refused any say and effectively have to accept that the club rules their man. As one police report put it rather dramatically, women are:

> ... little more than playthings. Women are generally victimized by forcing them into prostitution or street level drug traffickers and quite often physically abused. Generally, they are bought, sold, traded or given away within the club.

To an outsider it sounds pretty appalling and derogatory, yet within the clubs it's accepted by all, including the women. I even recall one bikie constantly using the term 'my bitch', when referring to his wife, with no apparent irony, humour or malice.

Yet, it hasn't always been that way. When the outlaw motorcycle clubs were in their infancy in the United States, women participated as full members, even becoming office bearers. The Hell's Angels, arguably one of the more adamant clubs against women's involvement these days, once had full women members. In the late 1950s Leila Sadiliek, the wife of the San Francisco Hell's Angels president Frank Sadiliek, was a full member and secretary of the chapter. Keata Zimmerman, the wife of the president of the San Bernardino chapter, was also a full

Hell's Angels member in the early 1960s. She was killed when her handlebars came off on a run in the late '60s.

The elimination of women as full members of the Angels appears to date back to the mid-1960s. When Sonny Barger took over the national presidency of the Hell's Angels Motorcycle Club in 1964 he immediately took the patches off the female members of the club. He argued that women were unable to defend the club as successfully as men, specifically in relation to the colours. He argued that during turf wars, when bounties were often put on the patches, women would make softer targets for rival clubs.

I've come across other arguments against women members, even one saying that eye contact with a female outlaw club member inferred different things to eye contact with a male member, making it difficult to protect the club; meaning that a stare by a woman member might be interpreted as a sexual come-on rather that a warning to a citizen to keep his distance. The same stare from a man would be pretty clear in its intentions. It's an odd reason for keeping women out of the clubs.

Another interesting argument is, I suspect, closer to the mark:

> An outlaw patch holder achieves a sense of personal satisfaction and authenticity by being able to stand up resolutely for club values, remaining true to these ideals under adversity. The fact that a woman could do the same would, by itself, devalue this sense of accomplishment. In effect, female membership in an outlaw club would blunt a man's experience of being set apart by virtue of his having achieved a special goal. In the outlaw biker community, rebellion as a road to independence remains a male venture. It's highly unlikely that women will ever gain equality in the social philosophy of the outlaw

motorcycle club subculture; females as equals would shatter the image of a biker as a rare breed of male independence and courage.
Daniel Wolf

The shift from integrated clubs to male-only domains had enormous consequences for the outlaw motorcycle clubs. It meant members attracted to the clubs usually had a certain view towards women and the role of women. The clubs are comprised of largely working class and lower class men who hold strong traditional warrior values. They're more openly sexist, placing strong emphasis on the masculine roles of protecting women, maintaining possessions and providing for the family. Women, in general, are expected to prepare the food, maintain the home, look after the man and raise the kids.

What has emerged from this is the strong view that marital relations represent the single greatest threat to the brotherhood and existence of the club.

Women, particularly women with whom one falls in love, pose the biggest threat to the brotherhood, as your time will be spent developing your personal relationship with your women and family rather than the gang.
Daniel Wolf

In fact, many of the younger, single club members believe marriage would mean the end of their membership:

When I get married and settled down, then I'm going to quit the club. There's just too much time required by the club to do a marriage justice.
Club member

In some clubs, such as the Coffin Cheaters, nominees who have a developing or relatively new relationship with a woman are advised to wait until the relationship stabilises before becoming a member of the club. If there's going to be friction between a member's partner and club commitments he may not be admitted. The clubs frown upon any outside distraction.

Along with politics, family and partners are major reasons for members opting out of the clubs. Many members have told me privately that if his partner put the ultimatum to him or an event occurred within his family, which required him to quit the club, he'd do so.

> The fact is that if Suzie [not her real name] put it to me that it was her and the kids or the club, I'd leave the club. I mean, you gotta keep these things in perspective.
> **Bandido**

> It happens all the time. For most of us, we like to think that we would stay with the club; but that wouldn't be me, man. I know I've got years invested in a terrific woman and kids that I love. For me, I'd leave the club.
> **Diablo**

However, most club members are in long-term relationships, and are able to balance club and family life. I'd estimate that 60 per cent are in a relationship of more than five years, with 75 per cent of those having had children with their partner.

> Twelve years, three kids with Carol [not her real name]. She's due for a trade-in but I can't find any of the newer models I like as much. A bit like a comfortable bike, you know?
> **Coffin Cheater**

I'm on my third marriage. The first lasted seven years, the second three and this one is going to last forever. She's a great ol' lady and I can't imagine life without her.
Rebel

A bikie has two possessions – his bike and his woman – in that order of importance. A wife or girlfriend has to accept she is second string to the iron maiden. She also has to accept that the club has the right to call her man in any time they want.

She does, however, have some rights. She can hang around the clubhouse when given approval by the men or go riding with her man, but that's about as far as it goes. She's certainly not permitted to attend club meetings nor have a say in the running of the club.

Club members are pretty protective of their women. Look out if another member or an outsider tries to make a pass at her. Jealousy can be a vicious thing. I know from first-hand experience. I scored a punch when I was apparently asking too many questions of one girlfriend at a clubhouse. We'd been speaking for roughly 30 minutes about the power she had in the club, and she was warning me about what she was allowed to say when out of nowhere came this punch, clipping me behind the ear. Unfortunately, it caught her square on the head. Her boyfriend threw the punch and I believe it was actually aimed at her. A big fight ensued and I never really figured out what the hell it was all about. I presumed he thought I was getting a little too familiar with her.

Physical abuse of females is viewed as taboo by the outlaw clubs in the same way as it is in the straight world, but for different reasons. While there's concern for the abused woman, much of the focus is on the club member. To abuse one's woman in public is regarded as a sign the member doesn't have control over his life and affairs, which could threaten his membership. There have been cases where members were asked to leave social functions because of the way they were treating their partners. Family violence is becoming a bigger issue in the clubs, with the Hell's Angels, Rebels and Bandidos looking to become involved in programs aimed at curbing abuse. Ultimately it's in clubs' interests for members to have a stable family home.

Perhaps the most controversial aspect of clubs' treatment of women is the 'property of' rocker worn on the women's leathers. Wives and girlfriends wear 'Property of' colours, with the name of the biker she belongs to on the bottom rocker. I've asked many club members about it, and their first response is always to justify it.

What's wrong with that?
Bandido

Yeah? They're our women and should be marked as such.
Satan's Cavalry

Most of the clubs say branding their women cuts out any confusion within the club, and also when the women come into contact with other clubs. It's pretty common for two clubs to get into a fight because someone has approached the wife or girlfriend of another club member. The clubs argue that if the woman is carrying the club colours and her partner's name, no other club member will touch her.

... other clubs got to know who they are messing with. Citizens too.
Rebel

We've found that it stops a lot of hassles. It just makes things clearer, that's all.
Club member

The clubs admit there is an element of showing class in the badges, of trying to offend and shock outsiders by saying someone owns a woman.

... it's nothing really. I think the whole thing is a joke. But you know how much the clubs like to get up the noses of citizens.
Hell's Angels affiliate (girlfriend)

The clubs certainly get up the noses of straight society when they start referring to women as 'mamas' or 'sheep', as the US clubs often do. These women belong to the club at large and are expected to consent to sex with any member at any time. They perform menial duties around the clubhouse, yet are also excluded from club meetings and club business. Some clubs permit mamas and sheep to wear colours with the inscription, 'Property of [club name]', embroidered on the back.

Few clubs have mamas or sheep attached to them. One club, the Rebels in Canada, had a mama who hung around for a few months until one of the wives heard she'd been trying to get her husband to have sex with her. Things got ugly when the wife assaulted the mama with a pool cue at the clubhouse. The club members thought it was a hell of a joke, but the mama was soon given her marching orders. She was actually palmed off to another club, much to everyone's relief. It turned out she was too much for the other club to handle and they tried to hand her back. But the Rebels had learnt their lesson, and refused to take her. She remains the first and only mama the Rebels have had.

Some women, referred to as 'broads' in North America, or 'cuties' and 'party girls' in Australia, are sometimes found at the clubhouses. They're not really closely associated with the club. They tend to want to take a walk on the wild side, so they attend a party or two, and then disappear from the scene just as quickly as they arrived. Just as not all clubs have mamas, not all members become involved with party girls.

> I've got no time to be playing around on Barb [not her real name]. She and I have been together for seven years and have three kids. I love her dearly and the last thing I need to do is have word get around to her that I've been playing with a party girl.
> **Coffin Cheater**

> When your ol' lady is into riding, you don't kick her in the teeth by riding by yourself. And you certainly don't kick her in the tail by packing someone else.
> **Former Comanchero**

Party girls are often seen by the clubs as a target to be cajoled, seduced and, if necessary, subtly coerced into having sex. It's unlikely the coercion would extend to blatant rape, as this would bring more heat on the clubs. The sergeant-at-arms or other club officials would generally bring an over-enthusiastic member into line when the woman is clearly saying no.

If a member manages to persuade a girl to have sex with him, and he doesn't consider her a long-term proposition, she'll generally be asked to consent to having sex with other club members. It's called 'pulling a train'; a term also used by the armed services and even male university fraternities in the United States. Some clubs also refer to it as onioning. As you'd imagine, what may seem like drunken fun at the time can soon turn into a traumatic experience for the girls. Therapists working in the trauma field frequently refer to females traumatised by these events; however, no official statistics are available.

There's a poem in the book *Some Biker Bitches Poetry* that sums up the sexual abuse of some women involved with the clubs.

Pass around Jane was not the same
when she found her call in life
Be a bitch, a biker's bitch
and learn to use the knife
She took her beatings like a champ
She learned to love and fight
She even found a peaceful place
to hide far out of sight
Commitment comes in many forms
how does one know what's right
Just ask Jane who felt the same
until she took her life.
'Pass Around Jane', Kimberly Manning

There have been some ugly incidents where clubs have been involved in rape. A simmering 30-year feud between the Hell's Angels and the Rebels was sparked over the rape of one club member's girlfriend. A major issue was whether the girl was identified as belonging to the member. The incident occurred in 1972 on a major run. Instead of wearing 'property of' inscriptions on their backs, the women had to wear a black armband if they were with a member. 'If you didn't wear a black arm band, you were fair meat,' said one bikie who was around at the time. It was alleged the girl was cajoled into taking her armband off by members of one of the clubs, and then virtually attacked by a number of the club's members.

One particularly nasty episode in the 1970s involved the Coffin Cheaters and the rape of the girlfriend of a rival club president. The case prompted the judge at the trial, in which five Coffin Cheaters members were convicted of rape, to say of bikie clubs:

They dehumanise their members, and those with whom they associate; they enshrine sacrosanct rules and customs, a code of conduct which is at its best puerile, and at its worst bestial, degrading and depraved in the extreme. Their attitude towards women and girls is at least as vicious and despicable as that of any cult, past or present, of which I'm aware.

The notion of sex abuse has fuelled the legend of small coloured patches that are said to indicate sexual achievement. Red wings are said to be awarded for having sex with a woman menstruating and white wings for participating in group sex with a girl. One US police report added fuel to the fire by describing each patch:

Eightball – Patch worn on colours, earned by committing homosexual sodomy with witnesses present.
Red Cross – Earned by committing homosexual fellatio with witnesses present.
Wings – An emblem worn by one percenters, as a pin or patch [cloth] attached to the colours. All wing earning must be witnessed.
Brown Wings – Earned when the wearer performs oral sex with a woman's anus.
Green Wings – Earned when the wearer performs cunnilingus on a venereal diseased woman.
Purple Wings – Earned when the wearer performs oral sex with a dead woman.

Add to this the notion of yellow wings for drinking urine and woolly wings, supposedly awarded for having sex with a sheep, and the outlaw motorcycle clubs would appear to be a depraved bunch of bisexual deviants of truly gigantic proportions. Imagine what must occur at parties to earn these badges! This is truly heady stuff – no pun intended.

There's no way a nominee would gain entry to a club if they engaged in this sort of stuff. If a person wearing one of the wings or other patches earned in those ways were to try to share a bottle of beer with any bikie I know they'd be lucky to escape with a simple bashing. But it does beg the question as to what the patches are really about.

Yes, this shit has been around for years [referring to the wings]. To tell you the truth Arthur, if a bloke were to do shit like that, I wouldn't vote for him to be a member of the club. I know Sonny [Barger] talks a bit about it in his book as something that went on in the old days, but I honestly think these days it's not on. Let's put it another way, if a guy wearing purple wings came up to me and offered me a joint, I'd definitely refuse it ... it's cop and media fantasy and that's all.
Hell's Angel

The issue of performing homosexual acts is hard to fathom. Homosexuality is definitely not encouraged among the outlaw motorcycle clubs or bikers. The clubs hate being portrayed by the gay community in displays such as the Sydney Mardi Gras with the leather caps and studs astride Harley-Davidsons. The clubs see it as a parody of their lifestyle.

Fuckin' garbage wagon poofters. There wouldn't be one amongst the lot of them that's had to fix a bike on a road in the middle of nowhere. They wear these trendy Harley gear and leathers that are a fucking disgrace.
Bandido

As you can see, it's a long shot anyone would be earning an eight ball or red cross patch and then wearing it around the club.

I haven't come across anyone wearing any of the wings or patches, so I can't tell you what they really mean. If they're out there, they are a bloody closely guarded club secret that only the most senior members would know.

On runs, at clubhouses and in club bars, sex-related party behaviour is the norm. That applies to general biker culture, not just the outlaw clubs. It's usually strippers or wet T-shirt contests and breast or tit contests. Sometimes there are macho contests such as biggest penis contests. Luckily I've never had the pleasure of witnessing such an event.

The wet T-shirt and tit contests are incredible phenomena in the bikie world. Interestingly, for a predominately male audience, it's not about the size or how much gear the woman gets off, but the mood of the audience that make these such popular events. I've seen tit contests where the girls get everything off, but the audience ignores them, whereas at others the excitement of the audience reaches fever pitch at the mere hint of flesh from the girls. The best contests become part of biker folklore. Often these involve reluctant women being dragged on stage to show their wares.

The best I can remember was the 1984 Tassie run held near Launceston. There was this one well and truly over the hill female who really made that event. She'd literally drag a woman up to the stage and then forcefully suggest that she join in the contest, 'helping' the woman remove her clothes. After she was able to get a few up on stage, they'd jump off and, as a pack; grab a woman to join in. Pretty soon, the stage was packed with women stripped to the waist. Then the woman who started the kidnappings removed the rest of her gear and proceeded to get the others to do the same. Pretty soon, there was a stage full of naked women, some getting in to the swing of things and some not. It was a hell of an event.
Satan's Cavalry Associate

The best I remember was, strangely enough, at an MRA rally held in Mansfield. The girls were really explicit. Not one of them had any clothes on at all and they were doing things like rubbing their crotches on stage supports and the like. Let me tell you, it really kept the blokes' attention. Part of it was the atmosphere. It was one of those situations where these rowdy girls and the blokes just seemed to hit it off.

Coffin Cheater Associate

The best I remember was when me an Sal [not her real name] were stuck in Cairns without enough money to get home. Sal entered the tit contest at a rally up near Cairns and really put on a show. She picked up $100, which was enough to get us back to Victoria. That was certainly the best for me.

Rebel

Professional strippers usually supplement the contests. I found myself backstage with the strippers at Broadford a few years ago, so I asked how they felt performing in front of a thousand alcohol-charged men braying for them to get their gear off. They were surprisingly calm and professional about it, explaining that the motorcycle club functions were among the least threatening, and the audience generally appreciated what they were doing. Of course, security was tight. Very tight. Any girl would feel safe under the wing of a Hell's Angel.

Michelle, an Adelaide stripper I interviewed, had to tackle the tricky issue of club politics in her work. I'd been told she didn't like stripping for the clubs, so I was keen to find out why. It turns out that wasn't the case.

Oh, no. I love stripping for the boys. My only problem is that I have a brother who is with the Rebels and it'd cause problems if I stripped for clubs which were not OK with him. It's OK for the clubs, they understand. For example, when I explained the situation to the Gypsy Jokers, they said they wouldn't want their sister stripping for the Rebels either.

Michelle has stripped for six clubs, including the Rebels, Finks and Descendants. The Finks got the nod as the club that treats the girls best, although she thought they were all pretty good. She said it was 'a respect thing' with the clubs.

'It's crap that the boys treat the women badly. I've literally had no problems with the clubs. [I've had] much more trouble with the suits and wog parties than the biker bashes.' I must admit that I interviewed Michelle in an Adelaide strip club and she was wearing nothing but cowboy boots and a belt. It was a very difficult interview.

The wheels are slowly turning for women and the clubs. The number of women riders is gradually increasing. In recent years, just under 50 per cent of those taking motorcycle lessons in Australia were women. Many become full members of the biker fraternity, participating in political associations such as the MRA. There are a number of all-women clubs in the US, including Leather and Lace, Motor Maids, Women on Wheels, Women of Harley, Devil Dolls and Women in the Wind. Motor Maids have been around since 1927.

Women of Harley has a chapter in Sydney, while another well-known club, with chapters in Melbourne and Sydney, is Dykes on Bikes. While members do not have to be lesbian to join, the majority are.

There has been at least one all-women Australian outlaw club, Women in the Wind. The club was based in Wollongong, and was active from about 1975 until the late 1980s. It claimed to be a 1% club, with a set of colours, entry requirements and badges similar to other outlaw motorcycle clubs. The only other reference to an all-woman club in Australia was a club called Against All Odds, which announced its arrival in the September 1989 issue of *V-Twin* magazine. I haven't heard of it since.

While the strong sexist attitude still exists in the outlaw clubs more women are being encouraged to ride on their own machines with the clubs. A point even Sonny Barger concedes: 'There are lots of women who ride bikes with the club right now – but none will ever be voted in as members.'

CHAPTER TEN SPILT BLOOD

Old age and treachery overcome youth and enthusiasm –
but not violence.
Hell's Angel

Violence is central to club life. It's implicit in the rules, the way members live, and their interaction with outsiders. The public usually only hears about bikies following a violent incident – a bashing, shooting, or the occasional bombing or murder.

I'd say 90 per cent of club violence is club versus club, protecting either a club's territory or its honour. In January 2002, the *Herald Sun* ran an article claiming bikies were involved in 23 national murders over the previous four years. According to my analysis of the murders, all but four of the victims were bikie club members or associates.

The internationalisation of the motorcycle clubs in recent years has seen a surge in amalgamations, with violence increasing significantly at the same time. Club violence arrived in Australia in the early 1970s, escalating in the early 1990s, following a worldwide trend that started in the US and spread to Europe.

That particular part of the world has been a hotbed of club violence in recent years, dating back to the arrival of the Bandidos into the Hell's Angels' stronghold in Denmark in the early 1980s. It triggered one of the most violent and sustained club wars ever seen. The first outbreak of lethal club violence was in 1981, when there was a gun battle between the Hell's Angels and the Bandidos at a Copenhagen airport, of all places. It triggered off a war between the two clubs for control of the territory, with 60 people killed.

The war culminated in an anti-tank missile destroying the Copenhagen headquarters of the Hell's Angels. The missile passed over the heads of police guarding the building, killing two and injuring 19. In 1987, a lawyer representing both clubs in various court proceedings was nominated by police and the clubs to negotiate a truce. The lawyer was successful and the international presidents of both clubs ratified the peace treaty that held for several years until the Outlaw Motorcycle Club arrived from the United States, sparking more inter-club violence.

Canada has been another hot spot, with 168 deaths associated with amalgamations and turf wars between the Hell's Angels and Bandidos from 1980 to 1998. They haven't finished, with turf wars continuing in the province of Alberta. In particular, large North American-based clubs such as the Hell's Angels and Bandidos are amalgamating with local clubs such as The Rock Machine, Grim Reapers and the Canadian Rebels, causing all sorts of turmoil.

Police are concerned that if the Alberta situation doesn't stop, the numbers killed will match the 40 people who have died in the raging biker war taking place in Montreal over the last five years.

There have been significantly fewer conflict-related deaths in Australia's outlaw motorcycle club wars. The bloodiest period was between 1995 and 1999 when there were 32 club-related deaths in Australia, compared with 24 deaths in the previous 10 years. However, when you adjust for population differences, Australia suffers about the same amount of club violence per capita as other Western countries.

Arguably, the most famous Australian bikie incident was the Milperra massacre which occurred on 2 September 1984, also known as the Father's Day massacre. Seven people died that day in a shoot-out between two clubs – the Comancheros and Bandidos – in the Sydney suburb of Milperra. It is a classic study of how amalgamations can provoke violence among the clubs.

The Comanchero Motorcycle Club of Australia was an outlaw club formed under the leadership of William 'Jock' Ross in 1973. The name Comanchero was chosen by Jock when he 'heard the name in a John Wayne movie'. Prior to its inauguration with an official constitution the club was a loose-knit group of riders who frequented the pubs in their territory along the New South Wales coast, just north of Sydney. In late 1973 the Comancheros were involved in a series of fights with another local outlaw motorcycle club, the Kings. The situation escalated so rapidly that the NSW Police strongly urged Jock and his members to leave the area or face the consequences. He took the hint, moving the Comancheros to Sydney's western suburbs near Parramatta.

Once established, the Comancheros rapidly became one of the more dominant clubs in western Sydney, due mainly to the aggressive recruiting style of Jock, who called himself the 'Supreme Leader' of the club. Indeed, he ran the club as though he was supreme leader, making members undergo weekly combat training to prepare for fights with other clubs.

In June 1983 the Comancheros instigated a dispute with the Loners, a small city-based club. The dispute began with a brawl in the Loners' territory at the Lone Star Hotel, culminating in one of the Loners threatening several Comancheros with a shotgun.

In retaliation, the Comancheros raided the Loners' club-house, where three Loners were beaten. However, Jock was determined not to let it rest there. He sent a message to the Loners suggesting they meet in a hotel to establish a truce. The Loners agreed; however, when they got there they found two carloads of Comancheros waiting and armed with baseball bats. They promptly attacked the unprepared Loners, who were beaten and forced to surrender their colours.

Handing over their riding gear with the club emblems meant not only the end of the battle, but the end of the Loners club. When the police arrived, the Loners said they didn't want to press charges. It was a wise decision, for to involve the police would not only have meant more trouble from the Comancheros, but possibly other clubs.

The Loners were effectively taken over by the Comancheros, with an offer for them to become a feeder club called the Bandileros. They had little choice but to accept. Under this arrangement members of the feeder club were scrutinised. If they made the grade they were offered membership of the mother club.

Throughout this process many Bandileros became Comancheros. The effective amalgamation of the clubs provided the Comancheros with the opportunity to expand their territory into the central city and enlarge the club's membership base.

However, it was not an easy marriage, as enforced mergers often prove. The relationship between the original Comancheros and Bandileros never really overcame the previous bad blood that had existed between the Comancheros and the Loners. There was tension from the start over Jock's military training methods, and the unusually formal ceremony of swearing in new members.

'Fuck, who is this guy?' asked one of the Bandileros after he'd been given his colours by Jock. 'If I wanted to march around the fuckin' backyard, I would have joined the fuckin' army.'

The tension spilled over during a dispute over the site of the Comancheros' new headquarters after the lease had expired at the old HQ. Jock favoured a western suburbs location, while the former Bandileros wanted to move closer to their old city stamping ground. The issue came to a vote, with the new members prevailing, 32 votes to 8. The new clubhouse was to be based in Lane Cove in the inner city. It was a severe blow to Jock. Following several weeks' consideration Jock announced he was splitting the Comancheros into two chapters, a city chapter and a western suburbs chapter.

After the club divided, relations between the two chapters deteriorated until communication between them was virtually non-existent. Meanwhile, office bearers of the Comancheros' city chapter went to the United States, where they made contact with the national president of the Bandidos Motorcycle Club. It was a strong club, allegedly with robust links to serious crime. At the time, they were prime suspects in three cases involving the murder of an assistant district attorney, the murder of a federal court judge in San Antonio Texas in May 1979 and a police officer in Louisiana in 1979. These were serious outlaws.

The Australians liked what they saw in the US and agreed to become an Australian chapter of the Bandidos. It has been alleged the American Bandidos were keen on establishing an Australian chapter to get their hands on a chemical called phenyl -2- propanone, or P2P, a major ingredient in the production of amphetamines. While it was illegal to import P2P into the US, at that time it could legally be brought into Australia. The allegation was that the local chapter could get their hands on the stuff, then smuggle it into the US. I have my doubts on this theory. I believe the Bandidos were keen to move into Australia merely because the chance arose through a group of keen Australians. Also, it gave them a chance to spread to another country, a move that would surely piss off the Hell's Angels.

Upon returning to Sydney, the city chapter informed Jock it was no longer a chapter of the Comancheros, but the first Australian chapter of the Bandidos Motorcycle Club. Jock immediately demanded the return of the Comanchero colours. The Bandidos complied. However, one set of colours had been sent to the US. The missing colours proved a very sore point with Jock. Within months the relationship between the Bandidos and Comancheros had deteriorated to the point where shots were fired at the Bandidos' clubhouse. A number of Comancheros were assaulted in return.

It all came to a head on Sunday, 2 September 1984 – Father's Day. A swap meet was being held in the grounds of the Viking Tavern, a hotel in the suburb of Milperra. The Comancheros had got wind that the Bandidos would be at the meet, so they organised an armed group, led by Jock, to meet them.

The Bandidos arrived, complete with their own arsenal, and a stand-off ensued. An attempt was made by some Bandidos to defuse the situation and get everyone to put their guns down, but in the powder keg atmosphere there was no hope. Scuffles broke out across the carpark, and then the first gunshot rang out. It was the signal for an event that shocked the nation. It was the first time Australians witnessed mass killings between bike clubs. Within minutes seven people were dead and 21 had been injured. The deceased included a 14-year-old girl, three Bandidos and three Comancheros.

Thirty-nine club members were subsequently charged and put on trial, with all but two found guilty of charges including murder, manslaughter and affray.

I caught up with a former Comanchero in late 2001. It was clear the episode had had a profound and devastating effect on him.

Well, I guess the last straw was the blue at the Viking Tavern. People think the Comancheros had three dead at the shoot-out. That's not true. We were one club. I blame these three for all the trouble that happened in the club [pointing to a picture of Jock Ross and two associates].

Jock used to rule by division. His tactics were to talk to each member and tell him what the others were allegedly saying about him. Naturally enough, we started to talk amongst ourselves and figured out what he was up to. It culminated in a vote where 32 of the 40 members of the club went a different way to Jock.

The whole thing, looking back on it, was so fucking petty. Politics, rules and power struggles – that's what started the feud. But we were actually, in the main, still mates with all the guys who decided to leave and eventually become Bandidos.

So, to cut a long story short, I feel like I lost six brothers at the Viking that day. Since then many, many others have suicided. Snoddy was the first to commit suicide, in Long Bay Jail. The most recent was Flash. He spent three days building a guillotine and cut his head off last week.

There are only three of us left now. Too fucking right I quit the club. I'm a biker not a bikie now.

The Milperra massacre had an immediate impact upon the Australian motorcycling community. The media portrayal of the event was similar to what I'd witnessed many years before in Monterey, and what had happened in Hollister before that.

The bikie clubs, which had a relatively low profile in Australia up to that point, found life suddenly changed after the shooting. Hotel owners and caravan park operators were suddenly very wary about admitting any club member, often refusing them entry onto their premises. One bikie recalls the times:

At the time I was riding in Darwin. It was unbelievable what went on as a result of the media beat-up ... particularly the bit about the alleged innocent 14-year-old girl who was killed by these mad bikie bastards. In the pub that me and a few mates were drinkin' in, the truckies and their wives came in the early evening. We were just settling in, anticipating a night's stay-over.

These guys, particularly their wives, would not shut up about the whole thing. They were talking like anyone riding a bike was a drug-crazed psycho who carried weapons in their bike's handlebars and the like. It was crazy shit.

It got so bad that I had my mates go outside and warm up the bikes while I told the pack of them a few home truths. I left in a hail of beer cans, bottles and bullshit after reminding them about the truckie who'd recently gone crazy and killed several people with his truck at Ayers Rock.

Getting back from Darwin was fuckin' unreal. The cops were everywhere. I remember the stretch of road from Brisbane to Sydney took us days. You'd just get on the road and a new set of cops would be on your arse. Basically, the cops were just tyre kicking. But they'd tie you up for ages. Near Goulburn it was really shitful too. Same thing. The police were a fucking nightmare to any two-wheel rider that didn't look like a sports type biker.
Club rider

The Milperra massacre may have been the worst of the battles between the clubs, but it certainly wasn't the first.

Probably the first violent death in the Australian outlaw clubs took place on the first, and only, Outlaw Run held in 1972. Organised by the Finks, with support from the Hell's Angels,

Rebels and Gypsy Jokers, it attracted more than 500 bikies from clubs such as the Nomads, Fourth Reich, Hell's Angels and Rebels. It was a dispute between these two latter clubs that led to the violence. The Hell's Angels took umbrage at the red and white colours of the Rebels, which they claimed were too close to their own colours. The president of the Hell's Angels took on the president of the Rebels in a fight. It's been alleged that every time the Rebel president, who was on his own, started to get on top of his rival, the Hell's Angels president received some 'assistance' from fellow club members who were watching the fight.

Nothing much came of that incident, until the Finks and the Mob Shitters became involved. These clubs joined the Rebels in going around to the home of the Hell's Angels president in Sydney to settle the score. An ugly fight broke out, which left the Hell's Angels president lying on the front path of the house in a pool of blood, severely bashed with a baby's pram. He later died in hospital. A 30-year-long feud ensued and even today the clubs still refuse to party together.

Another landmark conflict occurred in 1974 in Adelaide, an event seen as marking the arrival of inter-club rivalry in that city. It was all over a stolen transistor, worth about $10. At a party attended by a number of clubs, including the Iroquois and the Undertakers, an accusation was made that a member of one of the clubs had stolen the radio from the house hosting the party. It soon developed into a slanging match along club lines, with threats of violence. The Mandamas sided with the Undertakers.

The bad blood between the clubs festered until it was decided they should meet in a neutral location – a beach – to sort it out. The Iroquois enlisted the help of members of the Reapers, Finks and Mob Shitters.

It was supposed to be weapon-free; however, according to the Iroquois president, club members came along fully laden with shotguns, rifles, pistol, chains, mace, barbed wire whips and axe handles with chainsaw blades on them.

The Iroquois coalition arrived first and lined the road to the beach, ready to attack. But the Undertakers took them by surprise, arriving in cars. Rocks were thrown and bonnets bashed, until the Undertakers got out with their guns drawn. Shots were fired and an Iroquois member, Barry Bullshit, was hit in the chest. Old timers said the moment he was shot, the whole outlaw scene in Adelaide changed forever.

Barry survived, but 79 people were charged over the fight. As the former Iroquois president said, it was all over 'a stolen transistor worth 10 bucks and a couple of hurt feelings.' The Iroquois later prospected to the Hell's Angels, becoming its Adelaide chapter, while the Mandamas went with the Gypsy Jokers.

Another vicious example was the confrontation between the Coffin Cheaters and a small club, The Resurrected, in 1976. The two clubs were at a hotel in Melbourne where the Coffin Cheaters put a number of demands to the Resurrected, including the strange request that they change their name. When the leaders of the Resurrected refused, the Coffin Cheaters challenged them to a fight. They again refused and left the hotel bound for Morwell, where the club was based. A number of Coffin Cheaters jumped in a car and gave chase. It's alleged that while trying to run the rival president off the road, the car crashed, killing the Coffin Cheaters' president.

A few months later the Coffin Cheaters decided to mete out their revenge. They travelled to the home of the Resurrected's president, Pig, and handed out one of the most violent beatings imaginable. Pig's 19-year-old girlfriend was repeatedly raped. The pack then travelled to another club member's house to dish out more punishment. However, the occupants had been warned that the Coffin Cheaters were on their way so they were at least prepared for what was to come. Another club member was beaten while three girls hid in a bedroom. The Coffin Cheaters managed to break down the barriers where the girls were hiding, but were greeted by the sight of an 18-year-old girl holding a gun. She fired, hitting two Coffin Cheaters. One died on arrival at the local hospital. Eight Coffin Cheaters were charged with the attack. Six were convicted of charges including grievous bodily harm, aggravated burglary, malicious wounding, wounding with intent, theft and rape.

Rather than learning any lessons from these events, more and more violence has erupted over the years as clubs fight for control over territory through amalgamations. These amalgamations have been the major reason for the gigantic drop in the number of clubs from several hundred to just over 20 since 1985. Not only were countless clubs swallowed up by the larger clubs but many club members decided that things were getting too violent and dropped out of the scene.

Most club members are attracted to the clubs because of the bikes, the brotherhood and the notoriety, not the fights. But if it's a club decision to go out and become involved in a fight they have no choice. It's a rule of the club that they must jump in. The other major rule is that they don't back away, so they must keep slugging away until the sergeant-at-arms turns up and restores order. No one's really gung-ho about it. In organised stoushes over territory, many members approach it as something they must do. As one former president told me: 'In turf wars, the patches are feuding, not the people.'

Of course, there are some who enthusiastically tackle the violence, but most regard it as a hazard of the club because it's actually dangerous stuff.

I'm probably presenting a distorted picture here because the clubs don't spend all their time fighting. There isn't constant warring between the clubs. They manage to get along very well at many functions. They are there for a good time and will drink with each other. As one club member said: 'I do not have friends because they are outlaw motorcycle club members. I have friends who just happen to be members of outlaw motorcycle clubs.'

But it only takes someone to show a lack of respect for another club's colours, or to dish out an insult, and it's on. When the shit hits the fan it's like downtown Vietnam, 1964. It's serious stuff.

Many members tell me it's often the nominees that cause the problems between the clubs. Some guy trying to make a point to impress the full members will bring the whole club into the action. Sometimes it's a successful tactic for the nominee, with their willingness to stand up and fight admired by the club. Other times, he's seen as just an over-eager troublemaker who deserves to have his head punched in.

Many inter-club fights have an air of detachment about them. Sometimes two clubs can be involved in a heavy fight one week, but the following week they are back conducting business and inviting each other to their field days, without a hint of malice or a grudge.

After a fight between clubs the respective leaders will work out a truce, with nothing personal about it. It may take a few years but any animosity will generally subside.

The Hell's Angels and Bandidos' fight in Scandinavia was a good example. After a violent blow-up between the clubs, the two leaders went so far as to issue a joint press release saying it was a few members from each club who had been involved and not a club-sanctioned fight. The press release also said the members had been disciplined. It shows the level of the working relationship between the clubs, when the members can be fighting yet the organisations deal with each other on another level altogether. It also shows how sensitive the clubs are in that environment about attracting unnecessary heat.

The way clubs approach violence is interesting. There's a lot more verbal aggression in the overseas clubs, while the Australian clubs are more willing to get into a punch-up. Of course, there are more weapons in countries such as the US, so they tend to make a lot more noise, as the alternative can be deadly. One Gypsy Joker discovered the difference in club cultures on a visit to South Africa. When the Jokers came across another club he was more than happy to start some pushing and shoving so it would develop into a full-scale fight. The local club members watched in horror before they dragged him away. 'You don't do that here,' he was told. 'Everyone is armed, so they'll just shoot you.'

Australia doesn't have the same amount of gun activity among the clubs, with its limited access to guns, particularly after the tightening of gun laws following the Port Arthur massacre in 1996. But they're certainly out there.

In mid-2001, police found more than a dozen guns in the headquarters of the Gypsy Jokers in northern Adelaide. Most of the guns were reportedly found in a wall cavity.

Bombings are another popular calling card for the clubs, either as a weapon to injure or to warn someone they mean business. Bombings are one of the most dangerous aspects of club life, with most outlaw members realising they could fall victim at any time. Outlaw clubhouses need to be heavily fortified because of the constant threat of attack. Many clubs have had an unpleasant calling card arrive at their clubhouse. The Rebels in Adelaide had their clubhouse damaged by a bomb; the Bandidos' clubhouse in Geelong and Gypsy Jokers' clubhouse in Newcastle have also been bombed.

However, there was one major bombing incident that provoked strong speculation of being linked to an outlaw motorcycle club. What makes this case all the more intriguing is that one of the victims was not only an outsider but also a former policeman.

When former high-profile policeman Don Hancock was killed in a car bomb blast in Perth in September 2001 it didn't take long for the finger to be pointed at the Gypsy Jokers.

Eleven months before the bombing a Gypsy Joker, Billy Grierson, was shot as he sat by a campfire outside the small town of Ora Banda, 65 km north-west of Kalgoorlie, Western Australia.

A few hours earlier, Grierson had been thrown out of a hotel owned by Hancock following a fight at the pub.

Although Hancock denied involvement in the killing, his Ora Banda hotel and home were bombed a few weeks later. The Gypsy Jokers were blamed for the bombing, just as they were when Hancock and his friend, Lawrence 'Lou' Lewis, were killed after returning from the races 11 months later. Police believe the club planted the bomb while the car was parked at the races.

The episode put incredible heat onto the club, which was closely monitored after the bombings. For instance, about 60 police shadowed 30 club members as they rode from Perth to Kalgoorlie on the anniversary of Grierson's death.

At least two Gypsy Jokers were later charged with the murders.

The killings created a multitude of rumours and theories about who had killed Grierson, Hancock and Lewis. The Internet was abuzz with allegations that another club was involved in Grierson's death. None of it has ever been proven.

It's rare for outsiders to be innocently caught up in club violence. But it does happen, as was the case in Adelaide in 1994.

This case involved at least four Gypsy Jokers, flying colours, who arrived at the Flinders Hotel at Pennington, about 20 km from Adelaide on 19 October 1994. According to the statement of claim by one of the parties in a subsequent court case:

With the apparent deliberate intention of causing trouble the said gang members refused to pay for drinks, took drinks and cigarettes from customers and generally harassed and abused bar staff and customers.

Without provocation, one of the gang members assaulted the manager of the hotel and with other gang members commenced to throw beer bottles and ash trays around the front bar area.

A fight broke out between the bikies and security staff. One of the security staff was severely beaten, and a window was broken in the scuffle. The Gypsy Jokers eventually left.

The next night about 15–20 Gypsy Jokers returned to the hotel and bashed up a number of staff, including the manager, and a waiter, Minh Van Pham. These two suffered the most savage beatings. Pham was beaten unconscious and nearly died. His injuries included a fractured skull, a fractured ankle and index fingers on both hands, along with injuries to the knees and broken teeth. Permanent injuries included intellectual impairment and memory loss.

Police later laid charges and some members of the club were convicted. However, Pham sued the security company for professional incompetence. He argued the security company should have advised the owners and staff that retaliation by the club was likely after they had been thrown out the previous evening. If he'd known this he wouldn't have been there on 20 October. The matter was settled out of court, but it was widely believed Pham would have won the case if it had gone to trial.

It's the fear of unprovoked violence that frightens most people when they come into contact with bikies. However, despite the Pham case, an outsider would have to be very unlucky or very stupid to get into trouble with the clubs – like the two clowns who decided to taunt and abuse a reported 120 Coffin Cheaters and associates on the ferry *Spirit of Tasmania* as it sailed from Melbourne to Tasmania in October 2001. It's believed the pair, alleged to be off their heads on drugs, actually picked a fight with the club. The captain wisely decided to return to Melbourne to eject the pair before the club decided to do something to them. The Coffin Cheaters were cleared of provoking the men and were actually praised by police for exercising considerable restraint.

Sometimes trouble starts because the outsider is so terrified of the reputation of the bikies they make the first move. I know of cases where an outsider has gone for the trigger on the basis they presumed the bikie was going to attack them.

I'm often asked about the threat to my own safety because of what I do. I'm not really concerned. I've always expected that at some point I'd get seriously thumped. It may still happen. Perhaps something in this book will get me into trouble. (In fact, I have already been threatened by a club during its writing, and have had a warning from the police.)

The times I have got into trouble it's been with individual members, not a club thing. There was one incident where it got pretty scary, when a bikie took offence at me. What made matters worse was that he had four other bikies with him.

I was at one of the bikie concerts and had stumbled across a truck with a coffin on board full of ice and beer. I asked if I could take a photo of it. The guy who was standing there gave me the go-ahead, then disappeared. So I got up on the truck and started taking pictures. Before I'd finished some club members arrived on the scene. All they could see was a stranger standing on the truck hovering around their beer. I was actually taking a picture of my mate Rudi grabbing a beer out of the coffin. Not a good look in anyone's book. Before I could explain about the other bloke giving us permission, one of them was into it, threatening me with all sorts of things. He was only doing his job. It looked like we were pinching his beer, so why wouldn't he be defensive?

Thank God the sergeant-at-arms arrived just at that time. 'Hey Arthur, what's the problem?' he asked, almost casually.

Geez I was happy to see him. I told him what had happened, and that I'd fucked up.

The aggressive bloke realised what had happened and apologised. We then sat down and had a beer. One of those guys later quit the club and was able to give us extensive information on why he quit. Again, he was a victim of the politics of the club.

I've often wondered how much of that incident had to do with being a club member, and how much of it was about a bloke seeing someone pinching his beer? I suspect the same thing would happen at a footy club.

I guess the most dangerous time for me is when people don't know who I am when I start asking questions, such as the time Rudi and I showed up at one clubhouse uninvited. We really overstepped the boundaries by not knowing the chapter members well. We'd heard the club was expanding and were keen to find out what was happening to the smaller clubs being patched over. We asked what happened to the clubs that didn't join and how many people had decided to leave the clubs. That was the question that really got us into trouble.

We were pushed into a room by the vice-president, stood up against the wall and grilled. 'Who the fuck are you?' the vice-president yelled. I managed to score an elbow in the eye in the jostling, but nothing permanent. Rudi was able to do some straight talking to get us out of the fix. 'Look man, all we want to do is get the information to write a book, to tell it straight, not like what the cops want to hear.'

The president arrived soon after. Fortunately, he knew some people who knew us, and managed to calm everyone down. I'd have to say we deserved it. We arrived uninvited and were asking some pretty sensitive questions.

As a psychologist, a central focus of my studies is why outlaw club membership is associated with higher levels of violence. We know clubs are violent, with a clear connection to territory and its defence. But why must they use violence to defend their territory? All of us must defend part of our world every day. Why do the clubs feel they have to do it violently?

A study conducted way back in 1955 may give us a clue. Volunteer teenage boys from the same school were divided into three groups in a study on violence and aggression. One group was called the Blue Devils. It was given a clubhouse and encouraged to view the other boys as inferior. The Blue Devils were also encouraged to be competitive by the adult experimenters. The second group, the Red Hornets, were also given a clubhouse, encouraged to view the other boys as inferior and had their competitive behaviour reinforced. The third set of boys was not assigned to a group and were left alone or, in psychological parlance, untreated.

The experimenters were shocked at what they found. Aggression levels rose significantly among the members of the clubs, compared with the untreated boys. They had to pull the pin on the experiment when aggression levels rose to the point of violence against the other boys. Simply being a 'club' or 'club' member seemed to increase the propensity for violence.

Another classic study was a prisoner–guard study. An advertisement was placed in a local newspaper asking for paid volunteers to take part in a three-week psychology experiment. Volunteers were randomly assigned to one of two groups – either as prisoners or guards. The experiment aimed to analyse how authority relationships developed in two groups of people. The experiment had to be terminated after two weeks because of the degree of cruelty being displayed by the guards and the apparent psychological trauma both guards and prisoners were experiencing.

These research studies are just a few of the classic studies that illustrate what we now call the 'in' and 'out' group effects – the tendency for those who belong to a group to defend the 'in' group's values or attributes against those not in a group. Men, in particular, who join groups and defend their lot against outsiders feel they increase their chances of survival.

Another reason why club members are more likely to be violent is the 'risky-shift' effect. Put simply, people in a group are much more likely to make extreme decisions than they would as individuals. We've all seen the bravado of young men in a group, yet know that on their own they wouldn't say boo.

It's exactly what Justice Roden was getting at in his address before sentencing those convicted of the Milperra massacre:

> A fierce loyalty, and a propensity for violence, which rightly or wrongly typify the popular image of such clubs, are clearly indicated by the evidence in this case ... a need to belong, and to enjoy a close relationship and bond with others, can be readily understood. So too can a pride in physical strength and courage. But, like most admirable qualities, these can be carried to excess.
>
> The ugly side of loyalty seems to demand enemies against whom the loyal can be united. And the ugly side of physical strength and courage is seen when violence is unleashed against these enemies.
>
> When you have two groups like these, in conflict with one another, a Viking [Tavern] is always likely.
>
> As patriotism can lead to jingoism, and mateship can lead to cronyism, so bikie club loyalty, it seems, can lead to bikie club war.

Clubs and gangs of all kinds are becoming more violent. The street gangs in the first half of the 20th century were described as 'happy-go-lucky' people who joined for the camaraderie of gang life. There were fist fights with other gangs and petty crime but no evidence of guns or drugs. It was a different picture by the mid-

1990s, with widespread use of guns and drugs among the same urban street gangs.

The change can be seen in the US street gangs such as the Latin Kings and Gangster Disciples, where three generations of one family have belonged to the same gang. On rare occasions, grandfather, father and son are in the same prison. What emerges, even in these cases, is concern by the elder gang members that the gangs have become so violent compared to when *they* were active in the gang.

I came across an interview with a social worker working with gangs in Los Angeles who was a former 'gang banger' (gang member) with the Gangster Disciples.

> I'm really worried about the scene that the young face in the gangs today. In me and my father's era, it was fists and a few knives. But the knives were really only considered necessary for chicken shits or crazies. The main reason for a fight was an event would occur which would show disrespect or call for a challenge which was met gang to gang at a designated place and a punch-out followed.
>
> Today, it's drive-by shootings, assassinations, murder and mayhem. It is really scary. My son is in the Disciples and I really worry about that boy.

I see the same things with the motorcycle clubs. It used to be that you'd get thumped or maybe you'd get cut with a knife or hit with a baseball bat. Nowadays, there is an increasing chance of weapons being used in Australian club violence.

As clubs become smaller, more committed units they attract those people with more propensity to violence. With these people as members the issues of territorial defence, club honour, and even club dominance, take on a new level of hardness. Any action now warrants a violent response. There's also a bit of tit-for-tat among the clubs, with each retaliation needing to be more violent than the previous action. Once, a bashing would resolve a dispute within the clubs. Now, a more violent response is deemed the only way.

A lot of the blokes who are 1 per centers have limited patience, a fairly narrow outlook on the big perspective of the world. A lot of the blokes have copped it pretty rough and think no one's cared about them. They've got an attitude that they can now go 'bango' with other people.
Former club president

CHAPTER ELEVEN **THE OUTLAWS**

Outlaw *n.* 1. One excluded from the benefits and protection of the law. 2. One under sentence of outlawry. 3. A habitual criminal. 4. An untamed or intractable animal.
Macquarie Dictionary

Outlaw motorcycle clubs and crime. It's a natural fit. Or is it? The issue has dogged the clubs since their earliest days. Clubs are constantly accused of being criminal outfits, of forcing members to be law breakers to fit into the clubs. Is their bad rap in the media and by police justified? My answer? Yes and no. Before you brand me a fat-arsed fence-sitter, let me get one thing straight. In more than 20 years studying bikie clubs I've seen some bad things and met some bad people. But of one thing I remain convinced: Bikie clubs are not criminal organisations. But here's the rider: many club members are criminals. When these bad apples get up to no good the clubs are tarred with the same brush.

Most club members I've interviewed about crime are pretty

keen to change the topic. However, there's a strong view that crime among the clubs has been on the rise since the arrival of the big US clubs into Australia and the spreading federation of chapters under their umbrellas.

> To tell you the truth Arthur, I really hate it. There's this element that has moved into the scene that has moved the clubs right away from motorcycling and brotherhood to an emphasis on crime. I don't mean crime in the form of organised crime but crime as just gangsters. Crime as making money from their associations with the club rather than ridin' free in the wind ... I really hate these guys and what they've done to the lifestyle I love so much.
> **Lone rider**

> [In the club] there are those that have money, and these are generally the crims. Then there are those that have their knees and arses hanging out of their pants. This is the basis of the factionalism in the bigger clubs. And the crims generally try to buy their way by giving money to the real riders.
> **Former Comanchero**

You can point back to the alleged rape at Monterey that I was witness to all those years ago as the start of the outlaw element of the 1% clubs. Before that, they were merely considered renegades who got up to a bit of trouble. After Monterey they became a threat to society. When the incident hit the headlines the US police really started to pay attention to the motorcycle clubs. They found a new 'public enemy number one', as the Yanks like to say.

As a consequence, Attorney General Robert Lynch commissioned a report on the outlaw motorcycle clubs. The report was released in 1965, the year after the Monterey incident. It described the outlaw motorcycle clubs as a major threat to law and order. Governments readily accepted the report's recommendation that additional resources be allocated to police to rein in the outlaw motorcycle clubs. The pressure had an immediate impact. Membership dropped sharply as members were either thrown into prison or simply dropped out of the clubs to avoid constant police harassment.

However, the tactic backfired on the police, with the clubs swinging sharply towards the use of crime and violence. The members least likely to stay in the clubs were those who were most law-abiding, whereas the bad arses, formerly only a small percentage of the clubs, were now in the majority, setting the path and policies of the clubs. Throwing members into prison also failed to stem the growth of clubs, with a flood of members recruited in jail in the late 1960s.

These recruits were attracted to the new, more extreme, outlaw image. One club to undergo a major change was the Hell's Angels. Following the Monterey run, the club came under intense pressure, forcing the closure of the founding San Bernardino chapter. The San Francisco chapter was down to just 11 members when the *Lynch Report* came out in 1965. Suddenly, the club started to grow. New chapters were formed, and the Oakland chapter, led by Ralph 'Sonny' Barger, experienced a membership boom. It was clear the composition of the club membership was changing. With the police heat on, only those most committed to the outlaw life were joining the Hell's Angels and the other 1% clubs.

In Australia, it was another watershed event that put the focus on bikie clubs and criminality – the 1984 Milperra massacre. Until then, the clubs were basically regarded as counterculture groups who got into trouble now and then. Milperra made them criminals.

Is crime a major factor for those joining clubs in the 21st century? Unlike the other reasons for joining, which members are generally prepared to discuss, this is a more murky issue.

There's no doubt that crime is an element of clubs and it's certainly no disadvantage to be a criminal. In some ways it's a distinct advantage because the criminals of the club have access to resources and money, allowing them to give the sort of commitment often required by the hardcore clubs.

The fundamental question is whether outlaw motorcycle clubs are formed with the aim of committing crime, or whether only individual members commit crime.

The police have no doubts outlaw motorcycle clubs are criminal organisations whose reason for being is to commit criminal acts. So it would follow that the primary reason for joining a club would be to adopt a criminal lifestyle. After all, as the saying goes, 'birds of a feather flock together'.

However, police forces and crime authorities have had little luck using this argument to prosecute motorcycle clubs. There's never been a successful prosecution of an Australian outlaw motorcycle club as a criminal organisation.

A US study in 1995 analysed the crimes for which outlaw club members were imprisoned over the previous 20 years. While there were fairly high rates of incarceration for territory-related crimes such as violence, the number of convictions for 'organised' crimes, such as manufacturing and distributing drugs and extortion, was low. It's also interesting to note that the NATO listing of the top 100 organised crime bodies and entities in the late 1990s did not list any motorcycle clubs. In Australia the investigation in the mid-1990s by the National Crime Authority into the activities of outlaw motorcycle club, Operation Panzer, found the clubs were not a serious organised crime threat to Australia.

I don't believe outlaw motorcycle clubs are formed with the expressed purpose of committing crime. Being a member of an outlaw motorcycle club is about a commitment to a lifestyle, of being the biggest and toughest. Crime might follow, but the primary purpose is dominance over other clubs and the company of people who hold fundamental warrior values.

When it comes down to it, it'd be pretty difficult for a club to be a criminal front. For a start, assuming there are 15 to 25 chapter members with, perhaps, just as many nominees and associates – that's a hell of a lot of mouths to keep shut. It'd take extraordinary discipline on everyone's part to run a criminal operation such as drug manufacturing and distribution. They're just not sophisticated enough to do it.

Non-criminal members just wouldn't put up with crime. I know many of these blokes and if they didn't like what was going on they wouldn't meekly go along with it. They'd either put the criminals back in their box or tell the club to get fucked and leave.

Also, if you're going to commit serious crime you don't brand yourself outlaws, wear the most provocative clothes you can muster, and break every society norm (and most road rules) you can. It makes no sense. If you want to commit crime you put on a three-piece suit, not a set of outlaw motorcycle club colours.

Take drugs for example. The clubs are most commonly accused of manufacturing and distributing hard drugs. Yet to do this means keeping a very low profile and being almost invisible, something the clubs are not exactly known for. Individual members or groups of members have done it, but not an entire club, as far as I know. Most of those members have been busted pretty quickly as the police always have an eye on what the club members are up to.

Other aspects of bikie club life make it hard to stack up a case that they're involved in organised crime. For instance, outlaw clubs are voluntary organisations. People are free to join, provided they pass the initiation process, and they're free to leave, with or without the wishes of the club. Criminal organisations don't usually offer that freedom of choice. Once you've committed a crime it's not so easy to walk away.

The clubs are also accused of guarding their territories, or turf, so ferociously that it must mean they are protecting an exclusive drug distribution area. There's not much evidence of that. Club members who do get involved in the drug trade are not usually selling the stuff on the street. They neither know, nor care, where it goes so territory is not an issue.

However, for me, the ultimate test as to whether a club is dealing in heavy crime, such as manufacturing and dealing in drugs, is to look at the lifestyles of the club leaders. I've visited the homes of prominent Hell's Angels, Coffin Cheaters and other club leaders many times. I can say with utmost certainty that I haven't come across any opulent lifestyles. Invariably, the leaders live in working class suburbs in relatively humble abodes, albeit with fairly sophisticated security systems, by Australian standards. One senior leader of the Hell's Angels' Nomads chapter in Melbourne still had an outside toilet in 1995.

I've absolutely no doubt the homes I've visited were the legitimate dwellings of club leaders. I'd sometimes drop in on a club leader on no, or little, notice and find him there. I have never got the impression that the homes were any sort of front to convey the image of working class lifestyle when, in reality, the club leaders were living in more affluent suburbs. It conjures up an incongruous image – the club leader dressed in a smoking jacket, lounging by his jacuzzi in upper-crust Toorak, sipping Dom Pérignon Champagne, vintage 1953. He receives a call from me requesting a meeting at short notice. The club leader mumbles into the phone that he'll meet me at his 'house' in half an hour. He throws on his jeans and colours, jumps on his bike, roars over to his 'front' house in working class Preston or Reservoir, grabs a beer and a cigarette, jumps on the couch and manages to exude the relaxed air of a couch potato in time for my arrival. Like I said, the front house theory simply doesn't hold up.

Of course, there is the occasional exception. Alex Vella, the

Rebels' president, defies the image of the down-at-the-heel club leader, being a successful businessman in his own right. He's amassed a significant fortune initially by his career as a professional boxer and subsequently through investments over many years. A few years ago court documents revealed he owned a $700 000 office block, a home worth $500 000, industrial land valued at $380 000 and a villa in Malta. There were also two Rolls-Royce cars, a couple of Chevrolet Corvettes, and 41 Harley-Davidsons. He argued that he didn't make his dough through the club but through his investments and motorbike sales.

Occasionally you come across a club member who seems to lead a pretty good life, with the brand new bike and the ability to flash around a bit of cash. Most of the clubs have an 'ask no questions, tell no lies' policy. The Hell's Angels had to rethink that after Anthony Tait, its most famous US snitch, was able to fly about the country to any number of meetings, and have his own bike stationed in California, without any questions asked by the club. The club presumed he was making money from crime, so didn't question him on it, when it turned out he was actually being funded by the FBI in return for supplying information.

The 'ask no questions' attitude is also found in Australian chapters.

As I think about it, it's very rare for a member to ask another what work they do. Unless the brother is involved in the motorcycle trade or a trade which contributes to the customising of bikes, the matter just doesn't seem to come up.
Coffin Cheater

However, the wealth generated by the illegal activity of a member is not the same as a club operating off the benefits of crime. The Gypsy Jokers will proudly declare that every asset of their club has been earned legitimately, through raffles, runs and other fundraisers. This is despite an academic view that clubs should stand condemned for the actions of their members.

One of my overseas colleagues believes that if membership of a club leads to an increased ability to carry out crime, the club should stand condemned as a criminal organisation. I don't agree. Take the police and the clergy for instance. Being a member of these organisations provides increased access to targets of crime or enhances the abilities to cover up crime. Police have access to drugs and criminal networks, with nearly every police force having members charged and convicted of selling and distributing drugs from time to time. Yet, we don't say the police force is a drug-dealing organisation. It's the same with the clergy. Through their work they're constantly in contact with young and vulnerable people, a situation which a few religious figures have taken advantage of. Luckily, many of them have been exposed and found guilty of paedophilia. Yet, we don't brand churches as paedophile organisations.

The criminal element of clubs has been bolstered in recent years by a strong recruiting drive in prisons. With many club members involved in crime, virtually all outlaw motorcycle clubs have members in prisons. Outlaw motorcycle clubs not only survive in prison, they flourish. Following the Milperra Massacre, the fastest growing outlaw motorcycle clubs in Australia were the Bandidos and Comancheros.

The prison environment virtually requires inmates to join a gang purely to survive. That's why you'll have prison gangs, such as the Texas Mafia in the US, which is based entirely in prison. In Australia there are relatively few prison gangs. There are some Aboriginal gangs, complete with constitutions and tattoos (Aboriginals accounting for 13 per cent of the prison population), but these are different from the ultra-violent gangs of the US, such as the predatory toe-cutter gangs, that prey on other prisoners.

Outlaw motorcycle clubs attract members in prison for a number of reasons. When club leaders are imprisoned it's usually a big deal in the media, so they enjoy some notoriety and fame when they enter prison. It affords them luxuries there, such as a strong network of assistance and protection. Others see this and are naturally attracted to the club. Ironically, being a club member in prison is actually not as dangerous as it can be on the outside. Turf disputes between clubs are invariably put 'on hold' in prison, so opposition club members usually get along pretty well.

For up and coming club members on the outside, imprisonment can often mean a step up the club ladder if the club leader is also inside. They get an opportunity to rub shoulders with the leader that they wouldn't get on the outside.

Of course, the authorities take a dim view of such matters. The last thing they want is their prisons popping out more Hell's Angels or Bandidos. In some US prisons, to hinder recruitment, notorious gang and club members are locked into special segregation units where they're allowed no human contact. They have even built an entire prison to prevent inmates coming into human contact. It's designed specifically to counter the gangs. The closest we could compare it to in Australia would be the now defunct Katingal Prison in New South Wales and the notorious Jika Jika section of Pentridge Prison in Melbourne. Both these prisons within prisons were eventually closed after legal battles ruled that the institutions were too cruel. Nevertheless, the United States has continued to follow a policy of escalating punishment for its offenders.

In addition to these special segregation units there are prison farms in the United States for club members who became police informants. If a club member violates the fundamental rule of loyalty to the club his life is definitely at risk. Visiting these special prisons is very difficult. In most cases, a visitor will be photographed for identification. The inmate is shown the photograph and asked if they wish to see the visitor. Only then will permission be granted.

Bikies are pretty well behaved in prison. Remember, members join bikie clubs for their commitment to the biker lifestyle. You can't do much motorcycle riding inside the can. Therefore, they'll usually behave themselves in prison so they can get out as soon as possible. It's another reason why there are few turf wars in prison, even though most of them are inside for violence against other clubs. They also cause little trouble in the wider prison community. Other prisoners are usually intimidated by the reputation of the bikies so they're less likely to provoke the clubs.

A 1999 review of clubs in Californian prisons illustrates the point:

> The motorcycle gangs really pose no real problem in the state prison system. Known to be organised and industrious on the outside, they command very little attention from other gangs and authorities.
>
> The motorcycle gang members tend to distance themselves from the other white inmate gangs and mostly do their own time. Their years of methamphetamine abuse and spurts of unprovoked acts of violence tend to keep others at bay.

However, this conclusion stands in stark contrast to the claims of the Montreal authorities that outlaw motorcycle club members must be kept separated in order to prevent large-scale rioting and mayhem, as happened in 1998 when a turf war between the Hell's Angels and Rock Machine spilt over into prison. This is believed to be the only time this has happened, although in Australia NSW authorities were keen to see their prisons weren't the first, by sending Comancheros and Bandidos members to separate prisons to prevent any possible violence following the Milperra massacre.

However, the Canadian outlaw scene is particularly violent. The Canadian view of the bikie clubs as public enemies was bolstered by the brazen murder of two prison guards in separate incidents in Quebec in the mid-1990s. The first murder occurred in June 1996. The victim, Diane Lavigne, was in uniform and parked at a stop sign on her way home from work. Two unknown assailants riding a motorcycle and brandishing semi-automatic pistols approached her vehicle and fired, killing her instantly. The motorcycle clubs were widely regarded as having committed the murder, although there was no hard evidence other than the fact the murderers rode motorcycles. The media were pretty keen to point the finger at the bikies. No arrests were ever made for the murder.

In September the following year two prison guards, Pierre Rondeau and his partner, were driving a prisoner transport van in Quebec when they stopped at a railway level crossing. Two men in their 20s, armed with semi-automatic pistols similar to those used in the Lavigne murder, jumped out from behind bushes. The gunmen fired at Rondeau, who tried to jump from the van. Seven shots pierced the windscreen and driver's window, following Rondeau's path as he fell from the driver's seat. He was hit four times, once in the throat and three times in the chest. One of the bullets fired into his chest struck his heart, killing him instantly.

Montreal Police Chief Jacques Duchesnow was quoted as believing that the murder 'bore all the marks of a gangland execution'. In response, the Quebec Correctional Services Workers' union went on a 24-hour wildcat strike. The prison guards believed they were becoming the latest victims in an escalating war between the Rock Machine and the Hell's Angels. According to Rejean Lagarde, the president of the 2000-member union: 'It is clear that organised crime is behind all of this and the finger of suspicion at the moment is pointing towards the bikers.'

The media and police reported three theories as to why the outlaw motorcycle clubs might be involved in murdering prison guards. The first was that the killings were part of a dramatic new 'blooding in' process, where new members were required to kill a member of a criminal justice agency in order to gain entry into the clubs.

A second theory was that the outlaw motorcycle clubs were out to intimidate the prison guards so that jailed members would be treated better. The third theory was that the attacks were not random and the murdered guards had histories of run-ins with individual club members.

Quebec police didn't favour this final theory. They believed it was the uniform the victims were wearing that made them targets. Quebec Public Security Minister Pierre Belanger stated: 'These were premeditated crimes committed by professionals, whose goal is the destabilization of our judicial system.' It was six years before two Hell's Angels members were charged and convicted over Lavigne's murder. A third member died before he could be charged.

The Canadian experience stands in contrast to the experiences in Australia, New Zealand, South Africa, the United States and all other Western countries, where there seem to be few problems with outlaw motorcycle club members in prison.

Many may find my notion that clubs are not criminal organisations a difficult pill to swallow, particularly when there are plenty of cases where members acting as a group have broken the law. Usually club crime involves violence, with clubs in conflict with each other, or fighting back against police pressure, as was the case with the Gypsy Jokers' clash with police in early 2001.

However, increasingly the clubs are cited as major drug manufacturers. It's something the clubs are not happy with, as the next chapter will show.

CHAPTER TWELVE ON THE NOSE: CLUBS AND DRUGS

Drugs. They are truly the scourge of society. And despite their best attempts to escape from the confines of mainstream society, the outlaw motorcycle clubs face the very same scourge.

Outlaw motorcycle clubs have long been accused of being major drug manufacturers and distributors. In many cases, club members have been. The early bike clubs made a lot of money through drugs, particularly LSD when it was still legal in the 1960s. When it became illegal one would hope they tried to get out of production. But habits do die hard! I find the situation with drugs is similar to crime – the members do it, but it's not a club-organised thing. There's ample evidence that there is a fair amount of drug use by members. There's certainly a lot of powder and plenty of dope-smoking. Enough club members get called up before the courts on drug charges to prove that many are involved in the manufacturing and trade of drugs. However, within the clubs, it's treated as an 'ask no questions, tell no lies' sort of thing, where the issue of drugs remains pretty much under the table.

The only thing the clubs strongly oppose is the use of injected drugs. Most outlaw clubs have strong sanctions in their bylaws or constitutions against the injection of drugs. These include Hell's Angels, Coffin Cheaters, Satan's Slaves, Bandidos, Rebels, Comancheros and Gypsy Jokers. For example:

Any member found using the needle will lose his colours and everything that goes with them.

> No heroin is allowed in the club. Any member found
> using heroin will be bashed and thrown out of the club.
> **Bandidos bylaws**

These rules, like any of the rules, are enforced vigorously. Drug users aren't regarded highly in the clubs.

> You can't trust 'em. Their priorities are on things other
> than the club.
> **Coffin Cheater**

> Fuckin' hop heads. Those bastards are trouble for the
> club. They're not with the program. You get in a situation
> where you are on a run and a wired [high on metham-
> phetamines] brother goes off his head and starts kicking
> citizens. No way, man. They're just fucking bad news.
> **Rebel**

One Hell's Angel leader told me how much he hates drugs, and that they are not a big part of the club any more. Leaders of other clubs have told me they get pissed off when outsiders approach them looking for drugs, presuming that a bikie club would have drugs to sell.

Hard drugs are often a problem in some of the less disciplined clubs which don't keep control of their chapters. These clubs usually lack a good international or national sergeant-at-arms to ensure rules are enforced in the different chapters of the club. The large clubs also have nomad members who don't belong to any specific chapter yet pay their dues at various chapters. They are full members of the club with a fair bit of experience. They move from chapter to chapter and generally keep an eye on matters, offering advice to local members and nominees. These blokes would be the ones to crack down on any rampant drug use.

Many of the bikies are beyond using hard drugs anyway. They may have been into the LSD scene in the 1960s and '70s, but they're just too old for that sort of shit any more. Even the dope is starting to knock them around.

> I used to really like to smoke heads. Nowadays, I find it too intense. I prefer a bit of leaf if I'm having a smoke these days.
> **Satan's Cavalry associate**

However, drug use is a different issue from drug manufacturing. Many club members have been involved in manufacturing hard drugs. Clubs have faced extreme internal and external pressure because of it. One such case in the early to mid-1980s stands as a testament to the turmoil drug manufacturing creates for clubs.

The Hell's Angels Melbourne chapter was ripped apart and nearly destroyed by speed, a powerful drug that stimulates the central nervous system, speeding up messages to and from the brain. Hence its popular nickname.

There was no speed of any note in Australia in the 1970s. Yet by the late 1980s it had become the number one drug on the police hit list. Part of the reason for this growth lay with members of the Melbourne Hell's Angels.

It started with a visit to the Oakland chapter of the Hell's Angels by a member of the Melbourne chapter, Peter John Hill, in early 1980. Whether he went with the aim of learning how to manufacture speed, or merely came across it while there is unclear, but he allegedly arrived back in Australia with the basic knowledge and intention of manufacturing the drug.

Upon his return, a group within the club set about making speed. The members were Hill, Roger Wallace Biddlestone, Raymond Hamment, John Paul Madden and Terrence Alexander Faulkner.

The first thing they had to do was get the ingredients, the main one being phenyl -2- propanone or P2P. Due to a bureaucratic quirk at the time, P2P could not be manufactured in Australia, but could be imported – as long as you had a legitimate reason to do so. It had long been illegal to import it into the United States. The group faced the challenge of establishing a legitimate reason to get their hands on the P2P. It's alleged Faulkner had a relative who was an importer, who was able to identify and buy 200 litres of P2P from France for $16 000. More importantly, he provided a reason for bringing the chemical into the country.

While they awaited its delivery the group got to work setting up a speed factory – which was basically a laboratory to conduct the chemical process. While producing speed requires only a basic understanding of chemistry there are some risky steps involved. Many who undertake the process soon discover the major problem is the smell. It stinks unbelievably, so it's really only possible to do it on a remote property, as far from suspicious neighbours as possible.

A house was rented at Belgrave, in the Dandenong Ranges on the eastern edge of Melbourne. Slowly, piece by piece so as not to arouse suspicion, they took the equipment to the house – gas, glass heating equipment, gas masks, infrared lamps, etc.

While this was going on, Hill and Hamment jumped on a plane and headed back to the United States to find out more about the drug manufacturing process. A member of the Oakland

Hell's Angels evidently met them in San Francisco. They were taken to meet another Oakland Hell's Angel, Sergei Walton, who was to provide them with specific details of the process. It turned out that by the time they got there Walton was in the slammer for manufacturing and distributing methamphetamines. That was of little concern to the two Australians. They merely trotted off to the prison to ask him about the finer points of the speed-making process. You'd imagine that was a hushed conversation.

He gave the pair as much detail as he could verbally, promising to follow it up with written instructions.

Hill flew back to Melbourne, followed a few weeks later by Hamment. Some time after that, incredibly, a letter arrived from Walton, with detailed instructions on how to manufacture speed. It makes the mind boggle as to how Walton could possibly supply them with such information from prison.

The group still didn't have their shipment of P2P, but were keen to get the manufacture underway. They managed to get their hands on a small amount of P2P locally and began to experiment. In late 1980 the first batch of speed was produced. There wasn't much, but it was pretty good quality.

The initial trials revealed how nasty the chemical process was. They were forced to move from the semi-suburban Belgrave to a property called Greenslopes, at Wattle Glen in late 1980. The property, set in heavy bush, was rented by a woman who told the owner she planned to live there with her children. It was later revealed the woman was Rosemary Biddlestone, the wife of Roger. It wasn't the house that was of interest, but a bungalow and garage obscured from the road. The bungalow was to be the location of the factory. Its windows were covered with black plastic, the door concealed by fibro-cement and two air-conditioners installed.

Incredibly, six weeks after the club members took over the lease the owner of the property sprang a surprise visit to check how things were going. Evidently no one was about, so he had a quick look in the windows of the house. It appeared the only piece of furniture in the house was a refrigerator. He thought it a little weird, but as the rental cheques were arriving on time he didn't worry about it too much. The manufacturing of speed was relatively new in Australia so it would not have aroused the suspicion it may do today. It's not clear whether he looked in the bungalow.

Not long after Christmas 1980 the eagerly awaited P2P arrived from France. The group wasted no time swinging into full production. Doing the sums, you can see why they were so keen to get into it. The early experimental batches, which had been diluted by a third with sugar, sold for $22 000 a kilogram. Theoretically, with the P2P they had, they could make about 240 kg of diluted speed. They were looking at potential earnings of about $5 million before expenses. That's in 1980 dollars. Today's figure could be six times higher.

They gradually perfected the process and established a network. By the end of 1981 they were pretty good at putting the drug together, getting up to 95 per cent pure amphetamines.

The production and distribution process really hit its straps from that point. At first the market was mainly restricted to the local biker community, with speed enabling the bikers to party for hours on end. However, the Greenslopes drugs were soon being widely distributed throughout Australia. There's evidence the drugs reached New South Wales and Adelaide.

The amount of drugs produced in the factory in 1981 is unclear, with estimates ranging from 18 kg to 63 kg. The higher range would have netted the five Hell's Angel's about $1.8 million. That was the return from selling to dealers. The value by the time it was cut down and sold on the streets would have been much higher. Buoyed by the success of the enterprise, the group organised two further shipments of P2P.

It was later revealed the police were onto the gang as they were setting up the Greenslopes operation, even photographing the men in 1980 as they were buying equipment for the lab. But any attempt to move on the gang was thwarted by the gang's own anti-surveillance methods, including voice-activated tape recorders to detect any intruders in the lab.

In February 1982 police were able to enter the property, placing listening devices in the house and bungalow. Even though they were breaking in they carried a warrant so any evidence gathered could be tendered in a trial. The property was then placed under 24-hour surveillance. Little did the men know, photographers were sitting only 80 metres from the laboratory recording every movement. The surveillance lasted for five weeks until the lab was raided on 10 March 1982, after an earlier raid was aborted at the last minute.

The police arrested three of the men in the laboratory, with the others arrested soon after. They uncovered $18 000 cash, 3 kg of amphetamines, gelignite, a machine gun and a couple of pistols. They also found a device to re-seal cans. They were slightly puzzled by this until they realised what was going on. In return for providing the expertise to make speed, the group was allegedly sending P2P to the Oakland Hell's Angels. As importation of P2P into the US was banned the group was allegedly sending it in pineapple juice cans, after the juice had been tipped out. The cans were then resealed.

The men were soon out on bail, and back producing drugs while they awaited trial. What appeared to be a tight case soon turned into one of the longest-running sagas seen in Australia's criminal courts. There were three trials and one aborted in its infancy. The first lasted 75 sitting days, ending in a hung jury.

The second trial was aborted after a book, *Disorganised Crime*, mentioned that a machine gun was found at Greenslopes. Charges relating to the machine gun had not been presented to the jury during the trial. The judge of the case, Mr Justice

Hempel, ruled that a jury member who saw the book could have had their verdict influenced.

Another trial had to be aborted almost as soon as it started, before the final trial in which Hill agreed to give evidence for the Crown, saw all the men convicted. This was five years after the property had been raided. The legal battle swallowed 15 000 pages of transcript and there were about 600 exhibits. The cost of the trial is unknown but it's alleged some of the funds for the defence of the men were raised through advertisements in biker magazines calling for money. It was also believed money came from overseas Hell's Angels chapters.

Discontent over the drugs had been festering within the Melbourne chapter since Hill first visited the United States. The club split into two clear factions. One side saw it as an easy way to make money; the other faction was vehemently opposed to what was going on. There was a strong feeling in the club that the drug manufacturing was bringing too much police attention onto them. The split was not easily fixed, as there were high-ranking members and office bearers in both camps. Madden was actually the sergeant-at-arms and Biddlestone was treasurer prior to the drug blow-up. They were kind of the 'old guard' within the club, which made the split even more difficult.

The dispute within the club hit a low point after the police bust. Hill, Biddlestone, Hamment and Madden were back on the streets the day after their arrest on bail of $20 000 each. And they wanted answers. Hill and Biddlestone were convinced a fellow Hell's Angel had tipped off the police. Lie detectors were allegedly used to finger the mole. The pair believed they knew who'd squealed, so they put a contract out on his life. It was vicious stuff. A member found to have told the victim that the contract was on him was savagely bashed with a hammer, leaving him with serious head wounds. It was no surprise he soon quit the club.

The drug faction also directed its fury at the police who

busted the factory. A guy called Jim Jim Brandes flew into Australia from the United States allegedly to murder Detective-Sergeant Bob Armstrong, who led the Omega 2 taskforce that had busted the Greenslopes operation. Detective-Sergeant Armstrong was the officer who had broken into the lab to place the listening devices that cracked the case.

When Brandes arrived at Melbourne Airport there were some irregularities with his visa. Immigration officials decided to look through his luggage. In it they found press clippings on the local Hell's Angels drug case, manuals on explosives and phone tapping, a pair of thumb cuffs and details of Armstrong's activities. It seems as if Brandes wasn't the brightest spark, as the press clippings included details of a criminal trial in California in which he faced a charge of attempting to murder San Francisco policeman Bill Zurbe. Zurbe headed a similar taskforce to Armstrong, investigating the Hell's Angels in San Francisco. A cautious man, Zurbe would check his car for explosives each morning. One morning on stepping back to look under the car he stood on a pressure pad that activated a bomb, leaving him crippled. Brandes was acquitted of the attempted murder charge but that meant little to Australian immigration. He was put on the next plane home.

At about this time, in late 1982, a diversion hit the club, taking the club's focus away from the split between the pro- and anti-drug factions. A club called the Drifters arrived in Melbourne and attempted to muscle in on the Hell's Angels' territory. The move triggered a violent turf war. It escalated dramatically when a Drifter was dragged from his motorcycle and his colours taken by the Hell's Angels. Biddlestone's house, which was being used as the Hell's Angels clubhouse at the time, was later riddled with bullets. The dispute ended when two members of the Drifters were shot in the kneecaps and their clubhouse burned down.

However, it was the death of Madden that really fractured the club. Madden, who stood 190 cm tall, was not only the sergeant-at-arms of the chapter, he was also the enforcer for the drug faction of the club. Seemingly respected by both factions of the club and even, it seems, by the police, he was instrumental in maintaining order between the two sides and ensuring the rest of the Hell's Angels were not plotting against those involved in the drug operation.

In early 1985 Madden was on a run with the club at Kinglake, north of Melbourne. Witnesses say he had stopped suddenly in the middle of the road after his chain came loose. The 'crash truck' that followed the ride to collect anyone who broke down was right behind him. Madden stopped so abruptly the driver of the truck had no chance to stop or swerve and avoid him. Madden's skull was crushed by the impact and he died shortly afterwards in hospital.

It proved to be a huge blow not just for Hill and Biddlestone, as their watchdog had gone, but for the entire club, as they had lost the circuit breaker in the dispute. According to one policeman: 'They turned on each other once his stabilising influence was gone.'

There were about 40 violent incidents involving the club in the following two years. In one incident police believe a machine-gun massacre at the Hell's Angels' headquarters was averted only after those with the guns realised there were friends in the house who could be caught in the crossfire.

It was alleged that while this was going on, and throughout successive trials, Hill and Biddlestone continued to manufacture speed. In 1985 two drug-squad detectives, who were in Ballarat to give evidence at an unrelated trial, were about to check into their motel when they noticed two familiar names on the guest list – Hill and Biddlestone. They immediately high-tailed it, checking into another motel and calling in surveillance teams. Two weeks later a house was raided in Ballarat, as well as a room at the motel. At the house they found Hill, Steve Hardy – who was a member of the Adelaide chapter of the Hell's Angels – and an operating amphetamine lab.

The lab was smaller than Greenslopes and capable of producing only a kilogram of speed at a time. But it was of very high quality due to the involvement of an Englishman, Colin Fleet. Police branded him the mad professor; he appeared to have a brilliant, yet tortured mind. One of his major contributions was to develop a technique that dramatically cut the odour from the speed production process. He later committed suicide.

It appeared the Ballarat lab was the last straw for some of the other Hell's Angels. While awaiting trial, Hardy was invited to a party in Melbourne held by the Hell's Angels. Allegedly he didn't do much partying, as he was whisked away as soon as he arrived, and severely beaten before being run out of town back to South Australia. He was kicked out of the club soon after, although I'm not sure it was over his drug involvement.

Hill and Biddlestone then came in for some attention. The pair hadn't been going to weekly church, and had been warned that their lack of attendance was being noted. They were threatened with expulsion from the club. Hill took the hint and left the club, turning in his colours to a friend, who agreed to take them back to the club. Evidently not all the club paraphernalia was returned, so a posse was organised to visit Hill's house and re-claim the stuff.

Biddlestone decided not to follow Hill's lead and remained a member. As a member he was expected to join the other members in the attack on Hill's Warrandyte house. However, he refused to join them. He was bashed, in a taste of what was to come.

The raid on Hill's house went ahead in February 1986. The house was ransacked, causing thousands of dollars worth of damage. Hill, who was on bail at the time, was shaken by the attack because he believed his house, with its heavy security, was a safe haven.

There was worse to come for Hill. A few weeks later an abduction attempt was made on his wife while she was shopping in

Warrandyte. It was foiled only when Hill appeared with a shotgun and threatened the attackers.

By this stage, the dispute had got totally out of hand. In March 1986 the secretary of the Hell's Angels' Oakland chapter, Michael Malve, and a colleague, Michael Annalla, flew into Melbourne in an attempt to mediate the dispute. Their attempts were apparently in vain, for the violence continued.

The police decided to act in an attempt to quell the increasingly public feuding. They raided the Hell's Angels' Fairfield headquarters in May 1986, seizing a number of weapons and documents; however, no charges were laid.

By this stage Hill had gone to ground but Biddlestone was still going to the clubhouse. The dispute reached flashpoint in October 1986. It's unclear whether a specific event triggered it, but Biddlestone was savagely beaten. He was taken to a Ringwood house, handcuffed and beaten with an iron bar. He was then moved to a house in Fairfield where the beatings continued. After 15 hours of continuous physical abuse he was dumped outside the Austin hospital. His injuries were savage. One doctor's report said 'every major bone in his body' had been broken. (This was later found to be three breaks to an arm and multiple contusions.) He'd also been shot in the finger. The attack nearly killed him; his life saved only by being dumped outside the hospital.

With Biddlestone lying in hospital, Hill was finding the going tough. One of his few allies, Timothy Wurr, who was involved in the Ballarat speed laboratory, was attacked in his Ballarat home. Wurr and his wife were terrorised and two Harleys were allegedly stolen in the raid.

At this point it all got too much for Hill. He succumbed to pressure from both the police and forces within the club and decided to reveal all about the drug operation in a 120-page statement. Until that point the four surviving members of the drug syndicate had pleaded not guilty.

In March 1987, the last of the four was sentenced. Hill was sentenced to five years with a minimum of two, Biddlestone received six years with a minimum of three, Hamment was sentenced to six years with a minimum of four and Faulkner received four years with a minimum of two.

Hill was released from prison in late 1988, and is living under a new identity. Ray Hamment is still with the club and is currently a respected member of the Melbourne chapter. Hamment had two brothers with the club and was always uneasy defending the action of the breakaway group, when it was clearly opposed by his brothers. Biddlestone was pretty much destroyed by the whole experience, particularly the bashing. He faded from the scene and is now on a pension of some sort. I'm not sure what happened to Faulkner.

In early 1988 nine Hell's Angels members, including Ray Hamment and one of his brothers, faced court over the attacks on Hill and Biddlestone, with charges ranging from armed robbery, theft, burglary, unlawful assault and causing serious injury, to conspiracy to murder. The charges were sensationally dropped due to lack of evidence when Biddlestone refused to testify in court. 'I've been warned not to give any evidence in this case. I don't feel I can,' he told the court. He was convicted for contempt of court for his troubles. One of the accused was reported to have muttered 'piece of cake' after the charges was dropped.

I knew many of the Hell's Angels involved at the time, and I could see the anguish on their faces when I spoke to them. There was so much raw emotion surrounding the club. Hard men would become very upset when the subject came up.

Not many realised how close the club came to splitting completely. There has never been a situation as serious as this faced by any of the clubs that I know of – and all caused by drugs.

CHAPTER THIRTEEN THE BIG BLUE GANG

For outlaw clubs there is one battle that will outlive all other club wars. That's the war with the Big Blue Gang. If you think the clubs bear animosity towards each other, it's nothing compared to the hatred they feel for the police.

The clubs and the police have been at loggerheads since they were first labelled 'outlaws' after Hollister more than 50 years ago. They have become natural enemies, to the point the clubs regard the police as a gang, driven by the same motives as any other gang – power and domination. It's why they refer to the police as the Big Blue Gang. It may sound irrational for the clubs to think this way, yet in 2000 the *West Australian* newspaper published a picture of a police officer wearing an OMCG (Outlaw Motorcycle Gang) Taskforce badge with 99% clearly inscribed upon it. To the clubs, that signalled quite clearly the attitude of the police, even if it appeared the police misinterpreted the 1% badge as referring to the outlaw clubs being 1 per cent of mainstream society, not 1 per cent of the biker world.

In many ways, the police sometimes do live up to the notion of being the enemy by constantly targeting the clubs. Much of the focus is legitimate, such as attempting to cool a potentially violent inter-club situation. Or it can be intimidatory, when the need to be seen to be doing something overrides the rights of the clubs to go about their business unhindered. I saw it when I observed the police activity at the entrance to Broadford in the mid-1980s.

It can be a lineball situation. The Gypsy Jokers' clash with police in South Australia in early 2001 saw the club tailed back to Adelaide by 10 police. The club also had to negotiate seven police roadblocks. I'd argue that the government, via the police, was pretty keen to be seen by the public as doing something about the bikies. However, I'm giving the Australian police a bad name. Australian clubs, although they'll never admit it, are pretty well treated by the local authorities, compared to the heat the police put on clubs in the United States and Europe. Australian policing methods are quite different from those of the US and Canada, in particular. Much of that comes from the different structures of the Australian and North American police forces.

Police agencies of the United States are highly decentralised, comprised of literally thousands of different agencies. Often police of different agencies work within the same jurisdiction. Compare this to Australia, which has six state police agencies and a relatively small national police force whose primary mandates are the policing of the Australian Capital Territory, the Northern Territory and co-ordinating with International Police (Interpol). New Zealand and South Africa also have strong centralised police forces.

In the United States, local level police chiefs are usually elected whereas in Australia, Canada, the United Kingdom, New Zealand and South Africa police chiefs, or commissioners, are appointed by the elected politicians of the day.

It's these points of difference between the forces that lead to the most fundamental reason for the gulf in policing – funding.

Where public elections and pressure determine police funding, the clubs tend to be demonised to a greater degree than where allocation of police resources is largely an internal matter. That's why the US police public relations units dispatch sensationalist media coverage of outlaw motorcycle clubs as highly criminal units. They're more than happy for the clubs to be constantly portrayed as drug empires and criminal units, so the public willingly channels funds into keeping the scourge at bay. Canada, despite its centralised police force, seems to follow the US line in demonising the clubs. It probably has no choice. Being the United States' closest neighbour, the Canadian population would have much the same impression of the clubs as they do in the United States.

In Australia, South Africa and New Zealand the really heavy police attention is usually focussed on clubs only during turf wars or other sensationalist club crimes, as with the recent cases in South Australia and Western Australia.

On the whole, Australian policing is based on common sense and seems to be much more personal. Local police will invariably approach a bikie and say: 'We don't want you around here any more. If we see you again, we'll book you.' Some bikies will call this police harassment. Others will see it as a friendly reminder and hit the road, relieved they haven't been booked for something they perhaps should have been.

It creates a situation where there is less conflict and civil disobedience. In Australia, for instance, a bikie will stop and give his correct name. It's much different in North America. Almost all bikers in Canada and the United States will whip out a tape recorder the moment they're pulled up by the police, recording everything said before rushing the tape straight over to their lawyer to check if they have a case for police harassment.

The big problem in these cases is the Bill of Rights. In countries with a Bill of Rights, such as the United States, there is explicit protection from police harassment. There's no leeway for the police to deal with issues, as there is in Australia. Everything has to be done by the book for fear they'll wind up in court facing harassment charges. Without a Bill of Rights, Australian police don't feel they are forced into playing by the rules, and the public doesn't feel they have the right to challenge the police.

In Australia, Victoria is as close as you'll get to having Bill of Rights' conditions. The civil libertarian body, Liberty Victoria, keeps a vigilant eye on policing issues. Also, there is a much more libertarian ethos in the Victorian community compared to the other states. You only have to look at wash-up following the policing of one protest over a school closure in Richmond, an inner-Melbourne suburb in the 1990s. At issue was the use of pressure-point tactics used by the police against the protestors, where the police pushed their fingers into the necks of protestors to subdue them. The police took a pounding over the incident, not just in the court of public opinion but in the courts proper, with damages awarded to some protesters and police tactics heavily criticised.

Now, any time there is a public order event and the Victorian police use violence they are publicly pounded. The only time they are not is when there is a serious criminal event. I think, in the main, the Australian population, save for Victoria, is pretty apathetic in relation to the issues that the US holds dear, such as police harassment and tactics.

Even when Australian police could perhaps be excused for using a heavy hand against the clubs they use common sense. The mid-1990s was a very difficult time for the outlaw clubs, with enormous amalgamation pressure coupled with falling membership. The amalgamations produced a wave of violent incidents that shocked a nation which had heard little of the clubs since the Milperra massacre in 1984.

In Perth, Gypsy Jokers were feuding with Rebels, waging a

two-year war with periodic outbreaks of violence. In Sydney, Peter Ledger of the Comancheros was murdered. In Adelaide the Rebel's clubhouse was bombed and five members shot, then the Bandidos were subject to an arson attack. In Brisbane, a Bandidos'-owned business was fire-bombed. In Geelong, a Bandidos member's vehicle was also fire-bombed. So it went on, with more killings and bombings.

Australian police didn't attempt to fuel the fires of public concern by creating a public enemy of the outlaw motorcycle clubs. Rather, they did their best to provide mechanisms for the clubs to make peace while assuring the public that the violence was contained as much as possible to the clubs themselves. This was enlightened policing.

The US police response to similar outbreaks would be much different. Upholding the law is the only answer. A prosecution is more important than changing behaviour to prevent a crime.

A classic example is drugs. Australia's attitude to drugs is one of harm minimisation compared to almost all other countries, although many would argue that attitude has hardened in recent years in line with a more conservative view from Canberra. Australian authorities generally want to prevent drug use, with users given help to kick the habit. The United States regards drugs as an absolute evil, with law enforcement geared solely towards preventing their distribution. There is zero tolerance of drug users. You won't hear any debate about injecting rooms and treatment programs in the United States. The puritanical approach of the United States to drugs is evident the moment you set foot in the country. It's almost impossible to gain entry into the country if you have a minor drug conviction.

The US police are fully backed by the government, with every tool given to them to increase the chances of conviction. The bike clubs saw evidence of this when the *Racketeer Influence and Corrupt Organisations Act* was turned on them. The RICO Act is a piece of federal legislation that says being a member of a criminal organisation makes you a criminal. Prosecution under the Act carries a prison sentence of 5–10 years. It was a civil libertarian nightmare. It was introduced to control the Mafia in 1978, but the Hell's Angels was the first group they tried to prosecute, in 1979 and 1981.

The cases floundered because the courts found the Hell's Angels club was not organised for the purposes of commissioning crimes. Another US club has since been busted using the RICO Act. The international president of the Outlaws, Harry 'Taco' Bowman, was sentenced to life in prison in April 2001 on charges of conspiracy, racketeering and distribution of drugs. He was also convicted of plotting to murder rival club members, firebombing rival clubhouses and robbing and beating rival club members. The case heard allegations that the Outlaws controlled a large chunk of organised crime across much of the southern United States, with Bowman in charge of the operation. The prosecution was the culmination of a 15-year effort by the US government to pin the Outlaws and the only successful prosecution in 32 attempts to use Rico on the clubs.

Other countries have introduced similar laws. Canada introduced changes to its 1997 anti-gang laws in April 2001, to bolster a law that says a club is a criminal organisation if it is comprised of members who have committed a number of crimes. It also strengthened the legal definition of what's considered a criminal organisation.

It didn't take long before it became clear who the law would target. In May 2001 a Royal Canadian Mounted Police spokesman said the Nova Scotia chapter of the Hell's Angels would be a prime target under the law after it held a get-together in Halifax. 'It is illegal to belong to an organised crime group,' the spokesman said. 'That's what we are looking at now. So maybe this weekend, through our intelligence, it will help in charges of participation in a criminal organization.

'Their gathering this weekend is no criminal offence. There is no offence to celebrate. But if we can prove this is a criminal organization, which is what we're looking at, that's a different story.'

He did, however, acknowledge the difficulty in proving that the club was a criminal organisation.

'Although a conspiracy is quite a simple thing to define under the Criminal Code – the agreement of two or more people to commit a criminal act – to prove a conspiracy is ... very tough,' the spokesman said.

In the early 1990s Germany made it illegal for the Hell's Angels to fly its colours, based on the alleged crimes by its members. Its success was short-lived, as the German club chapters simply altered the colours slightly and continued on their merry way.

The move to bikie-specific laws has now spread to Australia, with the Western Australian government introducing very tough laws. Recent violent incidents involving the Gypsy Jokers were considered the last straw by the government.

WA premier Geoff Gallop, in introducing the legislation into parliament in late 2001, said the laws would be the toughest in the country. The legislation includes:

- new police powers enabling them to enter premises linked to organised crime without a warrant and to photograph, search and detain for questioning anyone found there.
- the ability to seize any document or item they reasonably suspect will provide evidence;
- substantial fines or jail terms for people who refuse to answer questions, produce documents or otherwise co-operate in organised crime investigations;
- wider police access to surveillance devices for investigations;
- new power to dismantle building fortifications;

- that unco-operative people brought before a Supreme or District Court Judge acting as a special commissioner must answer questions under oath or they could be jailed;
- that there will be no privilege against self-incrimination to avoid answering questions, and legal professional privilege cannot be used to stop documents being produced on request;
- that a special commissioner can require people to produce any documents or items considered relevant to an investigation;
- refusal to attend a hearing will be in contempt of court, with unlimited fines and/or jail terms able to be imposed at the discretion of the Supreme Court;
- false testimony can bring five years' jail;
- anyone trying to prevent a person attending a hearing faces five years' jail plus a $100 000 fine;
- five years jail plus a $100 000 fine for causing any loss, damage, disadvantage or other injury to a witness.

The legislation specifies more than 30 offences capable of triggering the new police powers, including murder, kidnapping, serious firearms offences, robbery, extortion, drug trafficking and explosives offences. At least two of the offences must be involved before the special powers can be used. According to the Premier, 'These are exceptional powers, so there will be safeguards, but I make no apologies for our strong stance'.

However, prior to its introduction, there were some political fears it was too draconian, and that the definition of who it could be used against was not tight enough.

One concerned MP said: 'The principal concern is that people not in the same league as bikies could get caught up in the net. It is a civil liberties issue. It is not about going soft on bikies.'

The laws are pretty heavy stuff and are set to test both the will of the clubs and the government. In creating these laws the government has created an expectation among the public that the problem will soon disappear. It will make the next WA state election interesting if the clubs are still visible and the laws have had little impact.

I don't think governments realise they may not crack many of the bikies. The fear of retribution by the clubs is greater than jail or a fine. 'It's better to go to jail than be killed,' as one club leader told me.

The South Australian, Victorian and New South Wales governments are also looking at new laws to target the bikies. It will be interesting to see how these states justify the precedent these laws set for civil liberties under Common Law, and how many of the original proposals become law. Only the fortification and seizure of assets aspects of the draconian Canadian anti-bikie laws made it through that country's review process and this is still to be tested in the Supreme Court.

The current mood spreading across Australia seems a dangerous exercise for civil liberties and an extremely expensive tactic to take in the light of the actual amount of crime the clubs are involved in.

However, these laws don't represent the first time Australian authorities have cracked down on the clubs. One famous case was the 1990 Hell's Angels' world run organised for down-under. It hit a major hurdle when police objected to members of the club being given permission to enter Australia. The stance was supported by the Immigration Department. The Hell's Angels claimed members without criminal records were among those refused entry. The Hell's Angels threatened legal action, but backed off and scheduled the run for two years later. By that time the Australian Immigration Department had had time to process the visa applications and there were few hassles. A couple of bikies with serious criminal records were refused entry, but most of those harshly dealt with in 1990 were allowed entry second time around. There was one case, however, of a prospect without a record who was taken into custody the moment he disembarked the plane and was sent back to the United States about four days later. It was never quite clear why this happened.

Another popular tactic for the US police is infiltration of clubs by undercover operatives. Again, the difference between the US and Australian police when it comes to this tactic is quite stark.

I find the Australian police infiltration technique much more interesting. The National Crime Authority, Australia's equivalent to the FBI, takes a much more up-front approach. For instance, the Gypsy Jokers have been in the news in the last couple of years for violent clashes with police, particularly in South Australia. This has prompted the NCA to assign an officer to monitor the activities of the club. The club is aware of the agent.

In rare cases, the club has actually been in contact with the agent. This was the case during the tense stand-off between the club and South Australian police in early 2001. The NCA agent could see that the club was ready to go down fighting so he became the go-between in the dispute, negotiating with both sides. He was able to organise the return of the club colours and badges confiscated by police, which proved a major break-through. It was a brilliant strategy, keeping communication open and heading off trouble before it spread to the public.

Another case was the Coffin Cheaters' run to Tasmania in late 2001. The police and the club liaised weeks before the event to set the ground rules for behaviour. The club made it clear it intended to be law-abiding while in the state. The Tasmanian Police then tailed the club throughout the 10-day ride with the full knowledge of the club.

The problems the police face in liasing with the clubs were highlighted when the club returned to Victoria. Victorian police command tipped off the club that about 70 police and officers from the Sheriff's Office would be waiting to search for weapons, drugs and outstanding warrants when the Coffin Cheaters disembarked from the Spirit of Tasmania.

The officers on the ground were outraged amid claims that 17 bikies wanted by police slipped through the net.

Assistant Commissioner (Crime) George Davis, who ordered the Coffin Cheaters be tipped off, was reported in the media as saying that he wanted to prevent:

> 130 drunken outlaw motorcycle gang members confronting 70 Victorian policemen in the middle of a public event with a number of other civilians trying to leave the boat.
>
> That wasn't highly probable but it was a possibility and one that wasn't necessary. The purpose of any policing organisation is to prevent crime as a first priority and if we've managed to do that I'm happy with the operation.

Mr Davis was hanged in the court of public opinion, with the media and commentators outraged that he could contemplate letting the club know what lay ahead. To me, it was another example of enlightened policing.

The clubs will reluctantly work with the police if it means the police will then leave them alone. One club in Queensland begrudgingly allowed the police to come into one of their functions to breath-test those planning to ride home. The police saw it as a chance to show the club they were willing to help them, not merely sit down the road waiting to hit them on their bikes. However, all the best intentions in the world didn't prevent some of the bikies being picked up for being over the alcohol limit.

Outlaw motorcycle clubs couldn't survive being completely

hostile to the police. They must conform to things such as liquor licences and the regulations that come with running public events, such as concerts.

Contrast that attitude to the FBI's Anthony Tait operation in the 1980s. Tait was the small-time bikie who rose to prominence within the US Hell's Angels, all the while passing information to the police.

Profiles of Tait present a complex and confused man, with an almost Dr Jeckyl and Mr Hyde personality, ranging from the worst acts of violence in the company of his fellow bikers, to complete moralistic disgust at the slightest notion of illegality. All wrapped up in a package that gave him the appearance of a mild-mannered public servant, with thick glasses and mousy moustache.

I find him one of the oddest characters I have come across in the biker world.

Tait had an odd upbringing. His father, Gordon, was an intelligence officer in the British Army, and spent some time in the Middle East seeking Israeli terrorists. He eventually settled in Alaska in the 1960s, where he felt the need to teach his son, who was not even in his teens, to survive in the sort of violent world he had experienced.

They stood on a corner, or on a ship, and Gordon told his son to take in the scene for a minute. He made him turn around and describe what he saw. Tait described more and more details. Gordon made his son count cars, differentiate makes and models, remember what else happened in the area when the car passed, what the driver looked like and wore. He made him look for anything out of the norm.

It seemed Tait was being groomed by his father for a life of espionage. Tait only had to find a target.

He tried his hand at the military, enlisting at the age of 17. But his father's training led him to believe he was well ahead of any training the army could offer. His military career was rather inglorious. He did a runner from the army not long after enlisting, returning after being absent for 27 days. Under US military rule, a soldier must be absent without leave for four weeks to be classified as a deserter. Tait escaped prosecution by a day, but was slugged with a charge of dereliction of duty after he went missing a second time. This time he scored a dishonourable discharge. That didn't stop him from applying unsuccessfully for a job as a CIA spy a few years later.

He moved back to his home town of Anchorage in 1974 where he worked as a bouncer at many clubs. He loved violence and had an intense dislike of certain groups, including pimps and drug dealers.

Not long after his discharge he told the police of some drug dealers on a construction site where he was working. It was his first experience as an informer, and it seemed to sit perfectly with his odd ideals. According to his biographer, Yves Lavigne: 'Among his goals in life were to create a better society where his idea of justice ruled, to ride the space shuttle – and to fuck a nun.' Charming!

Working as a bouncer put him in contact with outlaw bikers, notably the Brothers MC. After a few years of running into and getting to know members of the club, he was invited to hang around. He must have made an impression, as the club also offered him a Harley for US$2500 on the generous terms of paying it back when he could, even at as little as a dollar a week. The offer was made because he was considered such a high value potential member.

He was soon accepted as a nominee for the Brothers. At the same time he began to forge a relationship with the local police, asking if there was any intelligence work he could perform. He secretly harboured a desire to be a policeman, hanging around police bars, offering snippets of information so he could be in with that crowd. They were only too happy to take up the offer.

During his nominee period, the Brothers and Hell's Angels decided to do a patch-over. Under the arrangement, the Brothers were given the status as a nominee club, which lasted 18 months. The aim was that if it performed well it would be given full membership status and be authorised to form the Anchorage chapter of the Hell's Angels.

Like all nominees of the Brothers, Tait's colours were eventually changed from the Brothers to Hell's Angels as part of the arrangement. Throughout this time, Tait continued to provide information to the local police. However, when the Brothers became the Hell's Angels in 1982 the local police realised they were on to something. US police had never been able to crack the Hell's Angels, so the potential for Tait was enormous. They recognised the need for national intelligence, so they called in the Federal Bureau of Investigation. Tait was soon reporting to an FBI agent. While this was going on his nominee stage passed, and he was given his colours as a full member of the Anchorage chapter of the Hell's Angels.

Then he started to climb. After a few years he was the sergeant-at-arms of the Anchorage chapter. When he began representing the chapter at West Coast Hell's Angels officers meetings the boys at the FBI really stood up and took notice. They couldn't believe their luck. He was officially recruited as a fully-fledged FBI operative and paid for his troubles. By late 1984, he was being wired by the FBI for extensive taping of Hell's Angels' business.

A year previously he'd entered into a de facto relationship with a prostitute. In 1985, he allegedly assaulted her so she decided she would rat on him. She told the police that he had said he was a hit man for the club, killing people in California. He also told her he had won a Purple Heart for valour in the Vietnam War.

Within a month she'd also became an FBI operative. Their reasoning was that she could verify much of the information Tait was supplying. The irony was that while she didn't tell Tait she was working for the FBI, neither did she know or suspect he was doing the same thing. Incredibly, they were both reporting to the same FBI agent. Sounds like a crazy relationship, especially when she was quoted in the book on Tait's life as saying he 'wouldn't know when he was lying or telling the truth as there was no difference to him'.

The strange situation wasn't to last. After a few months Tait discovered his girlfriend was an agent reporting to his contact. He fell out with the agent but the couple continued to act as FBI informers after they realised they could live with the unusual arrangement.

His determination to continue the operation boosted his standing within the FBI even more. They began to give him more resources, building him a new identity as a tile salesman and providing him with free airline tickets to attend national and international meetings for the Hell's Angels. As the information flowed, the FBI even gave him money to buy a new Harley-Davidson, a monthly allowance and covered all his expenses. Any suspicion of his free spending was tempered by a presumption within the club that he was making money from drugs. Ultimately, he was given permission to commit crimes with indemnity in order to achieve maximum infiltration of the Hell's Angels. Because Tait was given to bending the truth, the FBI used extensive audio-taping and photographing in their surveillance operation of the Hell's Angels to back up what he was reporting. They also conducted random drug and lie detector tests on Tait.

After three years of information from Tait and his girlfriend, the FBI launched a full-blown operation called CACUS, swooping on Hell's Angels members across the United States. It resulted in the arrests of 38 Hell's Angels members on various charges ranging from conspiracy to commit murder to manufacture and distribution of drugs, possession of illegal firearms and conversion of government property. Twenty-four Hell's Angels were finally convicted. One of those was Sonny Barger on a charge of conspiracy to commit murder. The charge related to a turf war with the Outlaws Motorcycle Club. It was this war that forced the FBI to launch Operation CACUS. It has been claimed many more arrests could have been made had there not been plans to murder Outlaws members. Barger was convicted and sent to prison for five years.

The irony of this is that in one of Tait's covertly taped conversations, Barger says:

> We got to get one thing straight with everybody: what goes on in this room is 100 per cent legal. We don't talk about illegal things here. Because, if you're doing anything illegal, I don't want to know about it 'cause it's not club business.

The FBI continued to pay Tait while he testified in the cases, even giving him a US$250 000 bonus.

Tait is still alive, living somewhere with a new identity. He spent the first 18 months after the bust staying in a different place each night. Of course, he was clutching weapons each of those nights, and it's likely he is still doing so. According to his biography, he was last known to be 'an agent for a foreign service. He works from Africa to Afghanistan and enjoys himself thoroughly trying to make the world a better place.'

The Hell's Angels deny they have a contract out on him. However, they admit they'd like to have a 'chat' with him.

What strikes me as most bizarre was the cost of it all. The operation lasted more than three years and involved vast amounts of resources. In one case, light aircraft circled a house while Tait transmitted his conversations for recording. Two full-time FBI agents were assigned to the case for those three years as well as all the costs associated with payment for Tait and his girlfriend, and expenses. Throw in the new Harley Davidson as a 'necessary tool' for his work as informant, the $250 000 bonus, and the bills started to mount. The bust at the end resulted in a number of charges, including conspiracy to murder. But did it change the behaviour of the club or prevent any crime? I doubt it. The Australian method is more likely to do so.

Of course, that's not to say the Australian police don't operate covertly in local chapters. There have been at least three cases of undercover police joining Australian bikie clubs.

In one case, two Victorian policemen infiltrated the Bandidos in Ballarat after fruitless attempts by the police to negotiate a peace deal between the Bandidos and Vikings. It was decided the only option was to get inside the club to gather evidence that would blow it apart. The two policemen drifted into Ballarat under the guise of being unemployed. They started to bump into club members at pubs until they were invited around to the clubhouse for a party. They passed the test and were invited to hang around the club. Six months later they became prospects. Full membership on 12-months' probation was offered in October 1997. One of them eventually became the secretary-elect of the chapter.

There is the great story in John Sylvester and Andrew Rule's book *Underbelly 2* that when the national president of the Bandidos was shot and killed all the members, including the two undercover policemen, attended the funeral. As the members filed past the dead leader's body one of the undercover cops leant over the coffin and whispered: 'I'm a copper, you know.'

The violent death of the president and two other Bandidos forced police command to call in the undercover officers. The following month club members in four states were raided, with 19 people arrested. A fair amount of drugs and drug-making equipment, as well as weapons, were seized. Most pleaded guilty because of the evidence supplied by the undercover policeman. However, the main players spent less time in prison than the police spent undercover.

The process of joining a club makes it almost impossible to do that any more, with infiltrations leading to an escalation in admission requirements. Most inside information against the clubs comes from members turning rather than facing prosecution for their part in a crime. Peter Hill, in the Hell's Angel speed case of the 1980s, was a classic example.

The clubs believe the police unjustly harass them and that the politicians use them as a public whipping boy. However, most bikies believe the rank and file coppers are doing a job, and will treat them with the respect they themselves are shown. There isn't always animosity between the clubs and the cops. As one outlaw bikie told me, 'there's nothing wrong with the average cop, it's just the occasional arsehole who doesn't like bikies that makes life hard.'

CHAPTER FOURTEEN THE MILD WEST

I sat in the Qantas Lounge at Melbourne Airport, my mate Rudi by my side, pondering what I had got myself in to. It was 30 December 2001 and I was about to fly to Perth. However, this was to be no holiday. I'd been plucked from a lazy festive season on my farm and invited to ride with the Gypsy Jokers on their annual run. This was the most controversial run of Australian clubs at the time. It was on this run the previous year that the South Australian STAR Force commander had his jaw broken by a Gypsy Joker, and the run that saw the club negotiate seven roadblocks on their way home. It was also the run where the NCA had been forced to step in to retrieve a set of club colours from the police.

As if that wasn't enough to set the scene for a volatile time, I was about to lob into the hotbed of a murder investigation, where the West Australian Gypsy Jokers were not only regarded as public enemy number one in the eyes of the public and police but also the prime suspects in a couple of murders and bombings. As you can see, I wasn't exactly packing my sunnies and shorts in anticipation of lying on Fremantle beach.

The invitation had been issued some weeks earlier when I travelled to Perth to consult the clubs on the proposed West Australian legislation designed to crack down on the bikies.

The club's media spokesman, Ray Jennings, asked if I could come along and monitor the policing of the run. The club was expecting a fair amount of police provocation in the tumultuous atmosphere following the murder of former policeman Don Hancock.

Just prior to the run they stepped up the pressure by arresting Gypsy Jokers' national president Len Kirby for possession of prohibited drugs and other charges as part of the murder investigation. Other senior members of the club had been given the third degree by police, resulting in a spattering of arrests. The club's Perth and Kalgoorlie clubhouses were also searched as part of the investigation.

The appointment of Ray, who was not a club member, as spokesman in the lead-up to the run was a huge step for a hardcore club like the Gypsy Jokers. The mere notion of the club even communicating with the media was strange enough. In fact, it's clearly stated in the club's constitution that no statements will be made to the media unless approved by a total vote of the national membership. To have an outsider perform the task was incredible, although 20 years ago Ray had been a nominee for the club. After seeing the time commitments required of a member he'd decided not to pursue membership. However, he had remained mates with the Gypsy Jokers in the meantime.

As I was to later discover, it was not clear whether his appointment had the total support of the club. 'He had no authority to speak for the club,' I was told a few weeks after the run.

I believe the push for the front man had come from the Sydney, Wodonga and Adelaide chapters and the Perth chapter had reluctantly agreed. The Gypsy Jokers are strongly divided on geographical lines, with the eastern and western chapters actually starting life as separate clubs that merely happened to share the same name.

The intention was that I would travel behind the club and observe how the police operated. I'd done the same thing at a number of club events, including Broadford for the Hell's Angels. However, three incidents occurred in the lead-up to the run that made the club close its doors, batten down its hatches and prepare to handle the situation in the true Gypsy Joker way.

First, strip searches were alleged to have been meted out by the West Australian Police in Eucla to Gypsy Jokers travelling by vehicle across the Nullarbor. This really got up the nose of the club, which felt it was being discriminated against. However, given the history of the club, I found it hard to see them being too worried about it. The other incidents were far more serious.

The second incident led to a potentially dangerous confrontation in a public place. As the interstate Gypsy Jokers arrived at Perth Airport they were met by a large contingent of WA police. It was alleged that one of the senior police made a provocative statement to one of the Gypsy Jokers along the lines of: 'If you cunts are looking for a blue, let's get it on now'.

This, in bikie culture, cannot be shirked. If a challenge is made you have to take it on. However, fortunately cooler heads prevailed – as they were standing in the middle of a crowded airport. It was not the first time on the run that the Gypsy Jokers were forced to bite their tongues.

The third and final straw for the club also came in Eucla, where the police seized bikes being shipped across from the eastern states two days before the run was to start. The police methodically went through each of the bikes, cross-checking frame numbers with motor numbers and looking for weapons.

The club was furious on two levels. The first was that, like any outlaw club, no one messes with the bikes. It was a blistering sore for their bikes to be in the care of the police. Strangely, my queries to the police about the incident and threats of legal action by the truckie who was carrying the bikes seemed to help get the bikes there on time for the run.

The club was particularly angry that the bikes wouldn't reach Perth in time for the run, as Eucla is about 1800 km away. I believed at the time that the club had made a tactical error in not sending the bikes over earlier. They should have expected they'd be stopped somewhere along the way, especially as there are not too many alternative routes to Perth across the barren stretch of the Nullarbor. They should have followed the lead of the Coffin Cheaters who, a few years before, had sent their bikes to the start of their national run a few days earlier, giving the police time to check them without disrupting the run.

However, the police needed to think about what they were doing. If their intention was to delay the run they were about to make a huge mistake. If New Year's Eve rolled around and there were possibly hundreds of angry bikies wandering aimlessly around Perth, with police resources already stretched the potential for trouble was huge.

The most sensible tactic was to keep the club together so they could be monitored as one group.

These three events sent the club into a spin, and all sorts of weird stuff started to happen. The club went into what I call 1 percenter mode. They cut off all contact with outsiders, including me, pulled down the shutters and virtually got ready for battle.

The whole scene was becoming very ugly. When Sydney members arrived in Perth on 29 December things were already pretty well in a crisis state. That day, Ray Jennings was told he wasn't representing the club any more. It seemed one sector of the club objected to being described in the media as having asked for civil libertarians, independent monitoring and a media liaison person. There seemed to be a hell of a lot of tension within the club. However, it seemed strange that they'd want to get rid of their PR man just when they needed him most.

Ray countered by announcing he was pulling the pin. He released a statement saying that he was no longer speaking for the club because of threats made by the police. He told the media:

> If I show my face in Western Australia as the spokesperson for the Gypsy Jokers, even though I'm not a Gypsy Joker myself, they [the police] will get me. These threats need to be taken seriously.

I suspect he also feared repercussions from the club.

The moderates in the club seemed to be losing control of the situation. It was believed there was some bad blood within the club because one section of the club appeared to be presenting the Gypsy Jokers as 'chicken-shits who were afraid of the Jacks [Police],' as one member put it. Many didn't want that. My sources told me that years of harassment and recent events had left some WA members completely unwilling to compromise their hardline position.

I was told by one source that the WA guys had 'no regard as to the consequences of their personal actions with the police.'

'It's a perfect case of fuck the world,' they said.

Of course, as an outsider, I was one of those cut off from the club so I couldn't verify these sentiments. I was warned by three associates and one club member not to attempt to make contact with the club.

All this had happened before I left Melbourne, so I decided to take Rudi along with me for a bit of protection and advice. I also arranged to be in daily contact with a senior member of the Australian Civil Liberties Union, who is also a top Melbourne trial lawyer. I also organised Laurie Levy, a barrister from Perth, to give legal representation on the scene via the Civil Liberties Union if it was needed. It was time for me to batten down my hatches too, just in case.

The nature of the run had changed dramatically from the original plan. Talk was of full-scale war. I was heading over into what I thought was going to be a war zone, making me even more determined to go along to possibly observe a piece of Australian outlaw club history.

As I waited at the airport I spotted a bloke who I reckoned was a bikie. I chanced my arm and approached him, asking if he was with the Gypsy Jokers. 'Yeah, I'm going over for the run,' he said, casting a suspicious eye over me.

'It's pretty hot over there I hear,' I said, hoping he knew I was talking about the club dramas, not the weather.' He grunted in agreement.

'I hear the bikes are still in Eucla,' I said, clinging to the hope this would develop into a conversation.

'They won't find anything on or in those bikes,' he said, surprisingly giving me a wink and a nod as he said it. Looked like he knew something I didn't. I chose not to pursue that line. We talked a bit longer, trying to find mutual acquaintants and friends in the club, until it came time to board the plane. I judiciously let him go ahead so as not to appear too keen to be asking questions about the club and the run. On the plane he sat with a few other blokes who could have been members, so I didn't pursue the matter.

We arrived in Perth to be greeted by the banner headline in the *Sunday Times*: 'You [the Gypsy Jokers] are not welcome in WA'. The comment piece concluded: 'One piece of advice – if your run takes you near Cape Naturaliste, do the public of WA a favour and keep riding off the edge.'

There were cops everywhere at the airport. I could now see for myself what I'd been hearing over the previous few days. It was quite overwhelming. The Gypsy Joker who was on my plane was taken aside by the police and disappeared from view. I didn't hang around to find out what happened to him. I was glad to get out.

I'd arranged to meet Acting Detective Superintendent Jim Migro, the field commander of Operation Avalon, the name given to the monitoring operation. He insisted on coming to the hotel to establish ground rules for my involvement. I was uneasy about this, because there were about 50 Gypsy Jokers staying at my hotel. I didn't want them to see me with the top brass. He was actually waiting for me in the lobby when I returned from a short walk to recover from the flight. There goes my credibility with the club, I thought to myself. Luckily no one saw us.

Detective Superintendent Migro explained that, on orders, he was taking a big stick approach to the policing of the club, with 500 police assigned to monitor the run. I thought he was taking the wrong approach. This was exactly opposite to my philosophy, which is that if a truckload of dynamite is travelling through town you don't throw lighted matches at it. I told him I thought the best way to deal with the club would be to let them do their own thing and they wouldn't harm others. It's usually only when provoked that violence flares.

He explained that as far as the police were concerned I had no status. Rudi and I would be arrested if we came closer than 30 metres away from the searches we'd come to monitor. He did concede, however, that we could follow the very large police and media contingent accompanying the Gypsy Jokers, as would be the right of any citizen. We weren't even permitted to have the level of access to the police that the media did. This was despite our agreeing to report for the *Australian* newspaper and to film a segment for *A Current Affair*, deals done to cover the expense of going on the run. The club may have invited us but they certainly weren't paying our way.

It was clear from Detective Superintendent Migro's tone just who was in control. He made it very clear that, in his opinion, the history of spilt blood had set the stage for almost certain violence. I had to agree with him, particularly if his mood mirrored that of his men.

We spent the rest of the day organising a car and wondering how the hell we'd go about getting access to key players so we could do what we'd gone over for.

We'd lost contact with the club so we didn't know when the run would start. We presumed it was the following day as they'd want to be somewhere for New Year's Eve. But the destination was a mystery. That was no surprise; most club members had no idea where they were going until they arrived at the destination. It's a bit of an outlaw tradition for the top echelons of the host chapter to organise a destination and keep it secret from even the local chapter members. Part of the reason is to prevent small shops at the destination from inflating prices if they know the bikies are coming. It's also a ploy to keep the police guessing and not let them establish a strong presence in the destination town.

However, we did hear a whisper that the first day would be a short run of about 300 km, heading east. That made me nervous, as it was in the direction of Ora Banda, the small town where Billy Grierson was murdered. If that was the case the tension could be deadly.

While we waited I conducted a number of media interviews. I was a bit of a novelty in Perth, as no one had heard any other view of the bikies other than the police's. Perth is unique for a city of 1.4 million people, as it's a one-newspaper town. Much of the electronic media follows whatever appears in the daily *West Australian*, which makes for a pretty narrow range of views.

The clubs do themselves such a disservice with their policy of not commenting publicly. It gives the police free reign to make all sorts of allegations, which the media just lap up.

It's especially true in Perth where the legal system is based upon a completely different set of principles to most Commonwealth states. These principles are called code law. Only Queensland, Uganda, Singapore, South Africa (prior to independence) and a few other very repressive states use code law. The function of code law is to allow the state to step outside common law precedence and histories of decisions to make their own rules. The criticism of code law is that it protects the status quo of the powerful and their agents, such as the police, over and above the individual.

In the case of Western Australia and Queensland, code law was originally introduced to protect the soldiers, warders and police of the day from genocide and murder charges stemming from their treatment of Aboriginal people. The first white person to be hanged in Australia was found guilty of murdering an Aborigine, so these states moved to this form of law. Code law is a bit like the laws that are in force during a state of emergency in a common law state. People lose fundamental rights that have been established through common law, such as their right to legal representation or the right not to answer questions.

I was able to knock a few myths on the head in my meeting with Detective Superintendent Migro and the media interviews. One was that this run had been planned for the New Year period to maximise the amount of trouble for the police. I was able to explain that the run had been going for 15 years and had always been held at this time of the year. In fact, it's always been known as the Christmas Run.

I was also able to discuss the new legislation aimed at curbing the WA 1% clubs. I explained that it was, in part, actually aimed at people like me, who were on the edge of the clubs, and who would be forced to reveal any information disclosed to them, up to seven years after the fact, or face five years in jail. I was also able to highlight the fact that obstructing trains was one of the crimes that could trigger the new laws.

We got word late in the day that the club's bikes had arrived from Eucla, clearing that potentially dangerous hurdle at least. In fact, it was the guy I'd met at the Melbourne airport who told me. He certainly seemed to have a handle on the situation.

New Year's Day arrived and we still had no idea where the run was headed, or what time everyone was leaving. All we could do was pack our hire car and wait for word from the media. I did some more radio interviews and also had the chance to listen to some of the stuff the police were saying. What I heard sounded pretty inflammatory.

I heard one interview on radio station 6PR with Acting Commissioner Bruce Brennan, in which he set out the police policy quite clearly.

These people are self-declared 1 percenters. They put themselves outside the law, and if there are any criminals amongst them, we'll run the tape over them. That's the business we're in. We're here to look after the people of Western Australia.

He said the police intended to pull over club members if they were not known to them and ask them questions.

If that's considered a provocative act by some, then so be it. They can expect to be stopped and spoken to.

We will cut our cloth according to the measure. If they become unruly then we will police the situation within the parameters of the law. We won't go outside the law because if we do it makes us no better than they are. We will use the full force of the law. We will apply it sensibly and we will apply it rigidly.

As the words tumbled from his mouth we heard the Gypsy Jokers were on the move from their clubhouse. Luckily they headed south, not east as I had originally feared. We hit the road and were soon up with the action. The police presence was incredible. We estimated there were 400 officers present.

We stayed behind the main body of the run to observe the roadblocks and to see how the police treated the stragglers. Experience taught me that the edge of the group is where most of the action takes place.

We arrived at the first roadblock 20 km from Armidale. It was a painstaking process – breath-testing, warrant checks, detailed checks of the bikes, swags and rolls taken apart and the support truck searched. One bikie was crudely asked to take off his helmet so he could be photographed.

'Take off your helmet mother fucker,' one officer said.

'I beg your pardon, there's no need to speak to me that way,' replied the bikie.

'Come on fucker, we want your photo, take your helmet off. Or are you waiting for a blue?'

The Gypsy Joker, who would have been in his mid 50s, removed his helmet, steam almost coming out of his ears in anger, while the police photographer took a digital photo of him.

The 'haul' from the massive operation was two drink-driving arrests and a third man who was wanted on a warrant in South Australia. No drugs or weapons were found during the search.

After the club had cleared the roadblock, Detective Superintendent Migro gave a press conference. He said the police expense was justified by the fact that there were no other serious crimes detected. The media asked if the massive police presence wasn't simply making things worse by frustrating the bikies. Detective Superintendent Migro responded that there was no doubt in his mind that the tactics were appropriate.

I felt it was time to say hello to Detective Superintendent Migro. His reaction when he realised we were actually there monitoring what was going on was quite marked. His face changed and his body posture slumped. He realised then that the police were not going to have sole control over what was written about the run.

The media descended upon me, asking whether I saw the procedures as inflammatory and provocative. I had the clear impression the media was sick of having the government and police press releases controlling what was said. They appeared to be hanging out for someone to make an informed comment that might put things into context. I told them that most states had long since given up allocating massive financial resources for such operations as they inevitably produced little return. Simply, there's no return for your money and there is a high risk of frustrating and provoking the bikies into violence. I may have been a bit extreme in saying there would be provocation, driven by police agendas. At least I knew it was going to get some air-time. And I'd stepped in at the right time.

I later realised that most of the television crew left the run at lunchtime to head back to Perth, so the big roadblocks were staged in the mornings to get it on film. Any activity after lunch went largely unrecorded.

Any media that was travelling throughout the day stayed with the body of bikes. By staying at the back of the main body of the run we were getting a whole different perspective.

And there was plenty to see. Less than 45 minutes after the bikes cleared the roadblock the police started to randomly pull up club members. We came across three to four bikes getting the once-over, followed by another small group who were surrounded by police a few minutes further up the road. The last time I'd seen this sort of strategy was at the shemozzle that marked the 100th anniversary of motorcycling at Phillip Island.

An unusual feature of the run was its spread-out nature – there were lots of small groups. It was different from the close-knit runs the clubs usually conduct.

The convoy of bikes, media and police stretched about three

kilometres. It wasn't until well into the day that I got a true picture of how many bikies were on the run.

There were significantly fewer than I had anticipated. There are about 120 full members of the Gypsy Jokers nationally, yet I counted only about 70 Gypsy Jokers and a crash truck. If this was to be all the members to show it would be a pretty disappointing turnout. It was a totally piss-weak turnout. Because of the attitude of the club, I would have expected nearly every member to be there. The police were actually expecting 250. I suspected the hard arses and pisspots may have taken a different way, while the main body was designed to throw the police off. The backup truck was full of bikes, making me suspicious that many had not yet joined the run.

The low numbers gave the road show an even more surreal appearance. According to official sources there were 500 police placed along the run. There were huge numbers of police ahead, between and behind the Gypsy Jokers. They lurked in bushes filming the ride, and hung out at service stations and facilities to keep an eye on things. They even had sniffer dogs, a mobile lock-up and a booze bus.

Lunch was at Kojonup, which was wall-to-wall with cops. There was still no word on where we were going, but it was becoming clearer we were heading to the former whaling town of Albany, now a popular holiday spot.

We changed tactics and drove ahead of the convoy, monitoring the police presence ahead of the run. At one small town there were more than 20 vehicles with roughly three police in each vehicle. The cost of the exercise to the WA taxpayer was becoming clear. When the club hit Albany a few police vehicles led them into town, with a few more bringing up the rear. Then came the main police body – 54 police vehicles with about 185 members. It gave new meaning to the term Big Blue Gang.

The Gypsy Jokers headed to an industrial property owned by

God's Garbage and the police arrived at a billet nearby.

That night the stage was set for fireworks – both in the sky and on the streets. Rudi and I decided to cruise the town to watch the action.

Albany, like most seaside resorts on a New Year's Eve, was packed with revellers. It was the police's worst nightmare. I was very interested to see how it was managed.

Most of the Jokers gathered in town at the hotels and restaurants. It appeared that an extra 20–25 Jokers had turned up from somewhere, as I suspected they would. They may have come down from Kalgoorlie. We spent much of our time with the main group. It appeared the mood within the club had mellowed after the last few days of dramas, so we were finally able to speak to a few members.

They admitted the police attention that day had been frustrating.

'Well, we made it, and I think that's what counts in a situation like this,' one member told me. 'All those coppers made it difficult to sit back and enjoy the run, although it was still a run, so that was good.'

There were stories of their run ins with the police. One bikie told me:

I've got no problem with your average copper but some are just bastards. I was pulled over by one guy. I turned my bike off and he ordered me to turn it back on. I refused. He turned it on and started revvin' the bike until I grabbed the throttle and set her down gently and turned it off. Now that's the kind of stuff that, if it were done to one of the other members, would cause some serious trouble. Besides that, what right does he have to do it? That's provocation, man.

We watched with interest as a few women tried to move in to speak to club members. They looked full as a boot, so some of the Jokers gently told them they weren't interested. The only arrest, at 10.45 p.m., was a girl drinking on the street.

The club went to great lengths not to slip up in front of the police, particularly for drink-driving. They even had a system of designated riders, who would drop club members off at the hotels and take members back to the camp.

'We wouldn't dream of giving those arseholes the pleasure of finding any problems,' one club member told me.

One of the designated riders had a particularly busy night. He was breath-tested by the police 14 times.

We chatted to many of the locals, who admitted they'd never seen anything like it, the place crawling with police and bikies.

However, many of the young people in the town were really annoyed. With hundreds of cops cruising about they had no hope of sneaking in a few grogs or drinking on the streets as they usually did on New Year's Eve. I wonder if the club realised they were helping clean up under-age drinking in Albany as part of their visit. Every cloud has a silver lining.

I saw Detective Superintendent Migro later that night, and he told me it had been a quiet night. It had been a standard small-town New Year's Eve celebration.

We woke the next morning to a story in the *West Australian* that was to cause a bit of a stir. I'd been interviewed by the paper's police reporter the previous day. One of the points I'd made was that police sometimes need public enemies to justify increased powers. It was also useful at a time when the WA police were facing a royal commission into the alleged abuse of police powers and corruption. I also said if there was blood shed it would likely be due to police provocation.

The police appeared stroppy with us, presumably because of the newspaper article. A policeman came over to our car at one stage as we tried to film some bikes and took down the registration number. When we asked why, he responded aggressively, 'Cos, I can.'

I called Detective Superintendent Migro to see how things were going and he indicated he wanted to speak with me. He suggested we meet at a café somewhere and talk. We were near the Shamrock Café so I suggested we meet there.

We arrived first and grabbed a table outside. There also happened to be some Gypsy Jokers sitting nearby.

Detective Superintendent Migro and his media adviser arrived. He looked at Rudi and another associate who'd been doing some filming for us, and said he didn't want to speak to me in front of anyone. I suspected he also didn't want to speak in front of the Gypsy Jokers.

I was taken inside, only to be greeted by even more Gypsy Jokers, who were sitting even closer to our table than the ones outside.

Detective Superintendent Migro's first words were: 'This is not an official meeting, but ...'

I knew it was not going to be a pleasant conversation.

I was informed the police were not happy with the story in the *West Australian.*

'This is not the kind of thing we are going to take lying down,' he told me. 'If you don't do something about what you have said we are going to go after you. Specifically, we will hit your credibility.'

I was shocked by what he was saying. Without thinking, I found myself saying I would call the reporter and make some conciliatory statements.

As Detective Superintendent Migro rose from the table he turned and spoke to some of the club members. They made no bones about the fact they'd been eavesdropping on our conversation. One demanded to know why the police were monstering me for telling the story straight.

I went outside and sat down, the realisation of what had just happened starting to sink in. I then realised the club members from inside were standing beside me.

'Good on you mate,' one declared. 'Don't let the cunts change your story. Hang tough in there. You're the only one telling it like it is.'

I told him how much it meant to me for him to come up and tell me that. I decided then that I wouldn't retract what I'd said in the article.

Two South Australian Gypsy Jokers came over and joined us. We spoke for about an hour on the events of the club, and how our presence seemed to have an effect on the policing.

After a while three of the club members moved up the road, while two stayed with us chatting. A vehicle pulled up next to us. It was obviously a police surveillance vehicle. I could tell because its windows had been blacked out and it was being driven by a uniformed officer. They didn't even make a pretext of operating covertly. They just stopped directly beside us, presumably so they could film.

I'm not sure exactly who they wanted to film, whether it was Rudi and me or the members behind us. I thought it a bit coincidental after the warning I'd received in the café.

Rudi was decidedly unimpressed with the police, as he usually is. He had a bee in his bonnet about the inability of the under-cover police to avoid detection. He said he'd seen dogs' balls hidden better than them. They looked totally different from anyone in town in terms of dress. One of them was even seen carrying a police radio.

Once New Year's Eve had passed, it seemed a lot of the heat went out of the run. The mood of the club seemed to mellow as the day wore on; they rested sore bums and heads on the beach and did the tourist thing.

The change of mood was reflected in the media. Page 3 of the

West Australian the following day carried a picture of a few club members relaxing on the beach looking at a pretty girl with a child playing in the background. The headline read 'Gypsy Jokers Do The Holidaymakers' Thing', while the *Australian* headline read 'Jokers Play It Cool On Holiday Run'.

If I was correct in my assessment, the police were losing the public relations war. Instead of demonic bikies being told to 'Go Home, we don't want you in this state', the media was supporting the Gypsy Jokers' right to holiday like any other citizens.

Many of the police departed Albany on 1 January. However, those who remained continued to stop bikes for random searches. The only problems were minor traffic infringements, but there were fewer than six traffic charges.

There were a number of God's Garbage club members in town, but no friction between the clubs. This had a fair bit to do with the clubs being two of only five clubs to exist in Perth, along with the Coffin Cheaters, Club Deroes, and the Rebels, who arrived in 1998.

That night was fairly relaxed, with the designated rider system again operating successfully and no arrests made. I was surprised at how little the bikies were drinking. I even saw a few milkshakes being used to 'toast' the New Year.

The next day the club packed up and headed for Margaret River, about 350 km to the west.

At that point we thought our job was done so we headed back to Perth. We decided it was time to get out, particularly as the police had become less communicative with us. I hadn't withdrawn the statement so they'd become a little more belligerent, particularly when we tried to film anything. We left two local observers to carry on with the observations and report back to us.

The relief when we got out of town and away from the police pressure was palpable.

As we left, the club also hit the road. They hit the mandatory roadblocks but there were few problems. Some of the bikies even stopped to help a woman whose car had broken down. The *West Australian* report of that incident included the line from Commander Graeme Power that these incidents may have been a tactic of the club to show there was no need for the new bikie laws.

What he failed to mention was that save for the previous year's violence in South Australia, police had never had any problem with the Gypsy Joker run in all its 15-year history.

There was one report of a bizarre incident on that stage of the run. One club member stopped by the side of the road for a leak, only to find himself accompanied by a number of police. I caught up with him later on.

I've got a kidney infection and I was bustin' for a piss. I signalled to my mate to pull over with me near some bushes just outside Margaret River. Two squad cars pulled over with us and I went screamin' into the bush with three cops following behind, yelling at me. I said I was sufferin' from this problem and I got about two trees in and relieved myself. I couldn't believe it. Three coppers standin' around me while I pissed. I was tempted to ask them if they wanted to put it back in my pants after I finished but I knew if I did it was trouble, so I shut up.

The stay in Margaret River, again among many holiday-makers, went smoothly. There was some apprehension among businesses as the club arrived, with some businesses, including the Margaret River Hotel, closing their doors. It was reported that police convinced the hotel operators there would be no trouble and it re-opened later in the day.

There was, however, one incident on the final day of the run that had the potential of being the most serious. As with many of these things, unless you were there it's hard to decipher what actually happened from the conflicting versions. Unfortunately, the observers we had left behind missed the incident but were able to speak with some bystanders who had observed it and reported back to us.

Media reports simply stated there was a 'hiccup' when a club member fell off his bike near a police car in a hotel carpark. The club and bystander versions were significantly different:

> The cops tried to stop us going to the pub hoping we would go straight back to clubhouse, so we rode through their road block to the pub. They were trying to drag us off bikes and a cop car backed into one of the boys on his bike. Then it nearly got very ugly. There was a lot of pushing and shoving. We were outnumbered at least three to one so we retreated to the safety of the pub.

The run finished on 4 January, after five days on the road. According to club sources, on the way home many people lined the roads cheering the Gypsy Jokers and booing the cops. I've been told there is a video of this, although I haven't seen it. This surprised the Gypsy Jokers and angered the police. It seemed the Gypsy Jokers had clearly won the public relations battle.

All sides agreed it had been a very quiet affair. The police attributed this to their tactics.

Commander Graeme Power told the *West Australian*:

> This was a very successful operation. The Gypsy Jokers motorcycle gang is an exceptionally notorious group of people who have shown their propensity for violence in other places and it is due to the way we have handled this particular matter that there hasn't been any violence at all.

The bikies took a different view:

I can't see why the cops say that policing in big numbers is going to stop problems with us. Last year they had us outnumbered four to one and there was sure trouble there. This year, they claim to have us outnumbered five to one but we are convinced they are committed to provoking us. We expected to be provoked and we were ready for it.

I believe the presence of Rudi and myself as independent monitors had some impact in reminding the police of their responsibilities. One member told me:

The police have been pretty easy on us this year, Arthur. A lot of this is your presence because the cops have somebody who is watching the whole thing and telling it straight, not just running with the police media releases.

However, I believe the biggest factor accounting for the peacefulness of the run was the restraint of the club members. It was a testament to the leadership of the club that the members, who were set to explode in the days leading up to the ride, managed to ignore any police provocation. I believe it was widely understood that any antics would play directly into the hands of the police and the government.

The clubs are beginning to understand the implications of Western Australia's incredible new laws.

The laws were set to pass through parliament in February or March 2002. At the time of writing there were some rumblings over the laws within the governing Labor Party in Western Australia, with sources indicating concern over threats to basic democracy. The Independent members of parliament voted against the legislation when it was presented to the House for just that reason. It would also seem the charging of a number of Gypsy Joker members over the murder of Don Hancock and Lou Lewis had set back the cause for the new laws, with Law Society of WA president Clare Thompson saying the arrests showed the new laws were not needed.

Yet I fear irrespective of what happens in Western Australia, the trend toward tackling social issues with increased police powers looks set to continue across Australia.

CHAPTER FIFTEEN A DYING BREED?

We can't act like thugs any more. It's 2001, not 1972.
Hell's Angel

The outlaw motorcycle club of today is a different beast from the ones formed by ex-servicemen more than 50 years ago. The ideals are still there – brotherhood, partying, commitment and riding. And they still exist as a subculture of mainstream society, cut off from Mr Average. However, life is changing. The clubs face pressure from a number of areas, pressure that is throwing a heavy shadow over their future.

Is it a moot point discussing their future when, in fact, they have no future? The answer is no. The clubs are surviving. Some of the major clubs are even growing. The Hell's Angels, Bandidos, Outlaws, and Pagans have multiplied their memberships many times in the past 10 to 15 years, expanding over that time into European countries such as Sweden. However, the raw figures tell a lie. These clubs are growing through amalgamations. The actual number of clubs is not growing.

The number of members is dropping, particularly in traditional bikie countries.

A Canadian study found that the number of club members in Quebec increased from 600 to nearly 900 from 1970 to 1978. This period was characterised by the home-grown Canadian clubs amalgamating with existing US clubs, notably, the Hell's Angels and the Outlaws. Numbers then stabilised, with some 800 club members in Quebec by 1983. By 1990, there were fewer than 300 club members. There are no recent figures available but I estimate it would be a lower number today.

While no such study has been carried out in Australia, police sources confirm the number of outlaw motorcycle club members here has been dropping. In 1980 there were about 8000 outlaw club members in Australia. By 2001 it had dropped to 3000–4000.

The drop in club member numbers has been so dramatic since the mid-1980s that the clubs may be more accurately referred to as the 0.1 percenters. Perhaps I'm being a bit dramatic because the entire biker community is contracting. Australian motorcycle sales have dropped about 7 per cent since 1990 on a per capita basis, after receiving a short-lived boost when the Australian Motorcycle Grand Prix was re-introduced. It means the outlaw clubs have a smaller pool to draw from.

The decline can be put down to a number of factors – politics, amalgamations, police pressure, ageing, and changing life circumstances.

Earlier on I told the story of Robbo, the lone rider who fell in love with the biker lifestyle at Bathurst. He's now 47 years of age. Then there was John Smith, the former head of the God Squad. He's 60 years old. Sonny Barger? 64. What about Jock Ross the president of the Comancheros? 62. See a pattern? These are men active in the club world. And they're not getting any younger.

The 'greying' of the motorcycle population is a major issue for the clubs. There has been a consistent rise in the age of members since the early 1980s, when the average age would have been 25. The average age of an outlaw motorcycle club member today is late 30s.

Many of the more established clubs have senior members who are now literally unable to handle big Harley-Davidsons. These members either participate in club activities by riding a trike or travelling by car.

It's a problem in the wider biker community. In the past five years the number of deaths among motorcycle riders aged over 35 in the United States has risen nearly 60 per cent, compared with a 22 per cent fall among younger riders. Australian figures would mirror that trend. Part of that has to do with the average age of the buyers of bikes rising in the US from 25 to 39. Many of the new bike buyers are trying to catch the appeal of the bike from their youth.

> Many have been waiting for years to buy a superbike as a cooler alternative to the balding divorcee in his first Porsche, and common sense will not stop them.

However, some find they don't have the strength to keep a Harley upright when they come to a stop at the lights.

An experience in 2001 really rammed home the age issue for me. I was at the clubhouse of one hardcore club chatting to some of the club's leaders when some beers were offered around. The president and one of the founding members both refused due to medical conditions. Increasingly, members have diabetes or liver complaints, presumably after years of hard living.

The social functions also expose the effects of ageing. Only a few years ago I was at the Hell's Angels' Broadford concert, where many of the clubs were attending. I stood at the marijuana stand

and watched the bikies gather around. There must have been 30 blokes sitting there – and all would have been over 45 years of age.

They've even brought forward the evening fireworks at Broadford so the older members don't miss out before they hit the sack, as most of them get pretty knocked about after a couple of smokes. Unfortunately, the strippers don't usually come on until after midnight, which means many of the old-timers miss out on the highlight of the night, although a few are prone to say they saw the action when they were really tucked up in bed.

Another excellent US example of how age is catching up with the bikies was a report in the *San Diego Union-Tribune* of a run at Hollister in 2001 where bikers were 'complaining that the Hell's Angels booth would not give a senior discount on Death to Snitches T-Shirts'. The article also made the point that the ol' ladies were actually old. Another interesting point is that we are starting to see the memoirs of bikie leaders being published. When that starts happening you know times are moving on.

The age of the existing bikies is not the only worry. The new recruits are not coming through. Remember, the outlaw motorcycle clubs were formed by young men desperate to burn off their impetuous youthfulness by hanging around with mates and riding as fast and as dangerously as they could. It's rare today to find anyone admitted into the clubs under the age of 25. By that age much of the raw youthfulness has disappeared.

An important function of the clubs has always been to express non-traditional values, to rebel against the norm. It's this notion that seems to be on the wane. You can't blame young people, as they live in a different world from that of the 1950s and '60s when most of the existing clubs were formed.

Non-conformist lifestyles, on the whole, seem to be on the wane. However, there will always be young people wanting to rebel against society. Whether they choose to do it in a motorcycle club is the real issue. For much of the life of the clubs they've been seen as a natural outlet of rebellion. Today's youth have far more choice. The left-wing causes, such as environmentalism, are winning over more and more rebellious young people. The right-wing motorcycle clubs are not attractive to these people.

However, it's not just the motorcycle clubs feeling the pinch. Fewer people are joining clubs and organised activities than ever before. Membership of voluntary organisations has dropped 40–50 per cent in the past 30 years. The amount of time people devoted to voluntary activity is dwindling. Such is the pressure to maintain employment that people are spending longer and longer at work.

However the pressure is not just from work. We live in a different family environment from that of 30 years ago. Family demands are stronger. I was at a meeting with one club president recently, one of the toughest blokes you'd ever meet, when he suddenly declared he had to pick up his daughter from school. It was such an incongruous image, the president of one of the hardest clubs in the land, cutting short club business to race down to the local primary school. The advent of shared parental duties has not left the clubs untouched.

Wives and girlfriends are no longer so compliant that they will happily put up with the club taking away their man. He's expected to pull his weight around the house, which he can't do if he spends all his time down at the clubhouse.

This has certainly affected the clubs. Look at the reaction by younger club members, who openly admit that they'll probably have to give up the club when they marry. They fail to see how marriage and the club can mix.

The question of commitment is especially pertinent. The outlaw motorcycle clubs that are surviving are the ones that require less commitment from members. These clubs are likely to become the dominant clubs. We have seen evidence of this already with the growth of the Rebels compared to clubs such as the Gypsy Jokers, whose numbers are relatively small but whose entry requirements are relatively time-consuming and involved.

That's not to say that rapidly growing clubs such as the Rebels or Bandidos are not committed outlaw motorcycle clubs. They most definitely are. However, they differ from the Gypsy Jokers and Hell's Angels in that they don't require the level of involvement in the club and its activities that these clubs do.

To the Hell's Angels it's 'quality not quantity that we're about.'

The Rebels take the view: 'we're the biggest for a reason and that's because we're the best.'

It's not only the commitment to the clubs that appear to have a bearing on their membership, but also the way they operate. The rules have been shown to be a turn-off for many members. The hardcore clubs have a higher percentage of ex-members who blame their departures on the rigid rules.

There's also the issue of reputation. Being a bikie can have an enormous impact on reputation, both professionally and personally. Members have more to lose by being identified with an outlaw club. Jobs don't grow on trees any more, so they can't be chucked in on a whim because the lure of the bike and a long ride becomes too much. Employers are also reluctant to employ someone associated with a bikie club. With the cost of employing people today they can't afford to take a risk, no matter how minor.

Members are becoming much more conscious of the impact of membership on the reputation of their families, particularly their children. It only takes a child to be taunted in the schoolyard for that impact to hit home hard.

These are simply the 'outside' reasons for the clubs' membership crisis. There are also the structural issues within society that make the clubs less attractive. We are becoming isolated as more people work at home. Those who do work in offices increasingly travel in isolation. Work pressure doesn't permit the interaction it did in the past. It erodes our system until the concept of brotherhood and camaraderie diminishes. We are much more individualistic, concerned with getting ahead in life. We don't like taking risks that may see us either fail or make us stand out as different. It's made us a society of spectators, not participators.

This makes the outlaw motorcycle clubs seem archaic. Often they are referred to as boneheads, meatheads or Neanderthals. Society finds it increasingly difficult to deal with people who are different.

In some ways, this book is proof of this. People may read this because they are fascinated by the notion of a group of people who are so different. Many of those same people buy the Harleys and leathers and pretend they are bad boys on the weekend. They want to be *seen* as different yet they don't want to be different.

A recurring theme throughout these pages has been the constant pressure placed on the clubs by the police and governments. This pressure cannot help but be a major reason the clubs are facing a membership crisis. The constant attention of police wears down the members, while increasingly rigorous entry requirements drive many prospective members away. Clubs are almost being forced underground, making them more hardcore and more susceptible to criminal influence. Police have also reduced the number of club members through systematic campaigns of harassment and having the political mandate to control the public enemy, the 'Bikie Menace'.

Bikies are faced with a choice. Do away with the outlaw element of the clubs and ride their bikes unhindered without the rules and police harassment, or become 'heavier', shielding themselves away from the world. Some of the more successful and strongest clubs have chosen this path. However, many have chosen the former option.

Bikers are similar to other minorities under threat in society.

Their survival depends upon members having the political will to defend their lifestyle.

In recent years there have been signs that the political will to defend the lifestyle has abated. Membership in lobby groups such as the Motorcycle Riders Association and biker rights organisations such as the National Helmet Law Reform Organisation have declined dramatically since 1980. However, the passion is still out there.

Like it or not they [the Helmet Laws] are here. Maybe if some new, more awful helmet requirement or seatbelts or something stupid like that were to be introduced by the Government, then you would see all the political protest of the past come back. We are fair dinkum about our riding. It really pisses us off when these Volvo driving bastards try to introduce laws to ruin our passion and lifestyles.
Former National Helmet Law Reform Organisation member

The same political will has been lacking in the outlaw clubs. The recent advent of legislative moves to crack down on clubs in Western Australia and the proposed legislation to eliminate consorting among club members and to proclaim the clubs – particularly the Gypsy Jokers and Hell's Angels – as prohibited organisations in South Australia have created movement on the political front.

In South Australia, the clubs are closely monitoring the parliamentary sessions to gauge the mood of the politicians.

We have started to put a member into parliament sessions to monitor the hearings so that we can be aware of proposed legislation relevant to the club. It was inter-esting as we've seen members from other clubs in there

listening as well. In light of this, our club has gone to the other clubs in town and suggested that we pool our resources and start getting smart about how to protect ourselves from the legislators and police. I told them we didn't want to drink and party with them, all we wanted to do was to set up an ongoing meeting where the leaders of the clubs discuss issues relating to the outlaw clubs. People are considering it now and I think it will happen.
Chapter president

From this has come a proposal for the clubs to hire an outsider, a media spokesperson, to become the public face for the clubs.

Someone who looks like us but is not one of us. He would be answerable to us. The last thing we want is to set up someone who acts on his own about the clubs. He will be our employee and be expected to clear all statements with the clubs.
Club president

In New South Wales, the outlaw clubs have gone one step further and have set up a political party. The Hell's Angels was instrumental in establishing the Riders and Motorists Party of NSW. The party stood at the last state election and attracted 7027 primary votes. The Riders and Motorists Party of NSW has moved to enlist the support of mainstream bikers, to produce a broader movement. It seems to have borne fruit with indicative polling, according to the party, showing the primary vote is set to reach about 18 000 at the next state election. It doesn't sound much in a state with 3.8 million voters. However, in a parliament where the Labor Party majority is wafer-thin a block of 18 000 votes is vital.

The Riders and Motorists Party is finding itself feted by the major parties looking to do preference deals. It remains to be seen whether the bikies can use this to produce some benefit for themselves and produce a political climate that lets them not only survive, but also prosper. These moves indicate the clubs are uncertain of their future. They are trying to appeal to other interest groups by saying 'our problem is your problem.'

> We need legislation advisers and to start working more
> with civil liberties groups to make them aware of the cost
> that the proposed legislation is taking on the fabric of our
> society and the free Australian lifestyle.
> **Club leader**

The issue of riding a bike has become a major issue of the clubs as they ponder their future. Crunch time may not be far away.

For many years, Australian outlaw motorcycle clubs rode Japanese-made motorcycles due to the unavailability of Harley-Davidsons in Australia until the 1960s. It's now compulsory to own a Harley-Davidson motorcycle if you want to be an outlaw club member. However, the Harley-Davidson company is aiming its products at the professional white-collar market. They even advertise in the *Australian Financial Review*. I believe the company is uncomfortable with its association with the bikie clubs, despite the image of its products being built on the outlaw image of the clubs. Many yuppies riding a Harley have the notion they're a bit of a rebel, an image that comes from the bike's relationship with the clubs. However, that relationship has become a little rocky, with quite a push coming from the clubs to split from Harley-Davidson.

Anti-Japanese sentiment now appears to be on the wane. As the cost of Harleys continues to rise, the Japanese have released a swag of Harley imitations, right down to the throbbing engine note – and at half the price. To the layman it's getting almost impossible to tell the difference between these bikes and a true Harley-Davidson. Even the dedicated bikie magazines are reviewing the Japanese bikes. While it's in the charter of most of the hardcore bikie clubs that members must ride Harley-Davidsons, who knows, one day we may see a Hell's Angel hitting the road on a Kawasaki Drifter. That'd be a sight!

The new century is going to throw up many challenges for the clubs, and provide many opportunities. The New World Order of global economies has created many disaffected people in society. It's also created a lot of unemployment. We could be seeing the start of a new cycle of clubs, in the same way the modern outlaw clubs began on the back of the Great Depression.

More and more disaffected people will wish to rebel against a system that is alienating and isolating them. Joining an outlaw motorcycle club is one way to clearly communicate one's dissatisfaction with society.

However, the clubs will need to be different in both structure and attitude. The autocratic rules will need to be toned down. Young people are more questioning. They will not follow rules blindly. The clubs will also need to be more inclusive. Certainly, the pressures for equality among the sexes will continue to force change upon the clubs. Clubs that create auxiliaries for women or allow women into membership are likely to evolve in the next 50 years.

I also believe the police will be happy for the clubs to continue to exist. In a world where multi-billion dollar criminal transactions zap electronically across the globe in seconds, the police need easier and more tangible targets. Bikies are a lot easier to harass and prosecute than multinational pharmaceutical companies dumping banned pharmaceuticals in African countries or international drug cartels trafficking cocaine.

Massive police resources will continue to be devoted to policing of the clubs because law and order elections require a visible threat to the safety of the public. The outlaw motorcycle clubs are likely to be regarded as sent from the gods by politicians who campaign on law and order issues.

I spoke to the president of one club that has experienced some major police heat in recent years, and I got the impression it was starting to make the club feel vulnerable. He said there was a feeling within the clubs that they make themselves too visible a target, something that may change. The distinctive look and club patches may be toned down, or even disappear. According to some US reports, some clubs have moved to using removable patches so they can be quickly taken off when entering heavily populated areas or coming across police. This is a major change for clubs that consider the colours to be everything.

It's only those from within who can predict the future of the clubs. I've asked many club leaders whether they thought the clubs would be around in 30 years. All believe their clubs will still be around in 2030.

One senior Fink said the club thrived on the increasingly 'us against them' notion of society. 'The harder it gets, it brings out the camaraderie,' he said.

Some indicated that you could never change the people who are in the clubs. The clubs are their lives and they were going to live them. It was a theme I heard time and again. However, almost all admitted the clubs have to change.

We've got to move with the times and become a power in our own right in the new social order.
Senior Hell's Angel

Yes, we will survive, if we change with the times.
Chapter president

The clubs will change back to being more social clubs than outlaw clubs. The idea of trying to kill the bike scene is absolutely hopeless. Sure, they'll change things, curtail things, but it's a bit like trying to stop prostitution.
Former club president

Change seems to be the common theme. But can they change? In a way they already have. They've lost some of their outrage. They remain dangerous, yet strangely quaint in their uniforms. They scream out to be different yet all look the same with their colours and leathers.

The clubs have been changing since the 1% tag appeared at Hollister more than 50 years ago. In the beginning they were social clubs with a bad boy image. They gradually became bad boys. They will continue to change, most likely back to becoming social clubs again. They will remain the 1% of the biker world. As the biker world changes, so will the clubs. There will always be 1% clubs. The question remains: 1% of what?

AFTERWORD

I've already outlined how the outlaw clubs and the police have an intense dislike of each other. In the case of the Gypsy Jokers Motorcycle Club and those police who monitor their activities, I think the correct description would be loathing, even hatred. That's the picture that has emerged from one of the most infamous clashes between the two parties.

I have made previous reference to the Gypsy Joker's 2001 national run in south-eastern South Australia, where a fight between club members and South Australian police resulted in a number of police injuries and bikie arrests. In early 2003 I was finally able to get my hands on witness and police statements, which were released when police lodged a civil suit against a Gypsy Joker member convicted of assaulting them on 2 January 2001. Three members of the South Australia Police Special Tasks and Rescue (STAR) force (sometimes called STAR group) lodged the suit after the Gypsy Joker received a three-year $100 good behaviour bond on an assault conviction. It is believed to be the first time Australian police have gone after the bikies in this way, and certainly the first time that members of an elite unit such as the STAR force have felt the need to do so.

In piecing together what happened that night I have used witness statements wherever I could. However, none of the Gypsy Joker members provided statements, which is consistent with club policy and the bikie code of silence. Even the record of interview for the Gypsy Joker charged with assault records that he merely declined to comment. Therefore, much of the description comes from independent civilian eyewitnesses and the police who were present.

What the witness statements reveal is a startling picture of a police operation that got out of hand, along with a string of inconsistencies, contradictions and thinly veiled criticism by local police command of the STAR force's tactics. It also provides a unique insight into the level of loathing felt by both the police and the clubs.

The episode began when more than 100 Gypsy Joker members gathered in South Australia for the club's annual national run in January 2001. True to form, the destination of the run was kept a closely guarded secret. It was clear that this secretiveness played a key role in the late arrival of the STAR force at the scene the night the incident occurred.

STAR force commander Superintendent Thomas Rieniets reveals in his statement that he became aware at 10.30 a.m. on 2 January that 'a large number of Gypsy Joker Motorcycle Club members had travelled to Mount Gambier and were intending to stay in that area for an unknown time. At that time there was no problem; however, I was advised to be on standby should STAR group be required in the area.' At about 2 p.m. he discovered that 'about 120 bikies' were on the move, heading in the direction of either Beachport or Robe, two coastal towns about 350 km southeast of Adelaide.

Superintendent Rieniets' account of ensuing events reveals a number of contradictions when compared with the accounts given by local witnesses in the hotel that evening, as well as those of local police.

Rieniets stated that at about 6.25 p.m. he received information 'that the bikies were in Beachport and were taking over the hotel to the exclusion of other patrons, getting boozed up and committing numerous traffic and behavioural offences in the area'. He said he was asked to assist by Superintendent Bristow as the 'town was at the time under-policed for the problems occurring, with a great deal of tourists and holiday-makers in town. The request now being of a more urgent nature, given the behaviour of various bikies in Beachport.'

The request referred to had actually been made by Detective Senior Sergeant Edmunds Sudrabs, who was forward commander of police operations when the club was on the move. In his statement he outlined a number of alleged incidents that had been brought to his attention. These constituted traffic offences by the Gypsy Jokers, including riding around roundabouts the wrong way and failing to stop after being requested to do so by police, as well as smashing bottles on the road and confiscating the film from a tourist's camera.

However, the statement made by Superintendent Darrel Bristow, the officer in charge of the south-east area and the police commander while the club was in town, paints a rather different picture.

Superintendent Bristow gave a briefing to Superintendent Rieniets upon the STAR force's arrival in Beachport at about 10.50 p.m.

At this time there had been no major incidents with the bikie group, and police patrols had not encountered any difficulties in policing the town. I was aware there had been a patrol sent to a caravan park due to a report of bikies having entered the park, and also that a fire had

been lit on the foreshore of the bikie camp, in contraven-
tion of a fire ban. I was aware of liaison arrangements,
which had been put in place between police and the
bikies, which involved Detective Dewar. I directed
Detective Dewar to liaise with the bikies and for the fire to
be extinguished. This occurred and the fire was put out
immediately. Also during the evening I ensured the
Beachport Hotel was monitored, with Senior Constable
Zeitz regularly speaking with hotel management per tele-
phone. No complaints were received from the hotel.

This is a view supported by the hotel management, bar staff, local
drinkers and holiday-makers who were in the hotel that evening.
In all, 21 civilians provided eyewitness statements, including
locals who witnessed the incident from inside or nearby their
homes.

Debra Lee, a Beachport local, was in the hotel from about
5 p.m. to 6 p.m. when there were about 15 bikies in the hotel's
bar. 'There did not appear to be any problem in the hotel,' she
said in her statement. This was around the same time that
Superintendent Rieniets received a report of Gypsy Jokers 'taking
over the hotel to the exclusion of other patrons'.

Steven Bowering, who was visiting friends in Beachport,
arrived at the hotel at 9–9.30 p.m. that evening with his wife
and daughter. 'I would say for a front bar that the mood was good
and the behaviour okay. I don't recall any swearing or offensive
language. Some of the bikies were paying [sic] at the pool
table.'

Another patron, Bernadette Wray, described the scene that
night when she arrived at about 10 p.m.:

Inside the hotel I saw between 20 and 30 bikies in the bar
area. Some of the bikies were playing pool, others playing

music and the rest were basically in groups drinking either at the bar or at the tables. Throughout the evening we were in the hotel the bikies seemed orderly and were behaving themselves. We remained at the hotel having social drinks and general conversation.

It was not only fellow drinkers who painted a contrasting picture to Superintendent Rieniets' account. One member of the hotel's bar staff, Jennifer Taylor, started her shift at 4 p.m., working in the front bar. According to Taylor, there were 20–25 Gypsy Jokers on the verandah at the front of the hotel, another 20 in the front bar, and more were spread throughout the rest of the hotel. At the front of the hotel there were about 50 motorcycles parked on the road and a couple of motorbikes parked on the front grassy area. She pointed out that there were locals drinking among the Gypsy Jokers in the front bar.

> Generally the behaviour was fine. I would not say that any of them appeared to get overly intoxicated or drunk. In fact, I remember thinking that for the amount of alcohol that they had drunk during the afternoon and night, they did not seem too bad.

However, at 8.15 p.m. Superintendent Rieniets and nine other STAR force officers left Adelaide on two police planes bound for Beachport.

Taylor provided a comprehensive description of what happened in the hotel at about midnight.

> The hotel has a licence to operate until 1 a.m., but we usually close when it is no longer busy. At 10 to 12 there were about 20 Gypsy Joker members left in the front bar, more out the front under the verandah and I do not know

how many scattered around the hotel. There were also about eight locals in the front bar and two tourists playing pool in the front bar area.

Taylor said management decided to close the hotel at midnight, so last drinks were called.

> As I walked along the bar calling last drinks, one of the Gypsy Joker members said words to the effect of: 'You better get to the back of the pub when we go, babe, 'cause all hell is going to break loose when we walk out the door.'
>
> I said: 'What do you mean?'
>
> He said: 'The cops will have the place surrounded by now and they'll get us as we leave.'
>
> I said: 'No, surely not, they're still cruising past in their cars.'
>
> He said: 'You wait and see.'

At 11.45 p.m. Sergeant David Thomas, of the Mount Gambier police, was standing on the front lawn of the Beachport Police Station 'when I was approached by a STAR group member who asked if we had a caged car, to which I replied in the affirmative'. According to Sergeant Thomas, the STAR force member then said: 'You better get in it. We're going for a walk through the pub in a minute and we'll probably get a few arrests.'

Superintendent Darrel Bristow, the incident commander, became aware the STAR force was heading to the hotel only moments before they left the police station.

> I had not directed their attendance and was not aware of any disturbance at the hotel or that any other police officers were attending. I became aware of this as a result of Superintendent Rieniets coming to the front door of

the Beachport Police Station and saying: 'We are going for a walk down to the pub'.

A few minutes later, Jennifer Taylor turned to see a uniformed policeman standing in the front door of the hotel talking to Keith Allen, a part-owner of the hotel who was also working in the front bar that night.

The police officer was only there for about a split second when he suddenly turned around and headed for the front door. At the same time Gypsy Jokers members suddenly went everywhere, including en masse out the front door.

That policeman was STAR force leader Superintendent Rieniets. This is his account of what happened next:

At about 11.55 p.m. that same day after briefly discussing tactics with [Superintendent] Bristow and giving him a copy of my hand-written plan, I walked with the STAR members to the Beachport Hotel, some 85 metres south of the police station, my intention being to introduce myself to the licensee, speak to him regarding the closing time and to reassure him of our attendance should any problems occur. Prior to doing this I had briefed Rieke [STAR supervisor] as to the STAR group needing to be firm in their approach to any breaches of the law, yet at the same time bearing in mind that a large number of bikies were in the area and the potential for disturbances.

As I entered, two bikies moved to try to stop my entrance. However, I avoided them and walked towards a younger male person behind the bar ... I was about three metres from this person, not actually having spoken to him, when I suddenly heard a commotion behind me and upon looking saw most of the bikies suddenly rush outside ... There was lots of shouting and yelling. I could clearly hear the words 'Kill the fuckin' cunts' said on several occasions.

Outside the hotel were two STAR force officers, Senior Constable Benjamin Hodge and Senior Constable Andrew Thiele. According to the statement provided by Senior Constable Thiele, he asked one of the Gypsy Jokers to arrange for three motorcycles to be moved from the verandah to the road. 'This member stated, "No worries, we'll shift the bikes",' Senior Constable Thiele said.

However, things were less cordial when they moved to join Superintendent Rieniets inside the hotel. Thiele's statement continues:

There were approximately four members of the Gypsy Jokers Motorcycle group standing on the left-hand side of the front doorway. After Rieniets had entered the hotel, two of these persons moved across the doorway blocking the entranceway. I continued walking towards the doorway and I was approximately one metre from the front door when a person wearing a GJMC vest stepped out of the hotel and walked straight into me, thrusting his forearm into my chest as he made impact with me.

That Gypsy Joker was identified as Robert Darren Studar. Senior Constable Thiele grabbed Studar's arm to arrest him. 'As I took hold of his right arm to inform him he was under arrest, I saw a person out of my peripheral vision rushing at me from my left side.' This Gypsy Joker was identified as Stephen Williams. Senior

Constable Thiele alleged Williams punched him in the mouth. Senior Constable Hodge also said he had hold of Studar and was punched by Williams.

It was this incident that cleared the bar and saw Gypsy Jokers surge onto the street. Commander Rieniets ran out to see his officers grappling with Studar and Williams. He ran to Williams, caught him in a headlock and yelled: 'You are under arrest for assault.' He said that Williams, who was trying to break the hold, screamed: 'Fuckin' get off me. You're dead meat.'

Moments later, Rieniets said he felt a sharp blow to his head and could see broken glass flying over his shoulder. He then fell to the ground, fearing that his life was in danger as a number of kicks were aimed at his head.

Police flooded the area, until there were an estimated 40 police and 15 Gypsy Jokers involved in a clash, however some eyewitnesses estimated that as many as 40 bikies were present. After the initial confrontation, mostly what occurred was posturing by both sides, with police drawing batons and using capsicum spray. At one stage, two Gypsy Jokers retreated inside the hotel to ask for milk as they said they had been sprayed in the eyes by capsicum spray.

Jennifer Taylor said one club member grabbed a pool cue and started to head out the door. She told him to give her the cue, which he did. This is an interesting point as it demonstrates how facts can possibly become distorted. One policeman stated he saw a Gypsy Joker walking from the hotel carrying a pool cue, yelling, 'You've got sticks. We've got sticks too.' Commander Rieniets stated he heard someone yell, 'Get the fire sticks,' which he took to mean firearms. Whether these were three separate incidents or differing descriptions of the same thing is not clear. If it is the latter, it shows just how differently people can interpret the same incident – each one swearing that theirs is the correct version.

At the height of the encounter, STAR force members were

recalled to the station to don riot gear, but by the time they returned to the hotel the situation had died down. Constable Robert Martin, of the Penola police, stated that 'many [Gypsy Jokers] were yelling at police that they just wanted to get on their bikes and go'.

Constable Martin said he spoke to a club member amid the confrontation: 'He stated: "This is stupid. All we want to do is get out of here. We don't deserve this."'

Meanwhile, club member Studar, who had been involved in the initial confrontation, was brought into the hotel by another member for treatment to a cut on the back of his head.

Jennifer Taylor said she was administering first aid to Studar in the lounge when three police officers approached. 'The police started yelling at the two Gypsy Jokers, telling them to leave the area.' Taylor said 'something like "Excuse me. This man has got a bad injury and I am trying to fix it."' She said the police ignored her plea and ordered the men outside.

By this stage there were few Jokers remaining, with most having been ordered home by their leaders.

Studar jumped on a motorcycle as a pillion passenger without a helmet. He was grabbed by a STAR force officer and an argument ensued, until Studar was arrested for offensive language. It was this language, peppered with threats like 'We're coming back to get you cunts', that prompted police to later barricade the police station with vehicles in case the threat was made good by the club.

While being marched back to the police station, police claimed Studar attempted to grab the arresting policeman's firearm. However, Studar was never charged over this incident.

Constable Craig Arthur spoke about the incident to Len, the president of the West Australian Gypsy Jokers chapter. 'I said to him that trying to grab a police officer's gun is a "silly thing to do". He laughed and [said that] boys will be boys and he's just a lad. Of course he was gonna have a go.' Studar was released soon after as a result of negotiations between the club and police liaison.

Detective Sergeant Keith Reichstein described how three Gypsy Jokers approached the police station for the negotiations. One of these was Len, the WA chapter president. 'Detective Dewar and I spoke with the three, with Len doing all the talking. The gist of the conversation was that if the police would let the arrested person go, then he would guarantee his gang would cause no trouble during the night.'

Superintendent Bristow ordered Studar's release without charges. He was walked to the back of the station and handed to the three bikies. According to Detective Sergeant Reichstein, 'Len then stated all would be quiet for the rest of the night. This happened and the four bikies walked off. There were no further incidents during the night.'

According to club sources, Studar was released with the keys to all the lock-ups at the police station in his gear. The police were forced to go to the campsite to ask for the keys back. The club agreed to give them back only if the police would return some mobile phones that had been lost in the fracas. The police had earlier denied knowledge of the phones, but in light of the deal to return the keys were miraculously able to find them.

Meanwhile Hodge and Rieniets had been transferred to Millicent Hospital by ambulance, with Hodge flown to Adelaide the following day for surgery on a broken jaw.

The Gypsy Jokers stayed another night in Beachport before heading back to Adelaide. On the way they made a further one-night stopover in a small town and on their final day had to negotiate seven roadblocks manned by 100 police. This also included a dispute over confiscated colours at Murray Bridge and a strange incident that allegedly occurred at another small town.

The club had stopped at the town, when a local asked a member for a ride on his motorcycle. He obliged, taking the bloke for a spin, and then gave the bloke's wife a short ride. It has been alleged by the club that on this ride a carload of detectives came up behind the bike and ran it off the road. The member allegedly broke bones in his back and the woman was also injured. It is also alleged that the South Australian government is attempting to negotiate a financial settlement with this woman over the incident.

Steven Williams, the Gypsy Joker member who was alleged to have punched Senior Constables Thiele and Hodge at the Beachport hotel, headed back to Adelaide the day after the Beachport incident where he was charged with assault occasioning actual bodily harm, common assault and resisting police. Eight other members were charged with various offences, only to have all charges dropped.

In February 2002 Williams received an 18-month suspended jail sentence, reduced to a $100 three-year good behaviour bond. That's right. The entire episode resulted in a $100 good behaviour bond. It is not for me to speculate on the judgement, but it would appear to be a pretty light sentence if the case was proven. The three officers injured on the night launched civil action against Williams in early 2003. Officers Hodge, Rieniets and Thiele have claimed damages for physical injuries including broken bones, damaged teeth, neck injuries, soft tissue injuries and psychological injuries. I believe Williams has since declared himself bankrupt.

The club broke their silence on the incident in early 2003, accusing the police of provoking what happened that night. Club sources maintain that members happily accepted the hotel would close at midnight and that they planned to return to their campsite. They said if the STAR force had not attempted to enter the hotel the rest of the night would have passed without incident.

This does not excuse the violence of the members, but many in the club believe the police would have been well aware that they were walking into a highly charged environment of people who clearly did not like police and were more than likely to have been affected by alcohol.

The police, however, would maintain they are responsible for keeping the law and were well within their rights to enter a public place to ensure that the law was being observed. They would also say they have a responsibility to ensure everyone respected the law, so police were merely doing their duty when assaulted by the Gypsy Jokers.

And there can be no quibble with that. However, there are different styles of policing. For example, the 2003 Gypsy Joker run in Victoria travelled from Wodonga in the north-east to the popular ski resort of Mount Hotham then on to Lakes Entrance in East Gippsland for New Year's Eve with no incidents. Few in the holiday town would even have realised the club was in town. There was no open police presence, demonstrating once again the sensible policing policy of Victorian police when it comes to the clubs. And it would have been a damn sight cheaper than the South Australian debacle. Imagine the wages bill for the South Australian police, with some officers having worked shifts of three days straight. The mind boggles.

When I put these issues to the South Australian police for a response I received none.

It would seem to me that those police forces with special units targeting the clubs, such as the South Australian police force, often find they have trouble on their hands. In the South Australian incident, I believe the STAR force's actions on 2 January 2001 were bound to provoke a reaction in such an environment, and police command should have known that. As the old saying goes: 'If you go looking for trouble, you will surely find it.' And the police certainly found it that night.

April 2003

ACKNOWLEDGEMENTS

I gratefully acknowledge the significant and constructive input of photographer Chris Randells in better understanding the motorcycle clubs. He was particularly helpful in introducing me to members of several clubs. Thanks Chris.

Terry Johnstone was invaluable in helping me understand the clubs and introducing me to the scene in Queensland. I'm grateful to him and his wife Rose for years of friendship and advice. Yer me mate, Bear.

Rudi Grassecker is another friend and colleague featured in these pages. I am forever in debt to Rudi for his patient advice and staunchness in going along to many scenes, runs and clubhouses to gather information for this book. Thanks mate. You are my road mate forever. His partner Pat read earlier versions of the book and made me realise that I needed some help in writing the book. Thanks to you Pat.

My wife, Liz, and the children – Lucas, Zachary and Madeleine – have also allowed me to indulge my writing, having their father and spouse hidden away or on the road collecting information for the book. Thanks guys.

Special thanks to Ed Gannon for helping me write the book in a manner that was understandable to the average reader and for giving the book a clear Australian orientation.

Three academics have been incredibly influential in my writing of this book.

Lachlan Chipman, Pro Vice Chancellor at Monash University when I was at the Churchill campus. Lachlan will be surprised with my acknowledgement, as I'm sure he didn't think he did much; but Lachlan, you really gave me a hand when I needed one. The book wouldn't be possible if you hadn't had the ability to see there was some value in my work. Thanks very much.

A very special and key thanks to Professor Paul Wilson, Professor of Criminology at Bond University in Queensland. Paul showed me that a different form of writing, which is both academically respectable and interesting, was possible. Even back in 1980, he encouraged me to try to communicate my work in such a way. He's been very supportive of my work with the outlaw clubs and I thank him very much. Our visit to the Hell's Angels Melbourne chapter in the early 1990s was an event we will both never forget.

And finally, thanks to Professor Daniel 'Coyote' Wolf, Cultural Anthropologist and Rebel hang-around who was my only colleague in academia studying the clubs until his untimely death in 1999. You will be missed sorely brother. Ride free.

There are many bikers, bikies and riders who have specifically asked not to be mentioned in this work or in the acknowledgements of this book. You know who you are, my brothers. I hope I have done your passion some justice while, at the same time, telling the story the way I see it.

ENDNOTES

CHAPTER 1
'dirty stinking thugs... girls aged 14 and 15'. *San Francisco Chronicle*, 27 August 1964, p. 1.

CHAPTER 2
'They [motorcyclists] would ... other arguments combined.' Wolf, Daniel R., *The Rebels: A Brotherhood of Outlaw Bikers*, University of Toronto Press, Toronto, 1991, pp 32–3.

'About the last ...excitement of danger', James James, *WWII*, Leo Cooper Publications, 1975, cited in Carroll, *John Chopped Harleys: 50 Years of Rebellious Motorcycles*, Salamander Books, London, 1997, p. 21.

'boys got a ... drunk last night.' Thompson, Hunter S. *Hell's Angels*. Penguin Books, Middlesex, England, 1967, p. 74.

The media made ... shook Hollister *San Francisco Chronicle*, 7 July 1947, p. 1.

CHAPTER 4
'...being born and ... look for them.' Sonny Barger in Thompson, Hunter S., *Hell's Angels*, Penguin Books, Middlesex, England, 1967, p. 82.

'A biker who ... and drove off.' Wolf, Daniel R., *The Rebels: A Brotherhood of Outlaw Bikers*, University of Toronto Press, Toronto, 1991, p. 64.

'Rituals range from ... cases is a dog.' *An Inside Look at Outlaw Motorcycle Gangs*, Palladin Press, Colorado, 1992, p. 21.

CHAPTER 5
'We aren't about ... colours very seriously.' Veterans Motorcycle Club Australia, at www.geocities.com/veteransmc_australia/

'In 1993–94 in Sydney ... gangs in Australia.' Organised Crime Unit Gangs, Police National HQ, *The Fat Mexicans are Coming – A Preliminary Report on the Bandidos MC Merging with the New Zealand Highway 61 MC and Affiliates*, 17 June 1995, p. 16.

'An organised group ... crime or violence.' *New Oxford Dictionary of English*, Clarendon Press, Oxford, 1998, p. 526.

'Dedicated to the ... and motorcycle driving.' Lavigne, Yves. *Hell's Angels: Into the Abyss*, Harper, Toronto, 1996, p. 3.

CHAPTER 6
Satan's Angels Motorcycle Club Rules and Regulations and Hell's Angels By-laws in Wolf, Daniel R., *The Rebels: A Brotherhood of Outlaw Bikers*, University of Toronto Press, Toronto, 1991 appendix I, p. 352.

CHAPTER 7

'Q. What turns … their guide dogs.' Bull Bar, Haberfield, *Oz Bike*, No. 52, p. 31.

'This bloke breaks … anything about bikes' Alain Brainwood, Willougby *Oz Bike*, No. 52, p. 71.

'A biker was … a cop before.' Marcus, Croydon, *Oz Bike*, No. 45, p. 22.

'Q. What's the difference… on the outside.' Peg leg Pete, *Oz Bike*, No. 63, p. 81.

'Q. What's the difference … five years.' Hot Head Fowler, *Live to Die*, No.16, p. 12.

'Q. What's the difference… hold one cunt.' Tim, *Oz Bike*, No.67, p. 24.

The club was … keeping exotic animals. 'Bagger's Biker Post', www.bikerpost.com 11 January, 2001.

'Ken Part Owner … bouncer Full-time' Wolf, Daniel R., *The Rebels: A Brotherhood of Outlaw Bikers*, University of Toronto Press, Toronto, 1991, p. 257–8.

'Remember that you … rode in on.' Powers, Penny & Hays, *Chuck, Sit Down, Shut Up and Hang On! A Biker's Guide to Life*, Gibbs Smith, Salt Lake City, 1997, p. 69.

CHAPTER 8

'Their feelings strongly … state, "White Supremacy"'. *Inside Outlaw Motorcycle Gangs*, FBI report, Palladin Press, Boulder, Colorado, 1992, p. 8.

'I've also come … outlaw motorcycle clubs.' Lavigne, Yves. *Hells Angels: Into the Abyss*, Harper, Toronto, 1996, p. 92.

CHAPTER 9

'What I am … bitch by name.' Manning, Kimberly, *Some Biker Bitches Poetry*, Authors Choice Press Lincoln, 2000, p. 106.

'… little more than … or given away within the club.' *An Inside Look at Outlaw Motorcycle Gangs*, FBI report, Palladin Press, Boulder, Colorado, 1992, p. 10.

He argued that … for rival clubs. Barger, Sonny, *Hell's Angels: The Life and Times of Sonny Barger and the Hell's Angels Motorcycle Club*, Fourth Estate, London, 2000, p. 104.

I've come across … protect the club. Wolf, Daniel R., *The Rebels: A Brotherhood of Outlaw Bikers*, University of Toronto Press, Toronto, 1991, p. 152.

'An outlaw … independence and courage.' Wolf, Daniel R., *The Rebels: A Brotherhood of Outlaw Bikers*, University of Toronto Press, Toronto, 1991, p. 157.

'Women, particularly women … than the gang.' Wolf, Daniel R., *The Rebels: A Brotherhood of Outlaw Bikers*, University of Toronto Press, Toronto, 1991, p. 166.

She remains the … Rebels have had. Wolf, Daniel R., *The Rebels: A Brotherhood of Outlaw Bikers*, University of Toronto Press, Toronto, 1991, p. 158.

'Pass around Jane … took her life.' Manning, Kimberly, *Some Biker Bitches Poetry*, Authors Choice Press, Lincoln, 2000, p. 104.

'They dehumanise their … which I'm aware.' *Penthouse Magazine*, vol. 2, no. 1, January 1981, p. 36.

'Eightball – Patch worn … a dead woman.' *An Inside Look at Outlaw Motorcycle Gangs*, FBI report, Palladin Press, Boulder, Colarado, 1992, p. 16.

In recent years ... Australia were women. Berends, Lynda & Veno, Arthur, *A Qualitative Analysis of Motorcyclists' Experience of Accidents*, Vic Roads Report # 386, 1996, p. 86.

'There are lots ... in as members.' Barger, Sonny, *Hell's Angels: The Life and Times of Sonny Barger and the Hell's Angels Motorcycle Club*, Fourth Estate, London 2000, p. 102.

CHAPTER 10

In January 2002 ... previous four years. *Herald Sun* 9 January 2002, p. 3.

That particular part ... the early '80s. Bering-Jensen, Helle, *The Danish Biker Wars, Scandanavian Review*, Spring/Summer, 1997, Vol 85, Issue 1, p. 1.

However, when you ... other Western countries. Grabowski, P., *Trends and Issues in Criminology*, Australian Institute of Criminology Press, Canberra, 1994, p. 4.

The name Comanchero... John Wayne movie. Simpson, Lindsay & Harvey, Sandra, *Brothers in Arms: The Inside Story of Two Bikie Gangs*, Allen & Unwin, Sydney, 1989, p. 41.

'Fuck, who is ... the fuckin' army.' Simpson, Lindsay, Harvey & Sandra. *Brothers in Arms: The Inside Story of Two Bikie Gangs*, Allen & Unwin, Sydney, 1989, p. 82.

Most of the ... in a wall cavity. *Outsider's 1%er News.* www.chopperguy.net/~bikernews/, 3 May 2001.

'With the apparent ... front bar area.' Statement of claim, South Australian District Court Minh Van Pham V Consolidated Security Group Pty Ltd, 17 October 1997, p. 12.

A study conducted ... us a clue. Sherif, M., Harvey, O. J., White, B. J., Hood, W. R., & Sherif, *Intergroup Conflict and Co-operation: The Robber's Cave Experiment.* Norman Press, University of Oklahoma, Oaklahoma, 1961.

Another classic study ... prisoner–guard study. Zimbardo, Phil, *The Stanford Prison Study*, Collins, San Francisco, 1969.

'A fierce loyalty ... bikie club war.' Simpson, Lindsay & Harvey, Sandra. *Brothers in Arms: The Inside Story of Two Bikie Gangs*, Allen & Unwin, Sydney, 1989, p. 321–2.

The street gangs ... of gang life. William Whyte, *Street Corner Society*, Chicago University Press, Chicago, 1943 or Thrasher, Frederic Milton *Gangs: A Study of 1,313 Gangs in Chicago*, Chicago University Press, Chicago, 1927.

There were fist fights ... guns or drugs. Fleisher, Mark S, *Beggars and Thieves: Lives of urban street criminals*, The University of Wisconsin Press, Wisconsin, 1996; Klein, Malcolm, *The American Street Gang*, Oxford University Press, Ohio, 1996; Knox, George, *An Introduction to Gangs*, Wyndam Hall Press, Chicago, Illinois, 1995.

On rare occasions ... the same prison. Fleisher, Mark S., *Beggars and Thieves: Lives of Urban Street Criminals*, The University of Wisconsin Press, Wisconsin, 1996, p. 282.

I'm really worried ... about that boy.' Malcolm Klein, *The American Street Gang*, Oxford University Press, Oxford, 1996, p. 159.

CHAPTER 11

'Outlaw n. 1. one excluded ... or intractable animal.' *The Macquarie Dictionary Revised Edition*, Macquarie Library, Dee Why, 1981, p. 767.

While there were ... extortion, was low. Alain, Marc, *The rise and fall of motorcycle gangs in Quebec*, Federal Probation, vol. 59, no. 2, June 1995 pp. 54–8.

In Australia the ... less bikies around. National Crime Authority, *Operation Panzer*, NCA, Canberra 1998. (Report unavailable to public.)

The club presumed ... for supplying information. Barger, Sonny, *Hell's Angels: The Life and Times of Sonny Barger and the Hell's Angels Motorcycle Club*, Fourth Estate, London, 2000, p. 288.

One of my overseas ... a criminal organisation. Knox, George, *An Introduction to Gangs*, Wyndam Hall Press, Chicago, Illinois, 1995, p. 282.

'The motorcycle gangs ... others at bay.' Parry, Brian. *California Correctional News*, March 1999, p. 8.

'It is clear ... towards the bikers.' Quoted in Wolf, Daniel R., 'A Bloody Biker War.' *Macleans*, vol. 109, no. 3, March 1996, pp. 10–13.

'These were premeditated ... our judicial system', Quoted in Wolf, Daniel R., 'A Bloody Biker War.' *Macleans*, vol. 109, no. 3, March 1996, pp. 10–13.

CHAPTER 12

'Any member found ... of the club.' *Bylaws, Australian Bandidos*, 1983, reprinted in Simpson, Lindsay & Harvey, Sandra, *Brothers in Arms: The Inside Story of Two Bikie Gangs*, Allen & Unwin, Sydney, 1989, p. 230.

'They turned on ... influence was gone.' *The Sun New Pictorial*, 31 December 1987, p. 22.

'One of the ... charges was dropped.' *The Sun News Pictorial*, 5 March 1988, p. 16.

CHAPTER 13

'It is illegal ... the spokesman said.' *Outsider's 1%er News*. www.chopperguy.net/~bikernews/, 14 May 2001.

'These are exceptional ... Dr Gallop said.' Media Release, West Australian Government, 6 November, 2001, p. 3.

'The principal concern ... soft on bikies.' *Perth Sunday Times*, 28 October, 2001, p. 1.

'130 drunken outlaw ... with the operation.' *Herald Sun*, 9 November 2001, p. 3.

'They stood on ... of the norm.' Lavigne, Yves. *Hells Angels: Into the Abyss*, Harper, Toronto, 1996, p. 40.

'Among his goals ... fuck a nun.' Lavigne, Yves. *Hells Angels: Into the Abyss*, Harper, Toronto, 1996, p. 47.

'...wouldn't know when ... difference to him.' Lavigne, Yves, *Hells Angels: Into the Abyss*, Harper, Toronto, 1996, p. 81.

'We got to get ... not club business.' Ralph 'Sonny' Barger, recorded by Anthony Tait, Yves Lavigne, *Hells Angels: Into the Abyss*, Harper, Toronto, 1996, p. 178.

'an agent for ... a better place.' Yves Lavigne, *Hells Angels: Into the Abyss*, Harper, Toronto, 1996, p. 190.

As the members ... copper, you know.' Silvester John & Rule, Andrew, *Underbelly 2*, Floradale Productions Pty Ltd and Sly Ink Pty Ltd, 1998, p. 121.

CHAPTER 15

A Canadian study ... 300 club members. Alain, Marc, 'The rise and fall of motorcycle gangs in Quebec', *Federal Probation*, vol. 59, no. 2, June 1995, pp. 54–8.

In the past ... among younger riders. *The Australian*, 10 April 2001, p. 9.

'Many have been ... not stop them.' *The Australian*, 10 April 2001, p. 9.

'Another excellent US ... Snitches T-Shirts'. *San Diego Union-Tribune*, 22 July 2001, p. 6.

It seems to ... 3.8 million voters. NSW Legislative Council 1999 State General Election. State Electoral Office website. www.seo.nsw.gov.au

Reference abstract may cover more than one sentence if applicable.

INDEX